THE NEW TRANSIT TOWN

ABOUT ISLAND PRESS

Island Press is the only nonprofit organization in the United States whose principal purpose is the publication of books on environmental issues and natural resource management. We provide solutions-oriented information to professionals, public officials, business and community leaders, and concerned citizens who are shaping responses to environmental problems.

> In 2004, Island Press celebrates its twentieth anniversary as the leading provider of timely and practical books that take a multidisciplinary approach to critical environmental concerns. Our growing list of titles reflects our commitment to bringing the best of an expanding body of literature to the environmental community throughout North America and the world.

> Support for Island Press is provided by the Agua Fund, Brainerd Foundation, Geraldine R. Dodge Foundation, Doris Duke Charitable Foundation, Educational Foundation of America, The Ford Foundation, The George Gund Foundation, The William and Flora Hewlett Foundation, Henry Luce Foundation, The John D. and Catherine T. MacArthur Foundation, The Andrew W. Mellon Foundation, The Curtis and Edith Munson Foundation, National Environmental Trust, National Fish and Wildlife Foundation, The New-Land Foundation, Oak Foundation, The Overbrook Foundation, The David and Lucile Packard Foundation, The Pew Charitable Trusts, The Rockefeller Foundation, The Winslow Foundation, and other generous donors.

> The opinions expressed in this book are those of the author(s) and do not necessarily reflect the views of these foundations.

SPONSORS

The Center for Transit-Oriented Development seeks to use transit investments to spur a new wave of development that improves housing affordability and choice, revitalizes downtowns and urban and suburban neighborhoods, and generates lasting public and private returns. The Center was formed in 2003 to provide technical assistance, conduct research, assess performance and develop benchmarks, and to provide financial tools to bring transit-oriented development to scale in the United States. The Center works with transit agencies, nonprofit and commercial developers, financial institutions, and municipalities and regions, assisting them in realizing the promise of transit-oriented development to help meet the market demand for lively, mixed-use communities. The Center is led by Shelley Poticha, former executive director of the Congress for the New Urbanism. It is a project of Reconnecting America in collaboration with the Center for Neighborhood Technology, Strategic Economics, and the Congress for the New Urbanism. More information on the Center is available at http://www.transittown.org.

Reconnecting America is a new national organization formed to link transportation networks and the communities they serve. It expands the mission and scope of work of the Great American Station Foundation, which was formed in 1995 to assist communities with the revitalization of historic rail stations. Reconnecting America seeks to build connections between and among transportation networks and the regions and communities they serve in order to generate lasting public and private returns, improve economic and environmental efficiency, and give consumers greater transportation and housing choices. The organization does this through three core programs: Reconnecting America's Transportation Networks, a new Center for Transit-Oriented Development, and Reconnecting Rural America. To find out more, go to http://www.reconnectingamerica.org.

The Center for Neighborhood Technology (CNT) invents and implements new tools and methods that create livable urban communities for everyone. For more than twenty years, CNT has been working at the cutting edge of sustainable development—long before the term was coined—inventing programs and strategies that simultaneously achieve environmental goals and build strong communities. CNT's work has focused primarily on the Chicago region and its communities, but the tools and methods that help create healthy urban communities in Chicago are relevant in many other urban settings. CNT is now working in other urban areas, including South Florida, Los Angeles, San Francisco, Seattle, and Pittsburgh. For more information about CNT, see http://www.cnt.org.

THE **NEW**

EDITED BY

HANK DITTMAR AND **GLORIA OHLAND**

FOREWORD BY

PETER CALTHORPE

TRANSIT TOWN

**BEST PRACTICES IN
TRANSIT-ORIENTED
DEVELOPMENT**

ISLAND PRESS

WASHINGTON · COVELO · LONDON

ISLAND PRESS is a trademark of The Center for Resource Economics.

Library of Congress Cataloging-in-Publication data.

The new transit town: best practices in transit-oriented development/
edited by Hank Dittmar, Gloria Ohland.

  p. cm.

Includes bibliographical references and index.

ISBN 1-55963-117-1 (pbk.: alk. paper)—ISBN 1-55963-116-3 (cloth: alk. paper)

  1. Local transit—United States—Case studies. 2. Land use, Urban—United States—Case studies.
3. Transportation and state—United States—Case studies. 4. Urban policy—United States—Case studies.
I. Dittmar, Hank. II. Ohland, Gloria.

HE4451.N478 2003

388.4'0973—dc22

                          2003016783

British Cataloguing-in-Publication data available.

Design by Henk van Assen

Printed on recycled, acid-free paper ♻

Manufactured in the United States of America
10 9 8 7 6 5 4 3 2

CONTENTS

>

Foreword

Peter Calthorpe

At one time, urban development and transit were coevolving partners in city building; indeed, the urban center and streetcar suburbs defined a uniquely American form of metropolis. This form was at once focused on the city *and* decentralized around transit-rich suburban districts. Since World War II, however, this balance has been largely disrupted by sprawl and its soul mate, urban decay. Now a new balance is emerging between suburb and city. Infrastructure costs, environmental impacts, and strained lifestyles are combining with a new American demographic diversity to produce a more integrated form for our regions. For the past decade the transit-oriented development (TOD) experiment has been proving itself a match for these mounting challenges and new conditions. With this book, TOD is coming of age by defining a new synthesis for America's ever-evolving urban patterns.

> Transit-oriented development is regional planning, city revitalization, suburban renewal, and walkable neighborhoods combined. It is a cross-cutting approach to development that can do more than help diversify our transportation systems: it can offer a new range of development patterns for households, businesses, towns, and cities. But, as this book so rightly points out, it is in its adolescent phase. The concept is developing but the body of work lags a bit behind. The next stage will see its maturation expressed in differing regional, urban, suburban, and exurban forms.

> TOD is never a stand-alone phenomenon. It must be conceived within the context of at least a corridor and in most cases a regional metropolis. It is an alternative that provides choice not only in transportation modes but also, more fundamentally, in lifestyle. As we confront the regional issues of open space preservation, congestion, air quality, affordable housing, affordable lifestyles, and mounting infrastructure costs, TOD and its complex web of transit modes will become a more and more important strategy for sustainable growth.

> The original direction of TOD was limited; it focused on light-rail to the exclusion of other transit types. Now the modes have matured to include bus rapid transit, DMU (self-propelled light-rail), express bus, streetcars, commuter trains, and heavy-rail systems. There is no one best system; like the land use each generates, these systems are diverse and interdependent. And the range of development types implied by each overlapping system will add untold richness to the "regional cities" that are emerging.

> This book begins to clarify and detail this spectrum of development opportunities. The potential for inner-city revitalization as a result of transit investments and TOD is becoming clear, but can be enhanced. We have seen a return of regional retail to urban centers in some western cities partly as a result of transit development. Horton Plaza in San Diego, Pioneer Place

in Portland, and the Plaza in Sacramento are early manifestations of the nexus between light-rail and the return to downtown of regional retail. Simultaneously, residential renewal, even in decayed urban areas, is another manifestation of a larger movement back to urban living on the spine of transit. The Uptown District in Dallas was a startling early example of such a transformation.

> But the issue of gentrification must be addressed along with the hoped-for middle-class migration back to the city. In some places of extreme poverty, diversifying the mix of incomes is a good thing. But displacing whole communities by not providing an appropriate mix of affordable housing is a mistake. The greatest challenge for inner-city TOD is to balance the need for affordable housing with the need to diversify the city into economically integrated communities. Each place will necessarily go through a painful process to arrive at this balance.

> This issue of urban gentrification is connected to the suburbs. More affordable housing at transit-rich suburban locations not only can provide needed choices for inner-city poor but can also begin to support workforce housing throughout the region. Many suburban towns cannot provide housing that is affordable even to its own teachers, police, fire, and other service workers. Throughout the nation the average household spends 32 cents of each after-tax dollar on housing and 19 cents on transportation. Lower-income households spend up to 60 percent of every after-tax dollar on housing and transportation expenses. For these households affordable housing that puts them close to transit in job-rich sections of the region is essential to helping them make ends meet. TOD has a big role to play in satisfying this need in both the city and the suburb.

> TOD's capacity for inner-suburban renewal has been demonstrated but not exploited to its maximum potential. The first-ring suburbs, with their often-vacant industrial zones and moribund retail corridors, are perhaps the ripest areas for the positive impacts of transit. The land is readily available and the needs are clear. In these areas many underutilized rail lines coincide with brownfield industrial redevelopment sites just as old arterial and highway alignments coincide with decaying commercial corridors. Transit and TOD are often perfectly matched in these locations. The insights and studies presented in this book, which clarify existing economic and institutional barriers, are key to advancing the state of the art of TOD for these prime suburban infill areas.

> The final and perhaps most challenging area for TOD is in new-growth areas of expanding regions. These outer areas do not enjoy the natural benefits of the "location efficient" sites in the city and inner suburbs. The viability of density and mix is more difficult and the potential for transit ridership is often far in the future. But it is shortsighted to create a new ring of auto-oriented development at the urban edge; here an evolving strategy for both land use and transit is key. Such progressive planning should start by designating and reserving rights-of-way for transit, express bus, and commuter train service. These preserved rights-of-way could then be utilized when surrounding development has matured to support the transit system. And planning should allow critical areas to develop in a way that is receptive to adding density and more uses over time. Planning for phasing and land banking is essential.

> All of this opportunity will come to naught without long-term vision and hardheaded implementation strategies. One of the central problems addressed in this book is the lack of systemic leadership for comprehensive solutions. Individual cities and towns rarely coordinate with other jurisdictions, much less collaborate on complex new transit corridors and complementary land uses. If anything, the existing fiscal incentives cause them to compete. Current regional institutions, politically tied as they are to local governments, rarely advocate holistic solutions. Likewise, financing is a barrier to mixed-use projects and TOD because banks are structured to fund isolated single-use developments and are forced to underwrite them based on past successes rather than future needs. Add to this that many local planning, parking, and traffic standards contradict the goals of pedestrian-friendly design, and you have a short list of the challenges facing TOD.

> Luckily this book begins to provide answers to these challenges with more than mere assertions. Learning from the past decade's experience and focusing on the contribution of many experts, *The New Transit Town* clearly lays out the goals and means to accomplish a second generation of TOD. This book, along with the newly formed Center for Transit-Oriented Development, is a critical resource in a seminal time.

Acknowledgments

Hank Dittmar and Gloria Ohland would like to acknowledge and thank all of the people who have helped bring this book into being. First on the list are the contributors to this book, who not only contributed their individual chapters and expertise, but also collectively helped build our overall knowledge of the subject. Other people who helped us throughout the Transit-Oriented Development (TOD) Initiative that resulted in this book also deserve our thanks, including Matthew Baca, Janice Varela, Jacky Grimshaw, Mary Nelson, Rich Juarez, Josh Simon, M. von Nkosi, and Rod Diridon. Others who have contributed intellectually to our understanding of transit and development include Peter Calthorpe, Robert Cervero, John Holtzclaw, David Goldstein, Tom Downs, Bill Millar, Sarah Campbell, and Don Chen. Peter Haas and Albert Benedict are truly the cream of the crop at crunching numbers, drawing maps, and analyzing data. April Jones had the difficult task of collecting images for this book, and we thank both April and Laura Otis, who pitched in with the Congress for the New Urbanism image bank.

> The TOD Initiative was funded by the Surdna Foundation, the Turner Foundation, the Packard Foundation, and the U.S. Environmental Protection Agency (EPA). Of course, any mistakes are our own, and the recommendations herein are ours, not theirs. Ed Skloot, Carey Shea, and Hooper Brooks at the Surdna Foundation have been both staunch supporters and a challenging audience throughout. Thanks for sticking with us! Thanks also to Ned Farquhar, formerly with the Packard Foundation, and to everybody in the Smart Growth division at the EPA, especially Geoff Anderson.

Hank and Gloria wish to thank our fellow staff at Reconnecting America in Las Vegas, New Mexico, for putting up with us, as well as the Super Chief Café, of the same city, whose double lattes fueled many of our insights.

Hank wishes to thank his board of directors. He also wants to thank his colleagues on the board of the Congress for the New Urbanism for their vision and excellent practice. Above all, this book is for Kelle, Cole, and Clara Dittmar.

Gloria wishes to thank the Plaza Hotel in Las Vegas, New Mexico, and its excellent and caring staff. She also wants to give loving thanks and appreciation to her husband John and daughter Anabel.

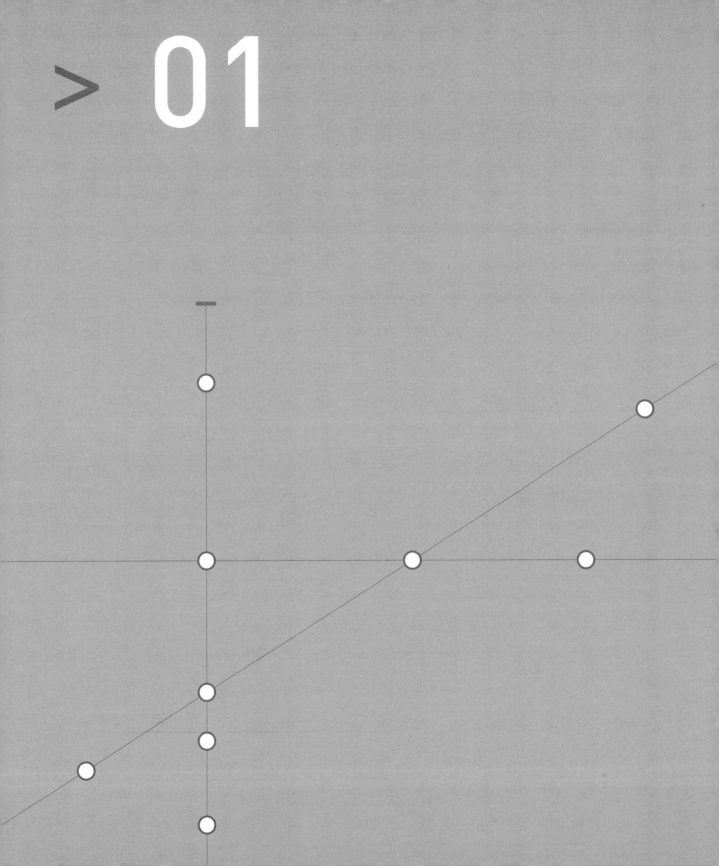

> 01

An Introduction to Transit-Oriented Development

Hank Dittmar with Dena Belzer and Gerald Autler

Debates about transportation and cities almost always generate more heat than light. First, there is the continuing debate about highways and transit. Transit proponents have been guilty of over-promising all sorts of environmental and social benefits from transit investment, without reference to the fact that transit is a specialized tool. Moreover, the sheer dominance of automobiles and highways makes any move toward more compact, transit-oriented land use of necessity gradual. For their part, highway and automobile enthusiasts tend to condemn transit by using national statistics and regional averages, without reference to the fact that transit is largely a tool for urban areas and works best as part of an integrated set of strategies involving transit, development, and other supportive policies.

> Another debate pits libertarians and smart growth advocates against one another over land use. The libertarians argue that today's growth patterns reflect market demands, ignoring decades of government intervention in planning and government subsidization of highways and automobiles. For their part, smart growth advocates tend to overstate the effectiveness of planning remedies and ignore the very real and persistent appeal of the detached single-family home in a suburb with good schools, not to mention the difficulty of changing entrenched lifestyles and habits. Transit-oriented development (TOD) has been touted as a panacea, with some arguing that all metropolitan growth can be accommodated through higher density infill development along transit lines—a physical possibility perhaps, but not viable in a democracy.

> This book tries to take a middle path. We believe that transit and transit-oriented development are essential parts of the toolkit for healthy metropolitan economies and improved quality of life. But we acknowledge that transit and transit-oriented development have their limitations, that autos, highways, and suburbs are also integral parts of the toolkit, and that a return to the era of streetcar suburbs is neither possible nor necessarily desirable. This book attempts to help fill a gap in the marketplace by evaluating the first generation of transit-oriented development, by setting some guideposts for the next generation, and by proposing some standards of practice. With this publication, we are trying to take advantage of three converging trends.

> The first trend is the resurgence of investment in America's downtowns. We are seeing the reinhabitation of our urban centers at a level that has not been experienced since World War II.

Census figures for the year 2000 and research by the Brookings Center on Urban and Metropolitan Policy and the Fannie Mae Foundation show that this urban rebirth is driven by demographic changes, including the rise in immigration, the aging of baby boomers, and the increase in nonfamily households. These changes add up to a growing market for smaller homes, and the increased popularity of cities. Urban centers are once again seen as attractive, lively places in which to live and work, and as hubs of intellectual and creative capacity.

> The second, and equally powerful, trend is the continuing growth and emerging maturity of America's suburbs, many of which are struggling to become cities in their own right. Suburban areas are increasingly diverse in race, ethnicity, and income, and are increasingly experiencing the pangs of rapid growth. Suburbs need to diversify land uses in order to build more solid revenue bases; they need to create urban centers and address the problem of traffic congestion along overtaxed suburban arterials. In addition, they need to respond to the desires of many suburban residents who have chosen not to move back into cities but who nevertheless want some urban amenities in their towns. In short, suburbs are increasingly being challenged to become more than bedroom communities.

> The third trend is a renewed interest in rail travel and rail investment. Virtually every major city in America is planning some form of urban rail or busway system, and states are joining together to plan and build high-speed rail systems linking metropolitan regions in the West, Midwest, Northeast, and South. In fact, the competition for limited federal funds is so intense that the wait for federal mass transit funding for a new project is estimated at almost fifty years. New rail or rapid bus systems have opened in the past ten years in such nontraditional places as Dallas, Denver, San Diego, Sacramento, Los Angeles, and Salt Lake City, with substantial system expansions underway in virtually every traditional rail city.

> At the convergence of these three trends is the potential for a substantial market for a new form of walkable, mixed-use urban development around new and existing rail or rapid bus stations. Changing demographics are resulting in a need for the diversification of real estate products, and the type of development known variously as transit villages or transit-oriented development is beginning to receive serious attention in markets as diverse as the San Francisco Bay Area, suburban New Jersey, Atlanta, Dallas, and Chicago. These transit-oriented developments have the potential to provide residents with improved quality of life and reduced household transportation expenses, while providing the region with stable mixed-income neighborhoods that reduce environmental impacts and provide real alternatives to traffic congestion. New research clearly shows that this kind of development can reduce household transportation costs, thereby making housing more affordable.

> Sadly, our review of the projects that are emerging across the country reveals that many of the first phases of these new "transit towns" fail to meet these important objectives. Somewhere between the conceptualization and opening day, many projects end up becoming fairly

traditional suburban developments that are simply transit-adjacent. Issues include unfriendly zoning codes and parking ordinances. Difficulties in dealing with the institutional complexities are also prevalent, with the chief confusion being the relative roles of local jurisdictions and transit agencies. Financing is difficult as well, with a lack of understanding about how best to finance mixed-use projects, and a lack of intermediary assistance for nonprofits and localities that want to pursue TOD projects that include affordable housing and involve minority-owned businesses.

>   The amount of hype around TOD far exceeds the progress to date, with many transit proponents selling new transit investments on the basis of future land-use changes. The result has been that transit opponents have begun to deride TOD as a failure by critiquing the performance of the flawed projects discussed above. This presents a particular challenge for the transit industry, because the long-term success of many projects depends on development trends over which the industry has, at best, only indirect control.

>   This book is an attempt to bring clarity to the debate by placing projects in a historical continuum, by creating a performance-oriented definition, and by analyzing and confronting the challenges that have been encountered. The research, which has been sponsored by Reconnecting America through its national Center for Transit-Oriented Development, is an initial step toward bringing TOD to scale as a recognized real estate product in the United States.

>   Over the past two years, we have been engaged in a collaborative effort with the Center for Neighborhood Technology, the Congress for the New Urbanism, Strategic Economics, and the Alliance for Transportation Research Institute to answer the question: What will it take to bring TOD to scale in a way that captures its potential economic and environmental advantages? Our work has involved a number of methods of inquiry, including a literature review, practitioner interviews, regional workshops, case studies, geographic information system analysis of travel survey and census data, and the evaluation of existing projects.

>   We seek first to understand the challenges faced, then to document the state of the TOD practice, and finally to assemble the resources necessary to assist cities, transit operators, and community groups who wish to undertake these kinds of TOD projects. In particular, we review the first generation of projects, document the progress made in defining the field, and attempt to advance the practice by defining principles to guide the next generation of projects being planned all over the country.

>   In our view, successful TOD needs to be mixed-use, walkable, location-efficient development that balances the need for sufficient density to support convenient transit service with the scale of the adjacent community. We intend to develop techniques to help assure that TOD also remains mixed-income in character.

Viewing TOD in Its Historical Context

Transit-oriented development should be viewed in a historical context. Transit has been around since the advent of the horse-drawn streetcar, and cities have always been at least partially shaped by their transportation modes—whether walking, streetcars, or automobiles. In fact, many of the urban design patterns that we seek to restore were common before the advent of the automobile; they simply arose spontaneously in cities for pedestrians. While TOD may not be a new thing, the challenge of adapting it to the auto-oriented metropolis is.[1]

THE EARLY TWENTIETH CENTURY: DEVELOPMENT-ORIENTED TRANSIT

The streetcar suburbs that existed before the 1900s evolved in a setting that no longer exists. Often, the streetcar lines and their adjacent residential communities were developed by a single owner who built transit to add value to the residential development by providing a link between jobs in an urban center and housing at the periphery, or by an entrepreneur who worked hand in hand with the developer. Indeed, the phrase "development-oriented transit" more aptly describes these places than does "transit-oriented development," since private developers built transit to serve their development rather than vice-versa. As part of this formula, streetcar stops often had small retail clusters to serve commuters as well as local residents. These small commercial districts are, to some extent, the precursor of modern TOD and represent a good balance between place and node.

>   Urban historian Sam Bass Warner's classic work, *Streetcar Suburbs*, characterized the way that transit and suburban real estate development worked hand in hand to decentralize the American city. The key to this was what Warner calls "a two part city: a city of work separated from a city of homes." Warner's study focused on Boston, but a similar model existed in Los Angeles as well. Planning professor Martin Wachs and others have chronicled the way that streetcar systems made the growth of suburban communities such as Glendale, Santa Monica, and Pasadena possible in Los Angeles between 1870 and 1910.

>   However, the interdependence between housing, jobs, and transit inherent in the early streetcar suburbs was broken apart by the automobile and, starting in the 1930s, roads, including highways, became the preferred transportation infrastructure in America. Development was no longer dependent on transit, the link between transit and development was broken, and developers got out of the business of building—or even thinking much about—transit systems.

THE POSTWAR YEARS: AUTO-ORIENTED TRANSIT

The postwar period saw a precipitous decline in transit use and the dismantling and abandonment of many rail systems. Buses became the primary mode of transit in most regions. Bus systems are subservient to the automobile, because they use the same streets and contend with the same congestion, but don't perform as well. And in most cases bus service has less influence on land-use patterns than fixed-rail transit. Transit became the travel mode of last resort and ceased to shape development, except in some of the commuter suburbs around older cities such as Boston, New York, and Chicago, which continued to function reasonably well as transit-based communities.

> As congestion worsened, a new generation of transit systems was planned and built. The San Francisco Bay Area Rapid Transit (BART) system, the Metropolitan Atlanta Rapid Transit Authority (MARTA), and the Washington (D.C.) Metropolitan Area Transit Agency (WMATA) all opened during the 1970s. These systems were built with a different rationale than their predecessors. They were built primarily to relieve congestion, their funding was provided entirely by the public sector, and little or no additional land was purchased by the transit agencies to ensure that there would be a link between these transit investments and future development patterns.

> These systems were also explicitly designed to work with the automobile, under the assumption that most people would drive to suburban stations rather than walk, bike, or ride the bus. What's more, they were viewed as primarily serving a regional purpose, and the individual stations were considered nodes within this larger system, with little concern about making them sensitive to the places in which they were located. Because of this, many stations were surrounded by large amounts of parking rather than being integrated into the neighborhoods they served; these large surface parking lots or structures created barriers between the station and the community.

> While these systems all play an important role—it is difficult to imagine Washington, D.C., without the Metro or the San Francisco Bay Area without BART—they are showing their limitations. Despite some success, they fall short of providing the full range of benefits that transit can stimulate. In general, they fail to contribute to neighborhood revitalization, to reduce automobile dependency significantly, or to encourage more efficient regional land-use patterns. In short, the idea that development should be linked to transit generally was not part of the philosophy of these systems.

TODAY: TRANSIT-RELATED DEVELOPMENT

Rail systems usually enhance the value of adjacent land, and transit agencies and the federal government see large-scale real estate development on property owned by transit agencies as a way to "capture" some of that value. While this return is not necessarily sufficient to pay the total cost of the rail investment, it at least partially reimburses public coffers. For this reason, transit agencies and the federal government have an interest in promoting intense development around transit stations. This "joint development" approach has been used with notable success in locations around the country, including downtown San Diego, Washington, D.C., and Portland.

> This form of transit-related development is problematic because it almost inevitably leads to a narrow definition of the relationship between transit and development. The emphasis of most joint development—which until the 1990s was virtually the only form of TOD pursued—

has been on dense, profitable real estate development aimed at generating revenue for the transit agency and the federal government. Projects were predicated on a purely financial rationale rather than a broad vision of how transit could work in tandem with surrounding development. As later sections explain, the goal of maximizing revenue from ground rents often works at cross-purposes with other goals. In other words, the "highest and best use" in financial terms is not always the best for either transit users or the neighborhood.

> There is increasing evidence that TOD can provide many other benefits besides capturing increases in land value. The last decade saw subtle but promising shifts in the landscape of transit and development, with the convergence of a number of trends: growing transit ridership, increased investment in transit (even in auto-dominated cities like Los Angeles and Dallas), frustration with congestion and sprawl, smart growth movements, New Urbanism, and, in general, a greater recognition of the advantages of linking development and transit.

> Architect and urbanist Peter Calthorpe, who brought together the notion of the pedestrian pocket with the idea of planning development around transit stations, largely sparked the new interest in development around transit. In both his design practice and his writing he advanced the concept of mixed-use development and density around transit, and was enormously influential among planners and local officials beginning in the 1990s. Calthorpe's book, *The Next American Metropolis*, written with associate Shelley Poticha, began to articulate the urban design principles associated with TOD:

- Organize growth on a regional level to be compact and transit-supportive.
- Place commercial, housing, jobs parks, and civic uses within walking distance of transit stops.
- Create pedestrian-friendly street networks that directly connect local destinations.
- Provide a mix of housing types, densities, and costs.
- Preserve sensitive habitat, riparian zones, and high-quality open space.
- Make public spaces the focus of building orientation and neighborhood activity.
- Encourage infill and redevelopment along transit corridors within existing neighborhoods.

> Sadly, many of the projects Calthorpe planned were either turned over to different architects or altered during the development phase, leaving much of his early TOD work frustratingly unrealized. Perhaps his efforts have most paid off in Portland, Oregon, where years of collaboration with Poticha and planner John Fregonese on regional and transit-oriented development planning have resulted in an impressive emphasis on walkable mixed-use development focused on the emerging transit and streetcar systems.

> The academic most associated with the concept of TOD is Robert Cervero, professor of planning at the University of California at Berkeley. Cervero's research has centered on the

relationship between transit and metropolitan development, and he has consistently stressed the relationship between urban form and the type of transit best suited to serving a particular urban form. In two books—*Transit Villages in the Twenty-First Century*, written with Michael Bernick, an attorney and former member of the board of directors of BART, and *Transit Metropolis*—Cervero used a case study approach to gather much new evidence about both styles of transit and styles of development.

>   Many of the projects in the United States that were studied and written about by Calthorpe and Cervero existed only as plans, or as transit-oriented zoning codes or design guidelines. Now, a decade later, we can look at the first generation of development projects around these new transit corridors to assess how well they lived up to their potential.

>   A closer look at TOD projects around the country shows that most still fall short of providing the full range of potential benefits. Projects that clearly could take advantage of being adjacent to transit to reduce parking still use standard parking ratios, indicating an underlying assumption that these projects will primarily be auto-oriented. Projects that contain a variety of uses still lack an "appropriate" mix—that is, the specific uses have not been selected to create an internal synergism but have only responded to more general market conditions. Residential projects rarely include units targeted at a mix of income groups or household sizes, but are focused on one particular market segment, be it subsidized projects targeted to lower-income households or luxury units for young singles and empty nesters.

>   Many of the examples examined in this book constitute good projects; most of them are significantly better than traditional development. However, the interviews conducted over the course of our study suggest that there is little understanding of the full range of benefits that can be achieved with TOD. This is reflected in both the physical design of most built projects and their mix of land uses. Many projects are relatively unambitious in what they hope to accomplish, or overly narrow in their view of the potential impacts of TOD. Even when the aims are broader, the fact that modern transit and development are built by several different actors introduces several additional layers of complexity.

>   Our goal is to bring TOD up to scale not just in name but in terms of the impact it can have on cities, the environment, communities, and individual lives. For this reason we must set the bar high and describe a vision of TOD that is ambitious without being unrealistic. Most current projects fall short of this vision, and as a result we have chosen to call them transit-related development, a name that acknowledges the connection they have made between transit and development while still recognizing their shortcomings. Not all projects in all places will or even can meet the standard by which true transit-oriented development should be defined, but without a benchmark there will be no way to judge the quality of projects or even to think clearly about the trade-offs that must be made when pursuing a project.

TOMORROW: TRANSIT-ORIENTED DEVELOPMENT

Transit-oriented development can realize its full potential only if it is seen as a new paradigm of development rather than as a series of marginal improvements. TOD cannot be and should not be a utopian vision: It must operate within the constraints of the market and realistic expectations of behavior and lifestyle patterns. However, the market and lifestyle patterns can and do change as a result of both policy choices and sociocultural trends. The automobile was not always the dominant form of transportation, and suburban living was not always the lifestyle of choice. These changes in American life have been fostered in part by government policy, such as the mortgage interest tax deduction and the generous subsidies for road infrastructure at the expense of alternative forms of transportation.

> Already there are clear signs that these trends are not permanent. Growth in transit ridership and renewed interest in urban living are two indicators that preferences may be changing. Federal transportation legislation in the 1990s has helped shift government investment priorities away from the automobile and toward alternatives, such as transit, walking, and biking. Transit-oriented development can respond to these changes by offering an alternative that is viable in the marketplace while still yielding social benefits. Transit-oriented development in the twenty-first century can be a central part of the solution to a range of social and environmental problems.

> As the environmental, social, commuting, and land-use trends described above progress, it is likely that the type of neighborhoods we envision will become increasingly attractive. Although defining a vision of transit and development that function complementarily is a crucial first step, it is not enough. The next step is to move that vision—in concept and reality—into the mainstream of real estate development. This requires an understanding of why relatively few projects get built, and why so many of those that do get built fall short of their potential.

Defining the Scale of the Market for TOD

One possible reason for the relative lack of success with TOD to date is the lack of definitions, standards, or road maps for developers to follow. However, some critics of the concept have suggested another reason: There is no market for more compact, mixed-use development near transit. After all, argue these critics, if people wanted it, wouldn't the market supply it?

> Our review both of the challenges to implementing TOD projects and of the market tells us that there is a serious mismatch between the potential demand for TOD and the supply, and this in turn informs us that there is a need to provide useful tools and models for practitioners.

> In order to better understand the challenges to implementing TOD, we conducted interviews with practitioners, staged workshops to examine and address site-specific problems, reviewed the literature, conducted economic analyses, and completed case studies. Our conclusions were summed up in a report by urban economists Dena Belzer and Gerald Autler and

published by the Brookings Center on Urban and Metropolitan Policy and the Great American Station Foundation. These conclusions can be summarized as follows:

·   There is no clear definition of TOD or agreement on desired outcomes, and hence no way of ensuring that a project delivers these outcomes.

·   There are no standards or systems to help the actors involved in the development process bring successful transit-oriented projects into existence. Without standards and systems, successful TOD is the result of clever exceptionalism, and beyond the reach of most communities or developers.

·   Transit-oriented development requires the participation of many actors and occurs in a fragmented regulatory environment, adding complexity, time, uncertainty, risk, and cost to projects.

·   Although transit adds accessibility and value to a place, transit alone is insufficient to drive real estate markets. When other market forces are not present, special actions are needed to ensure that projects to achieve regional land use or housing goals go forward.

>   Without a concerted effort to develop standards and definitions, to create products and delivery systems, and to provide research support, technical assistance, and access to capital, TOD will remain just a promising idea.

THE SHIFT IN HOUSING AND NEIGHBORHOOD PREFERENCES

Cities, once stigmatized as crime-ridden repositories of the poor, are now being seen as vital, resource-rich places, in part because urban density creates the opportunity for a more diverse mix of amenities than is available in one-dimensional suburban locations. A larger trend, however, lies just underneath this change in attitude. The demographics of the country are gradually shifting, and these shifts portend a fundamental change in the demand for housing and community. Four interrelated demographic trends are underway, which have been dramatically illuminated in the 2000 Census. Each has the potential to help us move from suburban sprawl and traffic nightmares to reinvigorated urban centers with high quality of life.[2]

Immigration

The most notable finding of the 2000 Census was the unequivocal diversity added to our nation as a result of immigration, principally from Latin America and Asia. Cities have traditionally been magnets for immigrants, and at least since World War II, most minorities have lived in cities. Although an increasing percentage of immigrants are choosing to live in the suburbs, and there is a significant trend toward minority migration to the suburbs, demographer William Frey projects that most of the immigrant population will continue to be concentrated in denser urban locations.

>   This urban concentration, along with the lower income levels of most immigrant and minority households, has historically meant that these households own fewer automobiles and drive less. According to Catherine Ross and Anne Dunning's analysis of the 1995 National Personal Transportation Survey, African Americans, Asians, and Hispanics are all more likely to use public transit or walk than is population as a whole. For immigrants, this may be due not only to income and poverty level but also to cultural factors, including the fact that they have lived in places where auto use was the exception rather than the rule. Consequently, as immigrants are assimilated into the population and their incomes rise, we can expect to see both higher numbers of drivers and a continued willingness to use public transit, particularly if its availability, quality, and convenience continue to increase.

"Empty Nesters" and "Echo Boomers"

The second demographic trend is the aging of the baby boom generation, and its passage from the child-rearing stage of the life cycle to the "empty nest" phase. Families that once demanded the single-family home on a quarter-acre parcel in a suburban location are now finding both the home and the location to be unsuited to this new stage of life. Evidence suggests that baby boomers have fueled much of the downtown population growth over the past decade, as they seek smaller homes in locations with a greater mix of amenities.

>   Marketing experts and demographers alike have trumpeted the preferences of Echo Boomers (aged 24–34) for exciting, dense, urban locations. Indeed, the much-publicized growth of new economy cities like San Francisco and Austin has been ascribed to their attractiveness to highly skilled young workers. A recent national study found that 57 percent of this generation preferred small lot housing and that 53 percent felt that an easy walk to stores was an extremely important determinant in housing and neighborhood choice.[3] In his influential book *The Rise of the Creative Class*, economic development expert Richard Florida makes a compelling case that the economically successful regions of the future will be those that attract technology and talent, and that "creative workers" are attracted to cities because they are centers of innovation. Florida notes, however, that this was not just a phenomenon involving young people and baby boomers. He also finds a clear correlation between child-friendly cities and creative hubs.

Nonfamily Households

The 2000 Census found that nonfamily households comprise 31.9 percent of all American households, a higher percentage than married couples with children at home, a group that now comprises only 29.5 percent of households. Ross and Dunning found that single adults with no children, and households of two or more adults with no children, were most likely to live in urban locations. These less conventional households are another force for change.

THE SCALE OF THE MARKET

These demographic trends add up to a growing market for smaller homes, town homes, and homes on smaller lots in vibrant walkable neighborhoods—all characteristics of transit-oriented development. In a recent study, Dowell Myers at the University of Southern California estimated that between 30 percent and 55 percent of the demand for new housing would be for residences in dense, walkable neighborhoods. He and his coauthor, Elizabeth Gearin, also found that almost 25 percent of the aging baby boomer demand was for town homes in the city.

The Transit "Boom"

In the past decade, new fixed guideway transit (light-rail, commuter-rail, subway, or busway) lines have opened all over the country, even—and especially—in cities that traditionally have not had much transit service. New light-rail systems have opened in San Diego, San Jose, Sacramento, Portland, Salt Lake City, Denver, St. Louis, and Dallas, often to better than forecasted ridership. At the same time, there has been a resurgence of interest in better performing bus services, with international successes like Ottawa, Canada, and Curitiba, Brazil, accompanied by experiments with dedicated busways in Pittsburgh and rapid bus demonstrations in a number of cities around the country. The result has been a huge increase in interest in transit system construction, with virtually every metropolitan area planning some kind of fixed guideway project.

> These are added to a large number of existing stations around the country. According to the American Public Transit Association, the station inventory includes twenty commuter-rail agencies with 1,153 stations; fourteen heavy-rail agencies with 1,009 stations; twenty-six light-rail transit agencies with 651 stations (with numerous additional street stops that don't meet the station definition); and fourteen other rail transit agencies with 71 stations (including monorails, cable cars, etc.). This count excludes the intercity bus industry, which serves over 4,000 communities, and Amtrak, which serves about 500 stations. Overall there appear to be about 2,400 transit and intercity rail stations together with a wide variety of intercity bus locations.

> The future demand for new transit starts projects appears tremendous. In an attempt to gauge the potential supply of transit, we reviewed the Federal Transit Administration's (FTA) 2003 *Annual Report on New Starts*. This report to Congress lists all pending and proposed projects around the country and makes recommendations about funding allocations for specific projects. As of 2003, twenty-five new start projects have full funding grant agreements with the FTA that commit the agency to a specified amount of federal support. These include projects in Atlanta, Baltimore, Boston, Chicago, Dallas, Denver, Fort Lauderdale, Los Angeles, Memphis, New Jersey, Pittsburgh, Portland, St. Louis, Salt Lake City, San Diego, San Francisco, San Juan, and Washington, D.C. Figure 1.1 depicts these commitments, which will add 131 new stations to the existing inventory.

> In addition to the projects in the full funding grant agreement category, FTA is monitoring an additional fifty-two projects that are in some stage of the federal approval process, either

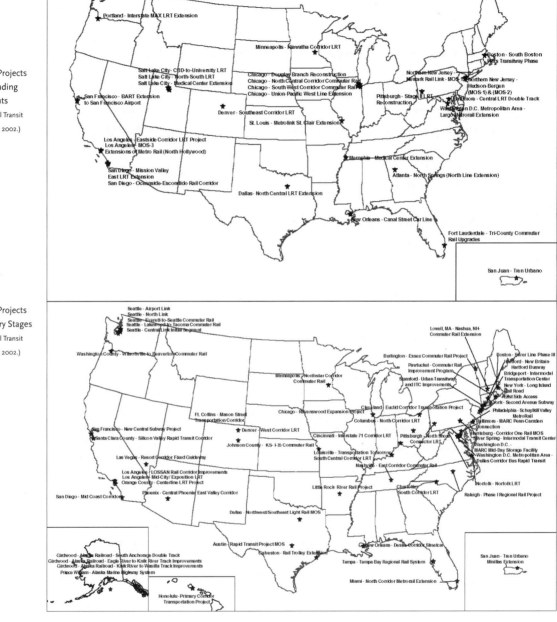

FIG. 1.1

New Starts Projects with Full Funding Commitments

(Source: Federal Transit Administration, 2002.)

FIG. 1.2

New Starts Projects in Preliminary Stages

(Source: Federal Transit Administration, 2002.)

pending a grant agreement, in final design, or in preliminary engineering. Figure 1.2 depicts the new transit start projects already in the federal approval and funding process. On top of these projects, there are an additional 151 new starts that were named in the last federal transportation authorization, the so-called TEA-21 legislation, for some level of federal funding.

> Of course many of these projects will never be built, and should never be built, as the demand or local financing capacity may not be there. The FTA has adopted a rigorous screening process to ration the relatively small amount of federal transit funds among the huge number of competitors and, fortunately, one of the key screening criteria is consistency with local land-use plans. As a result, many transit proposals now include some evidence of "transit-supportive existing land use, policies and future patterns." This provides both evidence of the degree to which ideas about transit-oriented development are taking hold and also evidence of the need for improved practices and standards, without which many of the new systems may fail to meet ridership projections.

TOD's Role in Meeting Metropolitan Growth Projections

Clearly, transit-oriented development has the potential to fulfill much of the unmet demand for more compact development that is expected to arise in the next decade. One analyst has attempted to answer a different question: Could TOD accommodate all metropolitan area growth? Writing soon after Peter Calthorpe's *Next American Metropolis* was published, and looking at actual growth patterns in the 1980s, Anthony Downs of the Brookings Institution used a methodology that assumed a 2,000-foot radius around transit stations, applied Calthorpe's density guidelines, and assumed the construction of radial transit systems in each metropolitan area. He found that "it might have been feasible to accommodate all of the population growth of the 1980s into combined TODs if large amounts of resources had been devoted to building a rapid transit system linking them together." Of course he notes that this would have been tremendously expensive, might have engendered resistance due to the higher density development, and hence concludes, "TODs should be viewed as building blocks that could be used to handle some significant part of growth."

> Many metropolitan planning agencies are now conducting scenario-based regional planning studies, and often one of the scenarios involves some degree of TOD. Salt Lake City's Envision Utah project and Chicago's Metropolis 2020 effort are examples of the ways that regions are attempting to get away from using trend-based forecasts and are using new approaches to mobility and development to meet a part of the demand for new housing generated by population growth. Maturing our approach to TOD will help these ambitious regional planning efforts become more than regional visions.

The Plan for This Book

The plan for this book is to provide the reader with both an orientation into the practice of TOD and an evaluation of the first generation of projects emerging around the country. We seek to learn from the efforts of the pioneers by presenting case studies of noteworthy efforts. At the same time, we have attempted to draw from the literature, from interviews with practitioners, and from the case studies a set of practical lessons about the pursuit of development around transit in key subject areas.

> Throughout, our goal is to provide a set of tools to allow practitioners to begin to deliver on TOD's promise of generating outcomes that are of lasting value to both communities and individuals, and of capturing value for the many actors involved in the process, including regions, cities, transit agencies, developers, community groups, and families. We are building toward standards for TOD and toward the creation of a standard real estate product that can be brought to scale. This is very much a work in progress, and our hope is that by suggesting directions for this work to follow we can set the stage for both continuous improvement and a more organized process of documentation and evaluation of the practice of TOD.

> The book is divided into two parts. The first part seeks to define the state of the practice and begins to set standards for key aspects of TOD. It is followed by a series of case studies that evaluate the practice of TOD around the country at both the project and the regional scale.

> We begin in the following chapter by seeking to refine the definition of TOD and to relate it to the structure of metropolitan regions with a typology that addresses issues of scale, transit service standards, land-use mix and density, and urban design characteristics. The goals are to embed TOD within the metropolitan structure that is emerging in this auto-oriented and postmodern era and to relate it to the neighborhoods in which the transit stops are located.

> Chapter 3 discusses the different actors involved in the TOD process—including cities, transit agencies, community groups, for-profit developers and lenders, and nonprofit community developers—and their roles. The chapter also examines some emerging ways of addressing the difficult challenge of delivering a project that meets agency and developer goals in terms of return and value capture while also achieving what may be very different goals for the community.

> Chapter 4 examines the regulatory environment for transit-oriented development and discusses the different approaches that cities have taken toward planning and zoning around transit. It takes a case study approach, analyzing a representative variety of transit-oriented codes in a variety of metropolitan settings.

> Concerned with the financing of TOD, chapter 5 serves both as a primer on the development finance process for TOD and as a guide for people who need to confront the challenges of financing walkable, mixed-use development around transit in a fragmented regulatory and institutional environment. Research for this chapter included exhaustive interviews with developers, city and transit agency staff, and lenders and investors.

> Chapter 6 looks at both traffic and parking issues, documenting the very real need for more work to determine specific parking and trip generation standards for TOD. Key problems are the accommodation of parking and the fact that parking standards for auto-oriented developments are being applied to transit-oriented projects without offsets for reduced auto use. Of course, this drives up the cost of these projects.

CASE STUDIES

Chapters 7 through 11 examine the state of the practice around the country through a series of case studies. Each case study examines in detail one or two projects in a specific region, seeking always to place that project within a regional context. The goal is to document the history of the effort, to report the outcomes, and to draw lessons that are applicable elsewhere. In selecting case studies, we consciously tried for diversity in both geographic spread and maturity of the transit system and the project.

> The case study in chapter 7 looks at a county in the Washington, D.C., region that has doggedly pursued an economic development strategy centered around transit . Thirty years ago, Arlington County, Virginia, was an inner suburb threatened by leapfrog suburban development at the fringes, and declining neighborhoods at the core. The county chose to use the new Metrorail system as a focus for development and density; it has succeeded in growing population, real estate value, and the tax base, as well as achieving dramatic transportation and environmental results. Our case study shows that the progress has not been without its challenges, particularly with respect to urban design, walkability, affordability, and historic preservation; still, the county has continued to confront these challenges, presenting a template for consistent local government action.

> Chapter 8 focuses on two successful projects in Dallas: the Mockingbird Station development near Southern Methodist University, and the Addison Circle development, a striking new downtown for the suburban community of Addison. The popularity of the new rail system in the Dallas/Fort Worth metroplex has generated a huge amount of interest in mixed-use walkable development, from urban neighborhoods like Dallas's Uptown and West End to suburban projects in Addison and Plano.

> The case study presented in chapter 9 discusses transit-oriented development in Atlanta, a region whose economic success appeared threatened by runaway sprawl, traffic congestion, and air pollution. In an encouraging example of corporate leadership, BellSouth decided to concentrate its many suburban facilities within walking distance of three transit stops on the MARTA system. Our case study looks at the challenges faced by MARTA, the city, BellSouth, the developer, and the project's neighbors as they attempted to accommodate this huge project at the Lindbergh station.

> Chapter 10, the case study of the Ohlone-Chynoweth project in the heart of California's Silicon Valley, focuses on transit's role in siting affordable housing, particularly in a booming regional economy where housing prices are skyrocketing. The case study illuminates the important role that local governments and nonprofit community developers can play in ensuring affordable housing is located near transit, as well as the challenges to ensuring that transit neighborhoods are mixed income in character. The chapter also looks at some of the design challenges faced when integrating transit into a suburban context and attempting to balance the station's role as both a place and a node.

TABLE 1.1—PROFILE OF CASE STUDY PROJECTS

PROJECT	DEVELOPER	DATE COMPLETED	LAND USES	TRANSIT	FINANCING	PARKING	RESIDENTIAL DENSITY
Arlington County Virginia	County plans Various private	As of 2000	17.9M sq.ft. office 3.0M sq.ft. retail 21,581 housing units	Heavy-rail Bus	Public/Private	(see pg. 142, this volume)	
Mockingbird Station Dallas, TX	Ken Hughes	2000	214,000 sq.ft. residential 183,000 sq.ft. retail	Light-rail Bus	Private	1.0/bedroom 3.23/1,000 gross sq.ft. retail	24 units/acre
Addison Circle Addison, TX	Columbus Realty Trust Post Properties	Phase 3 in 2002	1,800 apts. 86 condos 6 town homes 115,000 sq.ft. retail 342,000 sq.ft. office	Bus Light-rail planned	Public/Private	Phase 1: 1/bedroom Phase 2: 0.3/bedroom Phase 3: 1/bedroom 3.7 spaces/1,000 gross sq.ft. retail 3.2 spaces/1,000 gross sq.ft. office	100 units/acre
Mercado San Diego, CA	MAAC Landgrant Richard Juarez	Apartments in 1993	138,000 sq.ft. residential 144 apts. 118,000 sq.ft. retail	Light-rail Bus	Public/Private Affordable LIHTC	1.5/unit 3.5/1,000 gross sq.ft. retail	32.7 units/acre
Lindbergh Atlanta, GA	Carter & Assoc.	Phase 1 in 2003	388,000 sq.ft. residential 1M sq.ft. office 330,000 sq.ft. retail	Heavy-rail Bus	Public/Private	2.2/1,000 sq.ft. commercial less than 1 per bedroom	
Ohlone Court Santa Clara County	Bridge Housing	1997	135 units	Light-rail Bus	Public/Private Affordable	1.5/1.8/2.0 spaces for 1/2/3 bedrooms	22.1 units/acre
Ohlone-Chynoweth Commons Santa Clara County	Eden Housing	2001	194 units	Light-rail Bus	Public/Private Affordable	same	26.6 units/acre
1 Pearl Avenue Santa Clara County	Cilker Orchards	2003	182 units	Light-rail Bus	Private	same	41.4 units/acre

> Chapter 11 tells the story of Barrio Logan, a bootstraps effort at community revitalization in an inner-city Latino neighborhood near San Diego's downtown. The case study shows that existing affordable housing tools can be successfully used to create affordable transit-oriented housing, but that the tools for commercial development in lower-income neighborhoods and communities of color are less well developed. In particular, our review finds that attracting commercial developers and retail tenants to lower-income neighborhoods is complicated when the projects incorporate nonstandard features like walkability and transit orientation. This finding supports the need for more standard transit-oriented retail products as well as the importance of sustained community involvement and community capacity.

> Table 1.1 lists each case study and provides key details about development and transit.

> Chapter 12 attempts to draw some conclusions about the potential for transit-oriented development. It calls for a continued effort to set performance standards and argues that the benefits of such an undertaking will be profound and widespread.

NOTES

1   This section is based upon work by Dena Belzer and Gerald Autler for the Center for Transit-Oriented Development, published as "Transit-Oriented Development: Moving from Rhetoric to Reality," by the Great American Station Foundation and the Brookings Center on Urban and Metropolitan Policy (Washington, D.C.: Brookings Institution, 2002), at http://www.transittown.org.

2   This section is drawn from a chapter I wrote for *Sustainable Planet,* edited by Juliet Schor and Betsy Taylor (Boston: Beacon Press, 2002).

3   Federal Highway Administration. 2001. *Moving Ahead: The American Public Speaks about Roadways and Their Communities.* Washington, D.C.: Federal Highway Administration.

REFERENCES

American Public Transit Association. 2002. *Transit Fact Book.* Washington, D.C.: American Public Transit Association. At http://www.apta.com/stats.

Belzer, Dena and Gerald Autler. 2002. Transit-Oriented Development: Moving from Rhetoric to Reality. Great American Station Foundation and Brookings Center on Urban and Metropolitan Policy. At http://www.transittown.org.

Bernick, Michael and Robert Cervero. 1997. *Transit Villages in the Twenty-First Century.* New York: McGraw-Hill.

Calthorpe, Peter. 1993. *The Next American Metropolis.* Princeton: Princeton Architectural Press.

Cervero, Robert. 1998. *Transit Metropolis.* Washington, D.C.: Island Press.

Congress for the New Urbanism. 2001. *The Coming Demand.* San Francisco: Congress for the New Urbanism. At http://www.cnu.org.

Downs, Anthony. 1994. *New Visions for Metropolitan America.* Washington, D.C.: Brookings Institution/Lincoln Institute of Land Policy.

Federal Transit Administration. 2002. *Annual Report on New Starts: Proposed Allocation of Funds for Fiscal Year 2003.* Washington, D.C.: Federal Transit Administration. At http://www.fta.dot.gov.

Fogelson, Robert. 1967. *The Fragmented Metropolis: Los Angeles 1850–1930.* Cambridge: Harvard University Press.

Holtzclaw, John, Robert Clear, Hank Dittmar, David Goldstein, and Peter Haas. 2002. Location Efficiency: Neighborhood and Socioeconomic Characteristics Determine Auto Ownership and Use. *Transportation Planning and Technology* Winter:1–25.

Myers, Dowell and Elizabeth Gearin. 2001. Current Preferences and Future Demand for Denser Residential Environments. *Housing Policy Debate* 12,4:633–60.

Ross, Catherine L. and Anne Dunning. 1997. Land Use Transportation Interaction: An Examination of the 1995 NPTS Data. Prepared for the Federal Highway Administration.

Simmons, Tavia and Grace O'Neill. 2001. Households and Families: 2000. In *Census Brief.* Washington, D.C.: U.S. Census Bureau.

Sohmer, Rebecca and Robert Lang. 2001. *Downtown Rebound.* Fannie Mae Foundation and Brookings Center on Urban and Metropolitan Policy Census Note. Washington, D.C.: Brookings Institution.

Wachs, Martin. 1996. The Evolution of Transportation Policy in Los Angeles. In *The City: Los Angeles and Urban Theory at the End of the Twentieth Century,* edited by Allen Scott and Edward Soja. Berkeley: University of California Press.

Warner, Sam Bass. 1978. *Streetcar Suburbs: The Process of Growth in Boston 1870–1900.* 2nd Edition. Cambridge: Harvard University Press.

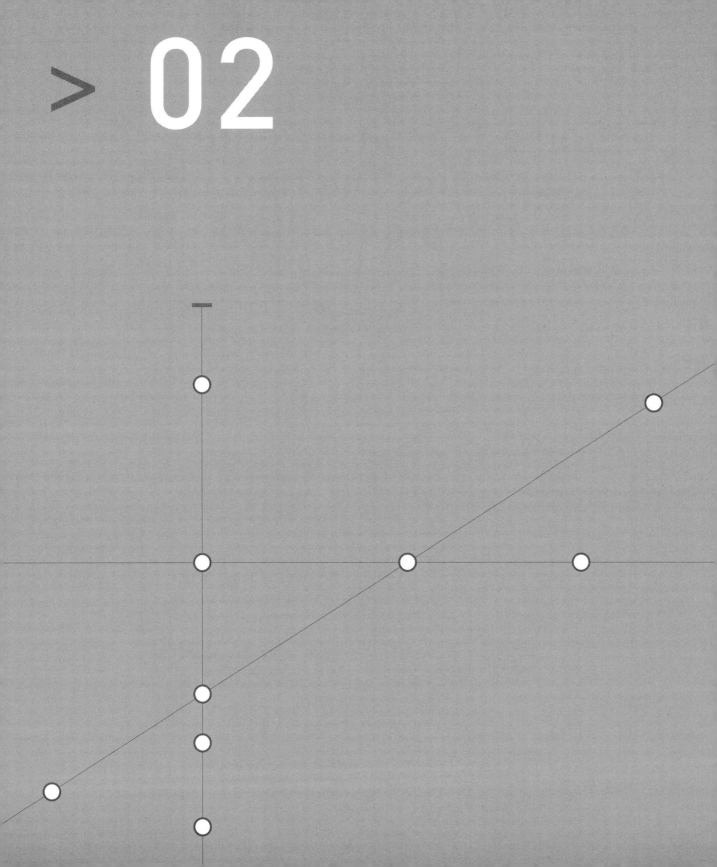

> 02

Defining Transit-Oriented Development: The New Regional Building Block

Hank Dittmar and Shelley Poticha

During the past decade there has been a tectonic shift in consumer preferences, employer location strategies, and transportation planning values. Sitting, as it does at the convergence of these trends, transit-oriented development (TOD) has the potential to form a new approach to development that builds on their synergy and results in places and regions that meet the demand for location-efficient mixed-use neighborhoods, supports regional economic growth strategies, and increases housing affordability and choice. TOD could be nothing less than the defining armature for a fundamental rethinking about how we build communities and how we make regional policy and investment decisions. Nonetheless, two questions persist: What are we aiming for? And what is TOD, anyway? Surprisingly, both questions have remained largely unanswered in the decade-plus effort to implement TOD.[1]

Defining Goals

Imagine a region made up of a network of great neighborhoods—places where residents of diverse incomes, ages, and backgrounds have the option to walk to nearby shopping, parks, and schools; where streets are safe to walk along and public spaces are beautiful, inviting, and frequented; and where people can choose to take a train or bus to their destinations as easily and conveniently as a car. Imagine, as well, a region where job centers are convenient for employees around the clock, where they can easily take care of errands during lunch, catch a movie after work, or even bike to the office. These job centers, even those located in suburbia, are linked to a network of neighborhoods and a revitalized downtown by high-quality, efficient transit.

> What this vision delivers is a new level of choice and freedom for those who want it. Families who want or need to save money can choose to live with one less car without sacrificing mobility and access. Individuals who seek out environments with active street lives and cultural scenes have a variety of options instead of having to choose the one or two great, but overpriced, neighborhoods that fit that description in most regions today. Employers who recognize that their

labor pool is dependent on attracting the "creative class," or who see an economic value in investing in around-the-clock districts, can locate their facilities close to transit. Further, transit agencies can begin to grow a sizable ridership base built on customers rather than parking spaces, and cities can create places that generate lasting public and private values.

> Achieving this vision will require new thinking about the way we plan our communities and transportation systems. In particular, we need to pay more attention to the pattern of development and the ways this pattern supports people and investors who want transportation options. It will require us to reconsider how transit is integrated into our communities and the quality of service that is provided, and to focus on the function and performance of entire places and systems rather than the individual elements. Finally, it will require us to define TOD to the extent that it is easily replicable but contextually sensitive.

> Achieving this vision, even with a revolution in our thinking, will be challenging. As we have learned from TOD history, the movement has been built on a legacy of ambitious promises and naive execution. An examination of projects that purport to be transit-oriented shows that many have been quick to embrace the term while falling short of delivering the concept's full potential. Defining TOD, and making the concept relevant to the many different types of places that make up vital and healthy regions, is the purpose of the TOD typology that follows. A clearer vision of exactly what TOD is meant to accomplish, coupled with a new approach to development, is necessary if TOD is to maximize its contribution to our social, economic, and environmental health. This effort is intended to use current market and social forces to drive toward a realistic yet nuanced approach to TOD. It is with this attitude that a redefinition of TOD is presented.

Redefining Transit-Oriented Development

The typical definition of TOD is purely descriptive: a mix of uses, at various densities, within a half-mile radius around each transit stop. Though the dimensions of TOD are well documented as the distances people are most likely to walk for a commute trip, there is little clear evidence that a prescribed set of uses or densities will deliver sufficient riders to support functioning transit systems.

> In fact, places like San Francisco demonstrate that TOD cannot be defined by physical form alone. San Franciscans clearly drive less than Bay Area suburban residents who live in relatively dense developments. The difference lies in the way that many San Francisco neighborhoods combine density with appropriate street patterns, access to transit, neighborhood amenities, and an adequate mix of nearby retail, and the fact that the demographic composition of the city is so varied. This contrasts with housing developments in many suburban cities that sit behind walls with only one entrance. Despite densities that are comparable to the city, most residents continue to drive for virtually all trips.

Similarly, locating a mix of uses within walking distance of transit does not necessarily create a place where a child can be dropped off at daycare on the way to the transit stop, where everyday errands can take place on foot, or where a business client can be taken to lunch without using the car. The types of uses located within TOD must be carefully matched with the function of the place and with the needs and desires of residents, workers, and visitors. Indeed, place making may be as important a factor in the success of TOD as access to transit.

> TOD ought to achieve a functional integration of transit and surrounding development, as well as a synergy among all its uses. What scale of development is necessary to make TOD work in different contexts? How much retail and what type is needed to serve the resident population and employees in different types of settings so that they are less car dependent? How can a project strike a balance so as to provide some parking but not so much that it puts a significant financial burden on the development or detracts from the overall pedestrian and transit orientation of the neighborhood? Planners have few answers for these questions.

> Although appropriate physical qualities (e.g., density, distance, and urban form) are essential to make TOD work, a focus solely on these characteristics can obscure the main goal of transit-oriented development, which is not to create a particular physical form but rather to create places that function differently from conventional development. The shortfalls presented by a purely descriptive definition of TOD have led us to augment the definition of TOD with a set of performance benchmarks.

A PERFORMANCE-BASED DEFINITION OF TOD

The term transit-oriented development should be reserved to refer to projects that achieve five main goals:

- LOCATION EFFICIENCY
- RICH MIX OF CHOICES
- VALUE CAPTURE
- PLACE MAKING
- RESOLUTION OF THE TENSION BETWEEN NODE AND PLACE

These goals do not simply represent an urban planner's wish list. Rather, they dovetail closely with the elements of "livability" as expressed in numerous surveys conducted to develop quantifiable "livability indexes" and similar tools. Many, perhaps most, of these indexes include such criteria as access to services and recreation, mobility choice, environmental quality, commute times, and health and safety (e.g., fewer traffic accidents, less pollution). Thus, there is significant overlap between the potential benefits of TOD and the quality of life that people desire.

2.1
New Portland streetcar
integrates seamlessly with
the Portland State University
campus.
(Photo: Mary Volm, City of Portland)

LOCATION EFFICIENCY

Location efficiency, or the conscious placement of homes in proximity to transit systems, is crucial to building a region that is both equitable and efficient. In a region that is dependent on owning a car, individuals with limited resources are at a particular disadvantage. Owning a car is the second largest expense, behind housing costs, for most Americans. For many middle-income households, owning a second car stretches household budgets to the point where home ownership is not an option. For people living in or on the edge of poverty, owning even a single car is often an out-of-reach luxury. However, communities with affordable housing within an easy walk of transit could increase the ability of those with limited resources to participate more fully in our economy.

Key components of location efficiency are:

- **Density**—sufficient customers within walking or bicycling distance of the transit stop to allow the system to run efficiently.
- **Transit accessibility**—transit stations and stops that are centrally or conveniently located within the TOD and service that allows riders to reach their destinations easily.
- **Pedestrian friendliness**—a network of streets within the transit district that is interconnected and scaled to the convenience of pedestrians.

These attributes combine to create a metric that enables one to predict travel behavior to a high degree of accuracy; therefore, evaluating the location efficiency of a site is a key part of defining successful TOD. Groundbreaking work on this topic was undertaken, and then largely forgotten, by the economist Bion J. Arnold, who prepared transportation and transit system plans for many growing municipalities in the early twentieth century. His work clearly predicted land value and travel behavior based on development density and travel access.

> Another, much more recent seminal work, Jeffrey Zupan and Boris Pushkarev's *Public Transportation and Land Use Policy*, published in 1977, examined the relationship between transit use, density, and urban design. They found that auto use declines and transit use rises as a function of both residential density and the presence of dense agglomerations of nonresidential floor space around the transit stop. Their work, which was conducted in the Tri-State region of New York City, New Jersey, and Connecticut, resulted in useful quantitative guidelines that have been relied upon by transit planners ever since. A few researchers have continued to explore the relationships between density, transit use, and automobile ownership. Larry Frank and Gary Pivo's findings in 1994 supported the standards promulgated by Zupan and Pushkarev in the 1970s. In 1996, planners Todd Messenger and Reid Ewing stressed the need for densities in excess of eight units per acre to support bus service on 25-minute headways and more than eleven units per acre to support 15-minute bus service frequencies.

> Advances in computing power and the development of geographic information systems have aided in the evolution of location-efficiency analysis. A team of researchers from the Center for Neighborhood Technology, the Natural Resources Defense Council, and the Surface Transportation Policy Project, led by physicist John Holtzclaw, examined millions of data records for auto ownership and use at the neighborhood level in three metropolitan areas (the San Francisco Bay Area, the Chicago region, and Southern California). Researchers analyzed a number of factors including income, household size, net residential density, transit accessibility, quality of the pedestrian environment, and the existence of neighborhood retail. Using this data, they developed an algorithm for predicting auto ownership and use and household transportation expenditures. The study found that "observed differences in density and transit can explain over

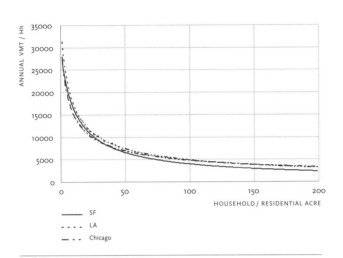

FIG. 2.1

Driving versus Residential Density

(Source: John Holtzclaw et al. 2002.)

2.2

A comfortable environment
for the pedestrian helps transit
succeed. (Photo: Congress for the
New Urbanism.)

3:1 variations in vehicle miles driven per household for a constant level of income and household size." Figure 2.1 depicts this relationship.

> The key variables for measuring location efficiency for a particular site, once household size and income were controlled for, were found to be

· Households per residential acre.
· Zonal transit density, which combines transit service frequency and proximity to the stop or station.
· Pedestrian / bicycle friendliness, which measures street grid and age of housing, with bonuses for traffic-calming measures.

RICH MIX OF CHOICES

Choice is the defining feature of the best neighborhoods. A well-designed neighborhood offers many activities within walking distance for those who do not drive (e.g., the young and the elderly), people who cannot afford cars, and people who choose not to rely on cars to get around. Providing a mix of uses within neighborhoods helps make communities more convenient, because several errands can be completed in one trip, and more affordable because a car is not needed for every trip.

> Similarly, a neighborhood built on the principle of choice provides community residents with a range of housing options—large single-family homes, bungalows, townhouses, live-work, and apartments—so they can find homes that suit their needs as they progress through life's stages and they aren't forced to leave the community. Young people just starting out can live alongside families and individuals who are nearing the end of their careers or enjoying retirement. In fact, most projects will fare better in the market if they accommodate a range of types and uses, because they are less prey to the ups and downs of market cycles. Integrating job sites with housing that is affordable to a broad group of households also helps solve transportation problems by allowing people to live close to work.

> Contrary to the assertions that are sometimes made, TOD is not about "forcing" people to live in a particular way. Rather, TOD offers a wider range of housing, mobility, and shopping choices than conventional suburban development (and much urban development). Rather than leaving residents with no other option than to live in a single-family home, shop at an auto-oriented retail center, drive to their workplace, and chauffer their children to activities, transit-oriented development can offer shopping choices that range from small specialty shops to larger retail outlets, and allow residents to get around on foot, by bicycle, or transit, which greatly enhances the mobility of children and seniors. Even a study that casts doubt on the ability of traditional neighborhood design to significantly reduce driving for shopping purposes finds that residents of walkable neighborhoods with nearby retail value having the option to walk and, in many cases, have chosen their residence in part because they want that option.[2] Another study supports the notion that traditional neighborhood street design has the potential to encourage walking.[3]

> TOD is about expanding, rather than circumscribing, options. Lower-income people with less money to spend on transportation, first-time homebuyers, and others inadequately served by most currently available housing options, such as single parents, the elderly, or the disabled, may particularly value the location efficiency of TOD. For that reason, a commitment to providing high-quality affordable housing in TOD projects seems particularly important.

VALUE CAPTURE

Since transportation is the second-highest consumer expenditure (after housing), success in creating effective transit-oriented development could mean substantial economic value capture. The challenges, however, to actually capturing this value are considerable. This is because success requires

- Frequent, high-quality transit service
- Good connections between transit and the community
- Community amenities and a dedication to place making
- Scorekeeping and attention to financial returns

TABLE 2.1—THE BENEFICIARIES OF VALUE IN GOOD URBAN DESIGN

STAKEHOLDERS	SHORT-TERM VALUE	LONG-TERM VALUE
Landowners	Potential for increased land values	
Funders (short-term)	Potential for greater security of investment	
Developers	Quicker approvals (reduced cost and uncertainty) Increased public support Higher sales values (profitability) Distinctiveness (greater product differentiation) Increased funding potential (public/private partnering) Allows difficult sites to be tackled	Better reputation Future collaborations more likely
Design Professionals	Increased workload and repeat commissions from high-quality, stable clients	Enhanced professional reputation
Investors (long-term)	Higher rental returns Increased asset value Reduced running costs Competitive investment edge	Maintenance of value/income Reduced life cycle maintenance costs Better resale value Higher quality long-term tenants
Management Agents	Easy maintenance if high-quality materials	
Occupiers (tenants)		Happier workforce Better productivity Increased client confidence Reduced running costs
Public Interests	Regenerative potential (encouraging other development) Reduced public/private discord	Reduced public expenditure (on crime prevention/urban management/ urban maintenance/health) More time for positive planning Increased economic viability for neighboring uses Increased local tax revenue More sustainable environment
Community Interests		Better security and less crime Increased cultural viability Better quality of life More inclusive public space A more equitable/accessible environment Greater civic pride (sense of community) Reinforced sense of place Higher property prices

(Source: Bartlett School of Planning, 2001, p. 29.)

Capturing value, accrued either to the household or the community, should be a key objective of TOD, thus allowing individuals to lead affordable lifestyles and letting communities reinvest the profits derived from their good work.

> A recent study in the United Kingdom used a case study approach to assess the economic, social, and environmental value of good urban design; it found a variety of benefits including lower maintenance costs, enhanced regeneration, and increased public support. Table 2.1 outlines the stakeholders identified in the study and the value capture each takes from the project. It provides a useful framework for our own examination of transit-oriented development, which can be considered a type of "good" urban design. It also defines the stakeholders in projects and indicates those for whom value capture means financial returns.

> For local governments, value capture can mean higher tax revenues from increased sales and property values. For the transit agency, value capture means both lease revenue from joint development and increased revenue from fare boxes. A third outcome for transit providers is reduced access cost. As the Arlington case study shows, TOD can dramatically increase the proportion of riders who access the system on foot, which is a much cheaper way to attract passengers than dedicating land for parking or operating feeder bus service. Developers are obviously looking for return on their investments, which can be stable longer in TOD communities. The sale of Arlington's Market Common project for $166 million in February 2003—the most expensive sale on record in the nation for some years—is convincing evidence of TOD's enduring value. In addition to the attributes for good urban design listed above, employers can capture value in reduced employee commute times.

> Transit-oriented development also offers value capture in terms of reduced household

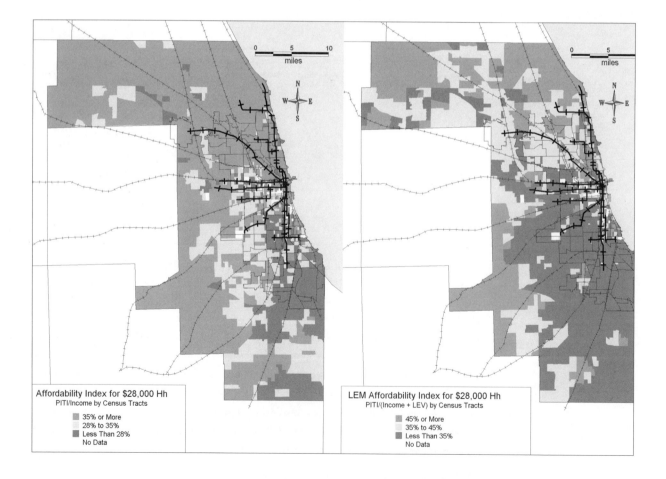

Affordability Index for $28,000 Hh
PITI/Income by Census Tracts
- 35% or More
- 28% to 35%
- Less Than 28%
- No Data

LEM Affordability Index for $28,000 Hh
PITI/(Income + LEV) by Census Tracts
- 45% or More
- 35% to 45%
- Less Than 35%
- No Data

2.3

Even regular transit users need access to the car, and car-sharing programs provide hourly rentals.
(Photo: Scott Bernstein.)

FIG. 2.2 [LEFT]

Affordability Index: depicts portions of Chicago region that are affordable for moderate-income homebuyers in normal circumstances and portions that became affordable when reduced transportation costs in transit-oriented neighborhoods are taken into account.
(Source: Center for Neighborhood Technology.)

expenditures on transportation and increased opportunity for wealth capture through home ownership. The Holtzclaw study referred to earlier calculated household transportation costs at the neighborhood level by using auto ownership and use records in each of the three metropolitan areas to impute costs for owning and operating a motor vehicle. The work demonstrated that households in denser, transit-rich neighborhoods have significantly lower transportation expenditures. Figure 2.2 depicts the portions of the Chicago region that are affordable for moderate income home buyers in normal circumstances and the portions of the Chicago region that are affordable when reduced transportation costs in denser, transit-rich neighborhoods are taken into account.

> For residents of TOD, capturing value involves two things: acknowledging that the value of accessibility is already reflected in the cost of housing, all other things being equal, and finding ways to give households in these neighborhoods credit for the transportation savings they experience from owning fewer cars and driving them less. A number of studies have demonstrated that proximity to transit tends to increase the value of a home, while proximity to a highway tends to decrease its value.[4] The Location Efficient Mortgage (LEM), developed by the Center for Neighborhood Technology, the Natural Resources Defense Council, the Surface Transportation Policy Project, and Fannie Mae, was a pilot project in three cities that attributed a portion of reduced transportation expenditures from living in denser, transit-accessible neighborhoods as additional income when qualifying for a mortgage. The program received modest support from Fannie Mae, which has since derived its own product, the Smart Commute Mortgage, which offers a smaller credit based solely on transit proximity in many more cities.[5]

> Capturing value for residents also entails providing amenities to enable the reduction of driving. These amenities include child care facilities at transit stations, such as at the Tamien Station in San Jose; bike parking and rental, as provided by the Bike Station in Long Beach and at other transit stations in California; and transportation demand management programs, which provide services to encourage transit use, such as guaranteed rides home from work.

> Even those living in location-efficient neighborhoods have the occasional need for an automobile. In response, a variety of schemes for car sharing have emerged, first in Europe and increasingly in the United States. Typically a variety of cars are purchased and distributed throughout neighborhood locations, and car-sharing customers or members of a car-sharing cooperative are able to access them on an hourly basis within an easy walk or bus ride of their home. This approach contrasts with auto rentals agencies, which are concentrated at airports or in downtown locations and require rental for a whole day. Car sharing is moving rapidly into the American market under a number of different business models, including hourly rental and member cooperatives. A recent survey found that car-sharing programs were being introduced in about a dozen American cities, including Chicago, Seattle, and San Francisco, and that mainstream car rentals were also considering adding the hourly rental feature to their product lines.

WALKING AND TRANSIT USE IN TRANSIT-ORIENTED COMMUNITIES

To explore the relationship between transit use and walking in transit-oriented communities, an analysis was undertaken of 2000 Census Journey to Work Data in three regions. Using GIS technology, we created half-mile-radius buffer areas around selected transit stops and examined the mode for the journey to work, along with some other variables including autos per household, median income, and persons per square mile. We selected four suburban town center stations in Arlington County, Virginia, two urban stations in San Francisco, three urban stations in Chicago, and three suburban stations in Evanston, Illinois. Table 2.2 depicts these findings, along with the comparable values for the county in which the stations are located.

> We found high levels of both walking and transit use at each of the stations, much higher than the levels in the county as a whole. The urban downtowns and the Evanston stops had particularly high walking rates for the journey to work, indicating that many downtown residents both live and work downtown and that transit supported that lifestyle. This is a fairly recent trend, as the moderate density at San Francisco's Embarcadero Station and Chicago's La Salle Station indicate. The level of walking to work was not high, however, at the four stations in Arlington County, where as noted in chapter 7, the pedestrian environment was neglected until recently. Arlington County is part of the capital region, and lies within easy access of the many jobs in Washington, D.C., which is surely a major factor in the large percentage of transit trips to work.

TABLE 2.2—JOURNEY TO WORK MODE SHARE IN TODS

COMMUNITY	TRANSIT SHARE	WALK SHARE	DROVE ALONE	AUTOS/ HOUSEHOLD	MEDIAN INCOME	PERSONS/ SQUARE MILE	TYPE
Arlington County, VA	23	5	55	1.4	63,001		County
Court House	37	8	43	1.1	55,567	13,988	Suburban Center
Clarendon	34	6	47	1.3	64,590	10,413	Suburban Center
Rosslyn	38	10	42	1.1	54,022	14,555	Suburban Center
Ballston	38	7	42	1.2	66,351	15,263	Suburban Center
San Francisco, CA	31	8	41	1.1	55,221		County
Church / 24th	34	6	38	1.1	64,841	29,148	Urban Neighborhood
Embarcadero	24	44	19	0.5	42,949	8,676	Urban Downtown
Cook County	17	4	63	1.4	45,922		County
LaSalle	25	37	25	0.7	61,092	10,580	Urban Downtown
Chicago/Fullerton	44	8	36	1.1	77,671	25,094	Urban Neighborhood
Chicago/Berwyn	38	5	42	0.7	32,711	32,567	Urban Neighborhood
Evanston/Davis	19	24	42	1	42,575	11,986	Suburban Center
Evanston/Dempster	22	14	49	1.2	52,971	11,067	Suburban Neighborhood
Evanston/Main	55	22	7	1.3	61,956	11,863	Suburban Neighborhood

PLACE MAKING

One of the greatest limitations of the current crop of TODs is that not enough attention has been paid to making them attractive and pedestrian-friendly places. Trips to the store, to visit neighbors, to the park, or to sit in a coffee shop and watch the world go by should be both negotiable on foot and a delight to those walking. If transit is inserted into a healthy pedestrian environment, then pedestrians can easily become transit riders. This assumes these healthy pedestrian environments also have some density and interconnected streets. However, if transit is not convenient, not appropriately frequent, or not linked with the desired destinations of local riders, then the transit-oriented aspect of the development will fail.

> A recent British publication, *The Urban Design Compendium,* makes a case for the importance of high-quality urban design in development and revitalization efforts. The authors argue that "many urban regeneration and development projects require public funding to help subsidize the costs of buildings, infrastructure and open spaces and to make the projects viable. The quality of design is becoming one of the most important criteria in determining whether a project should be eligible for public funding." The key aspects of quality urban design are defined as follows. These elements, though not specifically focused on TOD, form the basis for urban design decisions in places seeking to create healthy pedestrian environments.

Places for People

For places to be well used and well loved, they must be safe, comfortable, varied, and attractive. They also need to be distinctive and offer variety, choice, and fun. Vibrant places offer opportunities for meeting people, playing in the street, and watching the world go by.

Enrich the Existing

New development should enrich the qualities of existing urban places. This means encouraging a distinctive response that arises from and complements its setting. This applies at every scale— the region, the city, the town, the neighborhood, and the street.

Make Connections

Places need to be easy to get to and should be integrated physically and visually with their surroundings. This requires paying attention to how people can get around by foot, bicycle, public transportation, and the car—and in that order.

Work with the Landscape

Places should achieve a balance between the natural and man-made environment and utilize each site's intrinsic resources—the climate, landform, landscape, and ecology—to maximize energy conservation and amenity.

Mix Uses and Forms

Stimulating, enjoyable, and convenient places meet a variety of demands and provide amenities to the widest possible range of users. They also weave together different building forms, uses, tenures, and densities.

Manage the Investment

For projects to be developable and sustainable, they must be economically viable, well managed, and well maintained. This means understanding the market considerations of developers, ensuring long-term commitment from the community and local authorities, defining appropriate delivery mechanisms, and seeing this component as integral to the design process.

Design for Change

New development needs to be flexible enough to respond to future changes in use, lifestyle, and demography. This means designing for energy and resource efficiency; creating flexibility in the use of property, public spaces, and service infrastructure; and introducing new approaches to transportation, traffic management, and parking.

RESOLVING THE TENSION BETWEEN NODE VERSUS PLACE

A final element of transit-oriented development involves the tension that exists between the role of a transit station or stop as a "node" in a regional transportation network and the station's role as a "place" in a neighborhood. As a generator of travel, a transit stop attracts activity and is a desirable place in which to live, open a shop, or locate a workplace. At the same time, it is an interchange point serving a specific function in a regional network, which is in turn part of a metropolitan economy composed of employment centers and residential areas. The node and place distinction was made by Dutch professors Luca Bertolini and Tejo Spit in their book *Cities on Rails*. They argued that "the unique challenge of the development of node-places is the need to deal, at the same time, with both transport and urban development issues." A key node-place tension exists between the station's role as an access point for people arriving by train, bus, car, bike, or foot, and its role as a vibrant, pleasant livable place. Obviously design issues abound here, including the footprint of the station in the community, the degree of integration of customer services into the station itself, and the location and treatment of both parking and bus drop-off. At the core of TOD is the pedestrian, and ensuring that the walker has precedence over other modes is an imperative.

> Beyond urban design issues are considerations of the role of the node or station in the transportation network and the type of place it is in the region. While mixed-use development and jobs-housing balance are goals, some stations serve primarily as collectors for people traveling to work, while others serve primarily as destinations at the work end of the trip. Transit-oriented development can help to balance the use of the station somewhat, but it is unlikely in and of itself to alter the station's role in the regional network or metropolitan economy. In this case, mixed use around a predominantly residential neighborhood is likely to mean customer-serving retail and service businesses, such as restaurants and cafés, food stores, dry cleaners, and day care, with employment centers being targeted for the kinds of professional services that are needed—such as attorneys, tax preparers, and accountants.

> At the same time, stations at employment centers are unlikely to include single-family residential uses. If residential use is to occur, it will probably come about as the area evolves into a 24-hour destination, with entertainment leading the way and multifamily, live-work, and other specialized residential products following. Understanding the station's role in the transit system is key to planning for development around it, and one goal should be to balance the overwhelming peak hour nature of transit system travel by incorporating a mix of nonwork uses into most sites.

2.4

Brisbane's new busway offers
the permanence and design
quality of a rail system.
(Photo: Courtesy of Queensland
Transport. Photo by Les Dixon,
Corporate Image Photography.)

A New Typology for TOD

The standard definition of TOD, with modest exceptions, tends to force a one-size-fits-all set of
solutions onto the different types of sites served by transit and the different types of transit that
serve communities. Peter Calthorpe's work did identify "urban TOD" and "neighborhood TOD,"
and this approach recognized the differences between the types of places that ought to be located directly on a fixed transit line and those that were best located where only feeder
service was possible. Indeed, this approach substantially broadened our thinking about the
"catchment area" for "walk and ride" transit users.

> But regions are sophisticated places with a multitude of conditions to serve. The types of
strategies that might be appropriate in older neighborhoods close to downtown are certainly different from those that might work in suburban contexts, even with similar density goals. The
TOD typology discussed in this section is an attempt to recognize the important differences
between places and destinations within regions and then to identify appropriate performance
and descriptive benchmarks for these places. Our intent is not to define TOD narrowly, but to lay
out some of the complexity that must be addressed and simultaneously set boundaries for the
range of choices so they are both manageable and recognizable.

GENERAL TYPOLOGY OF TOD PLACES WITHIN A METROPOLITAN REGION

There is a danger in typologies that seek to strictly classify TOD. Many previous efforts have narrowly defined TOD as a set of numerical goals. However, transit systems and locations vary greatly in their characteristics and their suitability for TOD. We should not expect the same results from a project at the core of a metropolitan area and one in the suburbs, just as we cannot necessarily hope for the same outcome in Dallas as in Chicago. By focusing on quantifiable functional outcomes, our definition of TOD accounts for both different degrees of success and the limitations of individual places. Just as a project should be judged as more or less successful TOD, two projects with the same functional outcomes in very different places should to be assessed within the context of those places.

> Our approach is to use case studies of built projects and mature places to set loose boundaries on a range of TOD types. These boundaries are simply goals at this point; they will need to be revised and refined as more exemplary developments come on-line and their performance can be assessed. Thus, the following typology of places is put forward as a starting point for defining the common types of TOD and distinguishing them from each other in terms of their role and function within regional systems.

Urban Downtown

In recent years, regional and global economic dynamics have shifted a significant portion of jobs from central cities to the suburbs, causing the role of our downtowns to change. Downtowns are emerging as civic and cultural centers, rather than hubs of employment activity. People are moving back downtown, seeking proximity to cultural richness. This fundamental (and probably long-term) change has enormous implications for the character of central cities, the role of outlying areas, and the way transit systems serve these new metropolises.

> Several important considerations inform how urban downtowns relate to TOD. First, the history and size of a downtown is such that it is often served by several types of transit and is typically a primary transfer point for various modes. Second, as downtowns change and are reshaped, individual districts that emphasize different types of functions and uses often emerge. For example, South Beach in San Francisco has emerged as the city's new high-density neighborhood, complete with a range of neighborhood-serving retail uses within a few blocks of the city's financial district. Both South Beach and the financial district are considered within the boundaries of downtown, but have different functions and require different orientations to transit.

Urban Neighborhood

Virtually every region has a set of historic neighborhoods that surround the downtown and provide housing, shopping, and services for employees and their families. Often these neighborhoods were built on an extension of the downtown street grid and were served by streetcar or heavy-rail. Today, urban neighborhoods provide moderate to high density housing in settings that are quite livable: shopping is typically located along a central shopping street or key crossroads, schools and parks are integrated into the neighborhood, streets are designed for multiple purposes, and frequent transit is within a 5- to 10-minute walk. These neighborhoods provide affordability and convenience for residents, as well as a vitality that is attractive to urban dwellers.

> Urban neighborhoods form the backbone of a compact, transit-friendly region. In many regions, these neighborhoods could form a transit corridor, for either rapid bus or light-rail transit. By design, they provide a substantial amount of a region's high-density and (in some cases) affordable housing in settings designed to support healthy pedestrian activity. Since transit service is frequent, residents have remarkable accessibility to employment and entertainment opportunities throughout the region. The often historic nature of these neighborhoods, combined with an active street life, allows these places to become entertainment destinations in themselves.

Suburban Town Center

Suburbs are evolving in an entirely new pattern. Small towns engulfed by growth are becoming important job centers in the same way that central cities used to be. The result is the development of suburban town centers, which, while they may need to connect into the traditional radial system—for urban downtowns are still core job centers—may also have developed the need for their own connective tissue. Helping these suburban agglomerations evolve into vital 24-hour locations is one of the challenges that TOD can help address, and communities discussed in this book, including Addison, Texas, and Arlington County, Virginia, can provide hints on how to do it. Bedroom communities are maturing into places where there is a demand for high-quality shopping opportunities and transit connections to other nearby suburbs. Families living in residential subdivisions want their children to be able to walk to school or a park, not to have to drive them there.

2.5
Seven dwelling units per acre is considered the minimum density for transit service.
(Photo: Congress for the New Urbanism.)

2.6
Development at densities of 30 dwelling units per acre and higher can support both bus and rail transit.
(Photo: Congress for the New Urbanism.)

Suburban Neighborhood

This is a suburban community located on a light-rail or rapid bus line, with access to either a sub-regional center or to the urban downtown. This neighborhood offers the opportunity for some densification of land uses around the stop, with multifamily residential use close to the station and single-family detached housing farther away. Typically, if local transit is provided, it is either peak hour bus service, with infrequent service the rest of the day, or paratransit on-demand service. There may be neighborhood- and commuter-serving retail near the station.

Neighborhood Transit Zone

Typically, this is a transit stop (bus, streetcar, or light-rail) with limited neighborhood retail or office space in a largely residential area.

Commuter Town

A commuter town is a freestanding community outside of the conurbation, served by rail or bus commuter service to the downtown core. The station area can be developed as a "main street" center, with neighborhood retail, professional offices, and some multifamily residential housing within the core of the TOD zone. Typically, this type of community will support only peak hour service to the downtown and local paratransit service.

A NOTE ABOUT TRANSIT TECHNOLOGIES

In many cities there is a raging debate between advocates of light-rail and advocates of evolving types of bus service. Advocates of one mode or another tout their advantages with zeal, and dismiss other modes with disdain. The whole debate is based on a false dichotomy. The question should not be about a choice between bus and rail—it should be about which technology will best serve the community's vision of how it wants to grow. In most metropolitan areas, there is a need for a range of transit technologies—from car sharing and employer provided shuttles to local, express, and rapid bus service, to streetcars, light-rail, and commuter rail. The following are a few simple principles about transit service types.

Frequency: After density, the most important questions about transit have to do with service frequency and speed. These are the attributes that can most directly influence people to choose transit over driving. Autos are convenient, so to approach that convenience, transit headways must be reduced. Fifteen-minute headways begin to approximate the convenience of the car.

Speed: In order for transit to compete, journey times must be competitive with travel time by auto, including the time it takes to access the system. Because transit vehicles stop to pick up passengers, this means that running time needs to be faster than car traffic, and typically that can only be achieved by providing transit with a separated guideway—either a rail guideway, a busway, or a high occupancy vehicle lane. An exciting new development is the emergence of rapid bus systems, which combine attractive design features of light-rail—low floors, distinctive stations—with separated lanes and guideways and technologies that allow the bus preferential access at traffic signals. While these systems are still in the early stages, they may offer the speed of light-rail at lower cost. These rapid bus systems may be an attractive alternative for many communities that don't wish to develop at the densities needed to support light-rail. Other communities may view them as an interim step to building ridership and transit supportive development.

Regional Context: Transit systems in a region will employ a variety of methods to deliver service. A region with a strong downtown may still rely on a radial fixed route system to serve the downtown, but as suburban town centers develop, it may be important to serve them with more adaptive transit technologies, such as rapid bus, paratransit, and even car sharing.[6] The TOD typology that follows may help in understanding the role of different technologies in differing parts of the region.

Capacity: The heavier a transit technology, the more it costs, and the more people per hour it serves. The relationship to density is quite clear. Because of the larger capacity of each vehicle, rail operating costs, particularly labor costs, may be lower than those for bus, and rail systems commonly capture a larger percentage of their operating costs from the fare box than do bus systems. Two metrics can be used to combine cost and capacity: capital costs per passenger mile and operating cost per passenger mile.

Attracting Development: The evidence is quite clear that rail transit, all other things being equal, attracts more intense development and increases return on investment. Developers and employers can count on a rail line to be there, and rail has a more positive image than bus. The rapid bus technologies are so new that there is little evidence about their attractiveness for development. Most bus rapid transit projects cited as having land-use impacts are in other countries with different systems of planning and land use—Curitiba, Brazil, Ottawa, Canada, for instance. Systems in Ottawa and Brisbane have been shown to attract development. The most well developed system in this country is in Pittsburgh. The Pittsburgh West Busway has principally developed along a park-and-ride model rather than a transit-oriented development model, limiting opportunities along the corridor. An analysis by David Wohlwill of the Port Authority of Allegheny County found that fifty-four development projects valued at $302 million had occurred along Pittsburgh's four busways. The study, like many looking at development along rail lines, did not differentiate between development attracted by the transit line and development that would have occurred anyway. A similar study of the economic impact of the Dallas light-rail system found that "Between 1997 and 2001, the mean value of 47 office properties near DART increased 24.7%, compared with an increase of 11.5% for 121 properties not near the stations, giving the DART office buildings a 53% advantage."

> Developers and homebuyers alike seem to be attracted to the permanence of rail transit, and also to intangibles such as service quality. The more that Bus Rapid Transit can approach these features of rail in its design: clearly differentiated stations, dedicated guideways, attractive, modern looking vehicles, and speeds competitive with the automobile, the more it will succeed in providing an attractive development climate.

> The right answer to the bus versus light-rail debate is this: It depends on what the region wants to accomplish.

Applying the Typology

Transit-oriented development is about creating and exploiting synergies: between the community and the region, between jobs and housing, between levels of density and levels of transit service, between people and a vibrant community life, and among different generations, income levels, and people. At the heart of transit-oriented development is the pedestrian, and the purpose of mixed uses is to encourage the pedestrian environment. In successful transit-oriented communities in Europe, the share of trips made by walking is equal to or higher than the transit share, because the entire transit system supports the pedestrian. Pedestrian-oriented urban design tends to increase transit's share of all trips if the scale of the pedestrian improvement is large enough and transit service is of good quality.

> The typology should be applied regionally at first, and then used to understand each particular site. It should be used with care. We have attempted to cite only the lower bounds of densities in each case, for instance, and it should be noted that housing densities are expressed as dwelling units per residential acre, not as gross densities, and that densities should be highest next to the station and scale down as you reach the quarter- and half-mile radius around the stop. There is a direct correlation between increasing densities and increased transit-service frequencies. The densities, however, are derived from the literature and from the calculation of actual densities at TOD projects examined in this book.

TABLE 2.3—TOD TYPOLOGY

TOD TYPE	LAND-USE MIX	MINIMUM HOUSING DENSITY	HOUSING TYPES	SCALE	REGIONAL CONNECTIVITY	TRANSIT MODES	FREQUENCIES	EXAMPLES
Urban Downtown	Primary office center Urban entertainment Multifamily housing Retail	>60 units/acre	Multifamily Loft	High	High Hub of radial system	All modes	<10 minutes	Printers Row (Chicago) LoDo (Denver) South Beach (San Francisco)
Urban Neighborhood	Residential Retail Class B commercial	>20 units/acre	Multifamily Loft Townhome Single family	Medium	Medium access to downtown Subregional circulation	Light-rail Streetcar Rapid bus Local bus	10 minutes peak 20 minutes offpeak	Mockingbird (Dallas) Fullerton (Chicago) Barrio Logan (San Diego)
Suburban Center	Primary office center Urban entertainment Multifamily housing Retail	>50 units/acre	Multifamily Loft Townhome	High	High access to downtown Subregional hub	Rail Streetcar Rapid bus Local bus Paratransit	10 minutes peak 10–15 minutes offpeak	Arlington County (Virginia) Addison Circle (Dallas) Evanston (Illinois)
Suburban Neighborhood	Residential Neighborhood retail Local office	>12 units/acre	Multifamily Townhome Single family	Moderate	Medium access to suburban center Access to downtown	Light-rail Rapid bus Local bus Paratransit	20 minutes peak 30 minutes offpeak	Crossings (Mountain View, CA) Ohlone-Chynoweth (San Jose, CA)
Neighborhood Transit Zone	Residential Neighborhood retail	>7 units/acre	Townhome Single family	Low access to a center	Low	Local bus Paratransit	25–30 minutes Demand responsive	
Commuter Town Center	Retail center Residential	>12 units/acre	Multifamily Townhome Single family	Low	Low access to downtown	Commuter rail Rapid bus	Peak service Demand responsive	Prairie Crossing (Illinois) Suisun City (California)

> More research is needed into density, trip generation, parking generation, the relationship between the pedestrian environment and share of trips by pedestrian, bicycle, transit, and auto, as well as many more factors. It is our hope that Table 2.3 will serve as a guide for such evaluation. It is presented as a starting point for the next generation of TOD, drawing upon the performance-based definition presented in this chapter.

Conclusion

Given the proven demand for TOD, the timing is right to both expedite its adoption and improve its performance. However, in order for TOD to move from the demonstration phase to a commonly recognized series of real estate products, we must define TOD in terms of both functional characteristics—density, mix of uses, level of transit service, and street connectivity—and descriptive benchmarks—location efficiency, mix of choices, value capture, and place making. Only with a more rigorous understanding of the performance of the various types of TOD will we truly understand how to work gradually toward creating products that communities immediately recognize and thus expedite their permitting, that lenders can easily invest in, and that developers understand implicitly. Our goal is to define TOD so that it is easily replicable but still has enough flexibility that it can respond to the different realities of American communities. This TOD typology and the subsequent chapters are intended to further our collective wisdom in this area and move us toward this goal.

NOTES

1   Our work in this chapter benefits from an ongoing professional dialogue on transit-oriented development with Dena Belzer and Gerald Autler, whose paper for our project identified some of elements of a new outcome-based definition of TOD that we have built upon in this chapter.

2   Susan Handy and Kelly Clifton. 2001. Local Shopping as a Strategy for Reducing Automobile Travel. *Transportation* 28,4:317–46.

3   Jayanthi Rajamani, Chandra Bhat, Susan Handy, Gerritt Knaap, and Yan Song. 2001. Assessing the Impact of Urban Form Measures in Nonwork Trip Mode Choice. *Transportation Research Record*, forthcoming.

4   Robert Cervero and Michael Duncan. 2002. Land Value Impacts of Light Rail in San Diego County. At http://www.realtors.org/smartgrowth/.

5   For more details on the Location Efficient Mortgage, see http://www.locationefficiency.org. For more details on the Smart Commute Mortgage, see http://www.efanniemae.com/hcd/singlefamily/mortgageproducts/smartcommute.html.

6   Robert Cervero, *Transit Metropolis* (Washinton, D.C.: Island Press, 1998). Cervero developed this notion of adaptive transit, and remains a refreshingly clear-headed evaluator of the role of different approaches to delivering transit and their corresponding impact on urban form.

REFERENCES

Arnold, Bion J. 1905. *Report on the Chicago Transportation Problem*. New York: McGraw Publishing Company.

Bartlett School of Planning. 2001. *The Value of Good Urban Design*. London: Thomas Telford, Ltd.

Belzer, Dena and Gerald Autler. 2002. Transit-Oriented Development: Moving from Rhetoric to Reality. Great American Station Foundation and Brookings Center on Urban and Metropolitan Policy. Washington, D.C.: Brookings Institution. At http://www.transittown.org.

Bertolini, Luca and Tejo Spit. 1998. *Cities on Rails: The Redevelopment of Railway Station Areas*. New York and London: Routledge.

Calthorpe, Peter. 1993. *Next American Metropolis*. Princeton: Princeton Architectural Press.

Frank, L. D. and G. Pivo. 1994. Impacts of Mixed Use and Density on Utilization of Three Modes of Travel. *Transportation Research Record* 1466:44–52.

Holtzclaw, John, Robert Clear, Hank Dittmar, David Goldstein, and Peter Haas. 2002. Location Efficiency: Neighborhood and Socioeconomic Characteristics Determine Auto Ownership and Use. *Transportation Planning and Technology* 25.

Kretikos, Eleni. 2003. Market Common Fetches Rare Price. *Washington Business Journal,* February 28, 2003. At http://www.washingtonbusinessjournals.com.

Llewelyn-Davies. 2002. *Urban Design Compendium*. London: English Partnerships and The Housing Corporation.

Messenger, Todd and Reid Ewing. 1996. Transit-Oriented Development in the Sunbelt: Get Real (and Empirical). *Transportation Research Record* 1552:

Orski, Kenneth. 2002. Innovation Briefs. At http://www.innobriefs.com/.

Roberts, John. 1990. In *The Greening of Urban Transport*, edited by Tolley and Rodney. London: Belhaven Press.

Wohlwill, David. "BRT and TOD in Pittsburgh," Presentation at Railvolution 2002, October 5, 2002.

Weinstein, Bernard and Terry Clower. "DART Light Rail's Effect on Taxable Property Valuations and Transit-Oriented Development" (Denton, TX: University of North Texas Center for Economic Development and Research, January 2003), at http://www.dart.org.

Zupan, Jeffrey and Boris Pushkarev. 1977. *Public Transportation and Land Use Policy*. Bloomington: Indiana University Press.

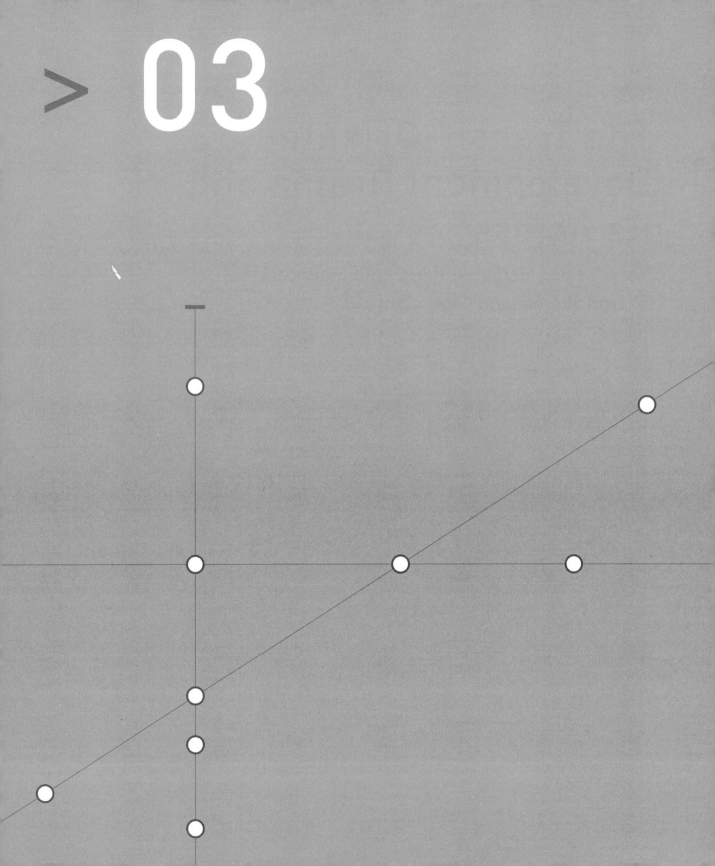

> **03**

> 03

The Transit-Oriented Development Drama and Its Actors

Dena Belzer, Gerald Autler, Judith Espinosa, Sharon Feigon, and Gloria Ohland

The Cast of Characters

In the late nineteenth century and the early part of the twentieth century transit and urban development were linked far more closely than they are today. At the very least, it was taken for granted that transit was needed to serve new development as cities grew, and in many cases developers actually took on the task of building transit lines to serve their projects. Rail lines were such an important part of the transportation system that they were, for the most part, privately financed and operated, and economically viable without subsidies. The automobile, meanwhile, was a much smaller force in society, and issues like parking had little or no importance. And the lack of zoning (which only became a significant force after the *Euclid v. Ambler* case in 1926) and other land-use controls meant that, for better or for worse, local governments played a much smaller role in regulating development.[1]

> Today, transit-oriented development (TOD) involves many different actors, with a much wider range of concerns. Transit agencies are responsible for building transit, often with the involvement of multiple public agencies; as subsidized public operations they often come under pressure to maximize their revenues and minimize their subsidies. Local governments are responsible for planning, facilitating, and shaping development while remaining accountable to constituents, and developers are responsible for generating returns for their lenders and investors.

> All of these entities—not to mention transit riders, neighbors, and the public at large—may have different ideas about what a particular project should accomplish. And these ideas have grown more complex. For example, the predominance of automobiles and low density development in most areas means that people expect parking (and often free parking) at rail stations,

office buildings, and shops. And transit agencies may see large revenue streams from ground leases on land they own as a good way to show that they are being "fiscally responsible."

> Like all other complex assets, no one agency or interest can make TOD work by itself. In order to fulfill its potential, TOD needs to have the benefit of goals, resources, and policies that are dependably and accountably aligned around the task at hand. This chapter focuses on the complex and often contradictory roles played by the various actors and provides some recommendations on how each actor could help reform the process and facilitate better projects.

Stage Fright

The large number of actors in TOD projects creates an obvious logistical challenge, that of coaxing a coherent and effective performance out of players who may have very different ideas about what that performance should constitute. Theatrical productions have directors, but, with few exceptions, no one has that kind of authority for overseeing TOD projects. Turf battles, tunnel vision, and disagreements about project outcomes—however legitimate these may be—are all part of the challenge.

> No single actor can completely set the agenda, and all players have the tendency to think too small when it comes to setting TOD policy. They often focus on what they perceive as their main function—running trains, for example, or encouraging development—rather than on larger goals. Even relatively progressive transit agencies, like Bay Area Rapid Transit (BART), which are actively engaged in creating station area plans, often do not link their efforts to the local jurisdiction's larger planning activities. For their part, local governments often fail to take on comprehensive planning initiatives around transit stations or, at best, limit their activities to pedestrian improvements and streetscapes without considering the broader land-use context.

> Dallas Area Rapid Transit (DART) has assigned a full-time staff person to facilitate development around its stations, but at the writing of this chapter in 2002 the City of Dallas had few policies in place to encourage TOD—not even provisions for reduced parking. In nearby Plano, in contrast, the city assigned a staff member to work on transit and TOD, produced a comprehensive downtown development plan and a parking management plan.

> TOD also often suffers from a wide variety of disparate views about what the project should accomplish. Each actor brings different goals, priorities, and interests to the table. A lack of definitional clarity exacerbates this problem because there is no widespread agreement about what TOD should accomplish from a functional standpoint. Should TOD aim to maximize revenue for the transit agency through lucrative ground leases? Or to minimize the use of automobiles? Should TOD be designed to maximize ridership? Or to help revitalize the station area? These sometimes incompatible goals can result in policies that work at cross-purposes.

The list below lays out some of the goals that may
be pursued by each actor in a TOD development.

TRANSIT AGENCY:

· Maximize monetary return on land;

· Maximize ridership; and

· Capture value in the long term.

RIDERS:

· Create/maintain high level of parking;

· Improve transit service and station access;

· Increase mobility choices;

· Develop convenient mix of uses near station; and

· Maximize pedestrian access.

NEIGHBORS:

· Maintain/increase property values;

· Minimize traffic impact;

· Increase mobility choices;

· Improve access to transit, services, and jobs;

· Enhance neighborhood livability; and

· Foster redevelopment.

LOCAL GOVERNMENT:

· Maximize tax revenues;

· Foster economic vitality;

· Please constituents; and

· Redevelop underutilized land.

FEDERAL GOVERNMENT:

· Protect "public interest" and set limits on how
federal investments can be used.

DEVELOPER/LENDER:

· Maximize return on investment;

· Minimize risk, complexity; and

· Ensure value in the long term.

3.1
Community stakeholders and
an expert panel meet to plan
the TOD at the Lake and
Pulaski in Chicago.
(Photo: Center for Neighborhood
Technology.)

3.2
Charrettes offer community residents a "hands-on" opportunity to engage positively around development issues.
(Photo: National Charrette Institute.)

3.3
The Chicagoland Transportation and Air Quality Commission produced a citizen's regional plan in 2002 calling for a network of TODs.
(Photo: Center for Neighborhood Technology.)

Many of these goals—such as maintaining a high level of station parking and maximizing pedestrian access to the station—are in conflict with one another. Even a single actor may have goals that are incompatible, or that require careful balancing if they are to be reconciled. A transit agency that prioritizes maximizing the monetary return on its land will probably make choices that lead to suboptimal results from the standpoint of location efficiency, favoring commercial development instead of housing, for example. This doesn't address the goals of constituents who may want to live in a mixed-use neighborhood surrounding the station, and it may lead to a project that generates less ridership than one with a better mix of commercial and residential development.

> Given the inherent complexity of TOD, the lack of an overall vision and streamlined structure for regulation and implementation is an enormous handicap. Projects must move forward in an environment of complex and sometimes contradictory regulations, lack of coordination among different actors, and the absence of a clear vision and the leadership necessary to implement it.

> There must be a better understanding of what TOD projects can and should accomplish, how goals must be aligned, and the role of each actor in the larger decision-making and development process. Without a clear functional definition of TOD—from which a coherent set of goals can be derived—there is no framework for weighing trade-offs and making choices about how to balance competing goals. Although competing goals can be a problem in any large project, the nature of TOD and the number of actors involved make the challenge even more significant.

Balancing the Tension between Place and Node

The role of transit in creating a link between individual places and the broader region means that transit-oriented development, unlike other forms of development, should explicitly perform a dual function as both a "node" within a larger regional or metropolitan system and a "place" in its own right.

> This balance is difficult to achieve, and is one of the main problems afflicting less-than-optimal projects. The need for balance affects virtually every aspect of the project, from physical layout and design to the appropriate development program. Some actors see their interests as connected to the station's role as a node, whereas others care more about the quality of the place. For example, a common complaint is that most transit agencies have little interest in stations as anything but nodes, even when agencies participate as property owners. And citizens who clamor for more parking (a node function) may be at odds with neighbors who complain about increased traffic in their neighborhood (a quality of place concern). All too often there are few or no advocates (and little or no money) to keep the idea of place on the agenda.

> The seemingly mundane issue of parking epitomizes the tension between node and place: Parking is tied to a station's role as a node in a larger regional system (since it facilitates station access for drivers), and there is often tremendous pressure to provide ample parking for riders.

Yet parking also complicates the political, financial, and design aspects of the project, and can conflict with place-related goals such as creating a pedestrian-friendly, mixed-use environment. Some transit agencies, such as BART in the San Francisco Bay Area, have required developers in joint development projects to replace all the parking that is lost when a project is built on a parking lot. When this requirement is combined with the number of spaces needed for the project itself, the developer can end up being responsible for building a very large and expensive parking structure. Because transit agencies typically charge little or nothing to park, the cost must be subsidized internally by other project components. The developer must then make the project profitable enough to cover these costs, which can skew the development program in favor of the most lucrative uses. Prioritizing commercial space may be the only way to make the project profitable, and housing—particularly affordable housing—often gets short shrift. Yet a balanced mix of land uses is precisely what is needed to create a good place.

> Because TOD must function as both place and node, all its components—trains, buses, taxis, cars, bicycles, pedestrians, housing, offices, and stores—must interact with one another. The synergy among these functions allows TOD to provide location efficiency and other desired outcomes, but the process necessary to integrate these parts into a single, well-functioning unit is extremely complex. It is essential that all of the users and actors in the planning and developing stages of new TOD projects cooperate in order to translate these goals into reality. One of the prime challenges, then, is getting all of these competing interests and uses to integrate seamlessly along the lines of the typologies that have been developed in the previous chapter in order to make our transit places and systems more enjoyable and better functioning parts of our communities. The remainder of this chapter discusses ways that each of the four main groups of participants in TOD projects can play active roles in reforming the development process so as to achieve optimal transit-oriented development.

Transit Agencies

Transit agencies often take the lead on TOD projects because they own land adjacent to their stations and view joint development as a way to increase ridership and generate revenues from ground leases. Coordination between the transit agency and entities doing station area planning—especially local governments—is essential for successful TOD. Moreover, as public entities and landowners, transit agencies should be willing and able to support long-term visions for their station areas and act as facilitators.

> Transit agencies should see themselves as more than providers of transportation services. This requires them to be full participants in the process of creating neighborhoods with long-term value by helping to develop station area plans that recognize the critical link between the station and adjacent land uses. In the long run, transit agencies can benefit from having stations that are parts of vital and economically healthy neighborhoods.

>   Transit agencies should also help plan for TOD at the systemwide scale and think at the regional level about the interplay between land uses around stations and how this affects access to and from regional origins and destinations. Although true TOD projects must balance their functions as a node and a place, the value of the system as a whole is enhanced if there is some degree of specialization at each station. For example, a park-and-ride station that functions primarily as a node can help reduce pressure on other stations to do so, thereby allowing the system as a whole to accommodate a certain level of automobile access without detracting from the ability of most stations to balance place and node functions. Any TOD project will be more effective if planned with other station areas in mind.

>   The case studies in this book on projects in San Diego (the Mercado) and San Jose (Ohlone-Chynoweth) describe how transit agencies worked closely with local government to plan for and coordinate development around transit. Transit agencies around the country are hiring full-time staff to promote and facilitate development. Denver's Regional Transportation District (RTD) hired a former developer to open a "one-stop shop" for developers along the agency's Southeast Line while it was under construction in 2002. The RTD was also conducting environmental impact studies as well as land-use studies along proposed routes for new rail corridors in order to compare the uses that were likely to occur along each route and determine which route would yield the best return on the investment by generating TOD. DART in Dallas reaches out to developers with marketing materials for each station area, providing information on demographics, land ownership, the characteristics of surrounding communities, and a basic market analysis.

>   BART in the Bay Area has been heavily criticized for providing too much free parking around stations, and for requiring developers to provide one-for-one replacement parking when TOD projects are built on station parking. But by 2002 BART was trying a new approach, promoting shuttle service to suburban stations, limiting long-term parking, charging for parking, and improving transit connections and cab service to stations. There was also a rapidly expanding car-sharing program that made cars available to members at or near seven stations, and a station car program that made electric cars available to the public to rent at one other station. BART was also reconsidering its one-for-one parking replacement policy and had agreed to a small loss of parking in order to accommodate its first transit village at the Fruitvale stop in Oakland.

Local Governments

When it comes to creating new TOD projects, local governments are in the best position to create and sustain the necessary long-term vision, to lead the planning process, and to assist with entitlements, land assembly, investment in key infrastructure, place-making amenities, and so on. Local government also has the broadest mandate of any actor: to promote the public good. When local governments do not recognize the opportunity stations afford them, the TOD process is vulnerable to the limitations imposed by fragmented regulations. It is unlikely other actors will be willing or able to give projects a broad scope when the local government fails to act meaningfully in key areas. Unfortunately, many local governments, even some that view TOD as a desirable goal, do not have a good understanding of the benefits of careful planning or a clear idea of how they can facilitate development.

> Developers nearly unanimously stress the importance of a good plan for providing a predictable environment for development. For example, the developer of two mixed-use projects in downtown Plano, Texas, says he would not have been interested had the city not done the planning and been willing to help assemble land and finance infrastructure and public improvements.

> Without a strong plan, developers have no guarantee that there is any agreement on a vision for the area or that the community will accept proposed development. Delays and uncertainty are more likely and, as a result, predevelopment work will cost more, the developer will require a higher return on investment, and the scope and creativity of the project will be limited. Transit-oriented development station area plans should include a conceptual land-use scheme and development program, identify key opportunity sites, provide design guidelines and a streetscape plan, and designate investment priorities for infrastructure and place-making amenities. Plans should also include a financing strategy that discusses how value will be captured and how it will be spent.

> Station area plans should take a comprehensive view of mobility, setting out strict guidelines around parking design and vehicular circulation so that cars do not interfere with pedestrian and bicycle access or make the station unpleasant for those who don't drive. Local governments should also create comprehensive parking strategies that link parking requirements to actual parking utilization and vehicle ownership levels. Parking ratios should reflect the area's transit service and enable people to live or work at the project without owning a car, or by owning fewer cars per household. Local governments should encourage and facilitate car-sharing and shuttle service to employment centers and neighborhood shopping centers (or beyond). Parking should be unbundled from other land uses such as housing—financially and perhaps physically—so that people pay for parking separately from other uses.

> In addition to comprehensive planning, it is also essential that the local government provides public infrastructure and amenities or developers may lack confidence that the public sector is committed to the area. Without a strong signal of such commitment, it is unlikely a station area will attract private capital unless the real estate market is extremely strong. And even if the real estate market is strong, it may be difficult for local governments to convince developers to build the types of projects needed for effective TOD without creating conditions of certainty.

> Finally, local governments can play a key role in encouraging development by paying for market studies and/or predevelopment activities, assisting with land assembly (since high land costs and fragmented land ownership patterns are often an impediment to infill development), facilitating deals, and so on. True transit-oriented development cannot occur on a single parcel,

yet property ownership is nearly always fragmented and assembly of multiple parcels can be difficult. If the local government does not play a leadership role, then the development program surrounding the transit station is unlikely to be of sufficient scope to be truly effective as TOD. Once a project begins, local government should conduct a careful review of design at all stages, and enforce design standards.

> When market forces alone are not strong enough to support good TOD, then local government becomes an even more critical actor, and strong public policy is an important tool for overcoming a neighborhood's disadvantages and attracting high-quality development. A local government that plays an active role in developing an area plan, providing infrastructure, and ensuring land supply can significantly alter the perceived market conditions. In the end, the most successful TOD projects will be those that involve a partnership between the public and private sectors.

> Municipalities and transit agencies need to work together to identify goals before physical planning begins or developers get involved. They should identify a timeframe and process for initial goal-setting, public involvement, and the selection of developers. Local governments should provide financial assistance to transit agencies and/or developers as an incentive for creating optimal projects, and should identify new revenue streams to support bond financing. Local government should make funding for key infrastructure, such as transit facilities or streetscapes, contingent on transit-supportive design.

Developers and Lenders

Developers and lenders provide the private capital and resources to build TOD. While developers share the local government's primary focus on place, they do not have a mandate to promote the public good. Their mandate is to meet the financial requirements of investors and lenders, and they focus on outcomes such as phasing, costs, revenues, income, marketability, property values, and overall return numbers. Lending institutions are less directly involved, and their focus is not on the TOD itself, but on how a loan fits into their loan portfolio and its marketability on the secondary market. They are concerned primarily with the performance of the loan and how well it matches standard underwriting criteria such as the debt coverage ratio, the loan-to-value, the track record of the developer, and parking ratios. The lender is focused on outcomes such as the net operating income, the value of the project, and invested equity as well as physical details such as square footage and parking spaces.

> Developers and lenders should become educated about the financial structure and performance of existing TOD and mixed-use projects. Phasing can work as a critical tool to examine assumptions and demonstrate market viability as well as respond to market change and limit risk. For instance, as the viability of reduced parking is proven and as a given project matures to the point where transit gains a greater share of mode split, parking in subsequent phases can be

reduced. Phasing should be used to test unknown markets. Portions of the project for which there is known demand should be built first, and may spark demand for less-tested products like higher density housing. Flexible design enables a project to react to market demands as the TOD evolves as well as to macroeconomic changes in the community and region. For example, as the TOD becomes more of a recognized place and destination, lively with people and activity, the demand for retail should grow. Building design should be able to accommodate more retail through conversion of ground floor offices to storefronts.

> As empirical data becomes available on traffic generation and parking demand at TOD projects, lenders should revise underwriting practices that require standard parking ratios so as to account for the reduced need for parking, thereby enabling project partners to capture the value of location efficiency. If suburban office parking ratios had been applied to office buildings in downtown San Francisco or Manhattan, there would have been no loans made in these very profitable markets. Lenders who do not account for location efficiency will fail to capitalize on what is a growing and potentially very profitable market segment. Lenders should also create loan guarantee pools to help TOD retail projects get financing, especially in revitalizing inner-city areas where projects have difficulty securing a major-credit tenant due to strict requirements such as minimum area median income. Without the revenue and credit security that a chain tenant provides, lenders are often reluctant to finance new retail development. Loan guarantees should fill the gap in the event of tenant turnover, slow lease out, or missing rent, and can eliminate the need for a major-credit tenant.

> The case study on Ohlone-Chynoweth TOD describes how the Ohlone Court and Ohlone-Chynoweth Commons affordable housing projects served to pioneer multifamily housing at a rail station in suburban Santa Clara County, California, stimulating investment in an adjoining higher density luxury apartment complex. Nonprofit affordable housing developers in Northern California have partnered extensively with transit agencies to build affordable housing near transit, producing several thousand units along both BART and Valley Transportation Authority rail lines. Lenders, including Bank of America, are willing to finance affordable housing projects with reduced parking ratios because demand will be strong even with fewer parking spaces. Lenders have also shown willingness when the developer can show community support; in Berkeley the developer of the downtown Gaia Building agreed to build a ten thousand square-foot cultural facility in exchange for a density bonus and reduced parking. There are ninety-one apartments and forty-two parking spaces.

> The case study on the Mercado project in San Diego describes the difficulties of financing retail in low-income neighborhoods, and shows how this problem was solved at a nearby TOD project where a community foundation was willing to be a "patient" investor. Because the foundation was willing to keep its investment in a retail center until it got off the ground, the project was able to attract additional financing even though it had no major-credit tenant. At Addison

Circle, described in the Dallas case study, ground floor office space was designed so that it could be converted to retail as the project evolved and the area densified, creating more demand.

The Community

Whereas transit agencies, local government, and developers represent a clearly defined set of interests, no single organization or individual or set of interests represents a community. Nearby homeowners may be most concerned about property values and traffic, whereas those who do not own property may be worried about gentrification. Parents may be concerned about the impact on local schools, a chamber of commerce may worry whether retail in the project will compete with existing businesses. The community is the most variable and sometimes volatile actor—"the wild card in the development game," noted one recent TOD study.

> This is why community involvement can further complicate projects that are already inherently complicated, and why the other actors are often reluctant to include the community. Moreover, the community does not have the same vested interests—financial investment or property ownership—as the other players, and for this reason may not be invited to the table until later. Setting up and managing a public outreach and involvement process always requires a great deal of time and effort and sometimes expense, which is a further disincentive to inviting community involvement. Plus, there's an inherent risk entailed in asking the community what it wants, because community members will have an opinion, and there can be dire consequences when input is invited with no serious intent to consider what has been said or to modify existing plans.[2]

> Because of the inherent difficulties, a whole industry has grown up around facilitating public involvement in planning. The amount of money spent, particularly when projects have been stalled because of public opposition or when the atmosphere is particularly contentious, can be significant. The public process that was staged to reach consensus on the eighteen-acre Pleasant Hill BART Station Area Community Plan, where efforts to build projects had stalled for almost twenty years, cost $240,000. Broader and more extensive processes—like the five-year Envision Utah project, which involved thousands of citizens in developing a comprehensive strategy for growth—can cost several million dollars. The bill is typically footed by the transit agency or local government, or shared with the developer; sometimes funding can be obtained from foundations.

> The case studies in this book on the Lindbergh project in Atlanta and two projects at the Ohlone-Chynoweth Station in San Jose illustrate the complications and costly delays—and, in the case of Lindbergh, a lawsuit—that can result when the community is invited too late or when community opinion is not weighted heavily enough. The single-family neighborhood surrounding the Ohlone-Chynoweth TOD had not been invited to participate in a joint development planning effort staged by the transit agency, private landowner, and several developers. As a result,

neighborhood residents were not aware of the extent of the plans. And while they accepted the first multifamily affordable housing complex that was built at the station—even though it pioneered both affordable and multifamily housing in a suburban single-family setting—the community felt blindsided when a second multifamily affordable project was announced, and their protests held up development for two years.

> In Atlanta the planning process was proceeding amicably with the community at the table when the transit agency suddenly announced it had found a very large corporate tenant for their joint development project at the Lindbergh Station. Not only would the density of the project increase considerably as a result, the agency announced, but there would also be thirteen thousand parking spaces. The surrounding single-family neighborhoods said that was too much development and traffic, and when the project went forward anyway, they filed suit—chilling developer interest in projects at other transit stations.

> The Arlington County case study, in contrast, illustrates the value of early, structured, and continued public involvement. The county took the time to educate the public about TOD and to build consensus with all stakeholders about its plan to build high density mixed-use development around five rail stations in suburban Arlington County. For thirty years the community has been actively engaged in county planning initiatives and the site plan review process for new development, and the county continues to encourage developers to consult with civic and neighborhood associations. The result has been a stable and predictable environment for both developers and the community, and as a result the Rosslyn-Ballston Corridor has attracted a tremendous amount of development at the same time that surrounding single-family neighborhoods have been preserved.

> Communities should not settle for less-than-optimal projects when they can improve project quality through their involvement. Transit agencies care above all about ridership, and developers are necessarily focused on profit. But community members should work to ensure that the project captures value for the community by raising the bar on design and by providing more housing, transportation, and retail choices, and public amenities like plazas, pocket parks, or community rooms. The community should also help argue for reduced parking standards—large parking structures are significant generators of traffic.

> Community involvement enhances the mutual learning that can take place during the planning and design process. Community members should help developers and designers understand what will work best in terms of the design and mix of uses as well as how to handle the frequently inflammatory issue of how best to integrate a project into an existing community. Because the community is the best and most important source of local knowledge, community members are the actors best equipped to help a project attain that intangible "sense of place" that will capture value for all partners. All partners will also benefit when the community is involved early enough that their concerns can be addressed up front instead of

after a project has been designed. Good design does not have to be expensive if it is done right the first time.

>   The community can serve as a politically powerful advocate for a project, especially if the project is pioneering some kind of development—like housing in a downtown, or multifamily housing in the suburbs—for which there is no proven market. Community support can also go a long way toward convincing lenders and retailers to become involved. It may be possible to attract an otherwise reluctant vendor, such as a grocery store, if community members are willing to come forward and say they will support the store.

>   The community has an especially important role to play in areas that have been bypassed by the market and that are not a high priority for local government or the transit agency. In these cases the community should take on the role of developer and planner and initiate projects that will benefit the community. In instances where this happens the community is often represented by a community development organization or other strong community group. This was the case in San Diego's Barrio Logan neighborhood, described in chapter 11, which was developed by a community services organization called the Metropolitan Area Advisory Committee or MAAC. It was also the case in the Lake-Pulaski neighborhood of Chicago, where an organization named Bethel New Life broke ground in 2003 on a TOD that includes a state-of-the-art "green" station building with a day care center and retail and nearby mixed-use development.

>   The City of San Diego was supportive of the Barrio Logan project, as was the City of Chicago supportive of Lake-Pulaski. But both cities had other priorities and pursued projects in communities where it was easier to attract developers. It took the long-term commitment of community organizations to keep the projects moving forward during the decade it took to get financing in place.

>   In Lake-Pulaski, the community first had to organize to stop demolition of the elevated rail line (the "L") and then created a neighborhood plan for development around the station that was saved. Along the way Bethel New Life bought land, developed housing, and negotiated with the city, developers, and the transit agency to realize their vision for the community. Bethel director Mary Nelson was able to put together financing in small increments, combining grants, loans, tax credits, and willpower to make the deals work. It was not easy to convince developers or the city of the benefit of developing the neighborhood as the assets were not readily apparent. But the community was successful in championing the redevelopment vision.

>   Communities have also served as effective champions of transit-oriented development at the regional level. A citizen-led coalition called the Chicagoland Transportation and Land Use Coalition came together because they were tired of being excluded from transportation decisions and they believed transportation funding was not being spent wisely. They wanted more transportation choice and projects that minimized the impact on the environment and in communities, reinvestment in existing neighborhoods, and investments that enhanced quality of life

for all residents. Transit-oriented development was at the juncture of all their concerns, and their conclusion—that investment and development should be channeled into existing communities around transit—was supported by a business-driven coalition called Metropolis 2020.

Conclusions

When all of the actors who play a role in creating good TOD are reasonably aligned in their goals and policies, and commit to sustained efforts over time, the outcomes are encouraging. The case studies on Arlington County, Virginia, on Dallas, and on the Ohlone-Chynoweth project in San Jose all describe the successful efforts of local governments to plan, promote, and facilitate TOD. The story of Arlington County, where the local government used TOD as a redevelopment tool in a low density commercial corridor, establishing and then refining a consistently supportive policy framework over three decades, is particularly compelling. There has been an enormous amount of development and investment around stations, which has generated very high transit ridership and little traffic, has been supported by developers and the community, and has preserved surrounding low density neighborhoods.

> The City of San Jose and the Valley Transportation Authority have successfully worked together in mostly suburban Santa Clara County, California, to address the jobs–housing imbalance and critical housing shortage by channeling new development, especially housing, and densifying existing development around public transit. Although the City of Dallas itself has not promoted or facilitated TOD, the suburbs surrounding Dallas have been vigorous in their efforts, resulting in the transformation of very low density Plano and an excellent TOD project in Addison.

> There is opportunity for involvement that this chapter has not discussed. For example, regional governments have also helped encourage TOD by funding planning efforts. In the San Francisco Bay Area, the Metropolitan Transportation Commission not only funds planning but also provides capital grants for transportation and streetscape projects that support TOD. State government in California has also provided incentives for TOD by incorporating smart growth and community reinvestment into the investment criteria used by the state's Infrastructure and Economic Development Bank, for example. These programs are discussed in more detail in chapter 5.

> Good TOD is not magic. Rather, it is like theater: it requires a good script, strong vision and leadership, and actors who are committed to working together. When these elements are in place, the result is greater than the mere sum of the parts. TOD works best when it is an ensemble piece.

NOTES

1   The information and conclusions in this chapter were drawn from the work of the TOD Initiative, a project of the Great American Station Foundation, which involved a number of organizations and individuals who began investigating the state of TOD practice in 2001. The TOD Initiative held a series of workshops on TOD, conducted a review of the literature and extensive interviews with practitioners, which resulted in several papers and case studies that became the basis for this book. The material in this chapter came from one of these papers—"Transit-Oriented Development: Moving from Rhetoric to Reality," written by Dena Belzer and Gerald Autler and published by the Brookings Institution in 2002—as well as the research conducted for other chapters in this book. The paper is posted at the Center for Transit-Oriented Development's website, www.transittown.org.

2   The authors would like to thank the following developers and facilitators who were interviewed: Bill Lennertz and Steve Coyle of Lennertz and Coyle (Bill Lennertz also heads the National Charette Institute), Gianni Longo of ACP Visioning and Planning, Michael Dieden of Creative Housing Associates, Richard Juarez of Urban West Development Consultants, Joshua Simon of the East Bay Asian Local Development Corporation, Victor Dover, and Kristen Pickus.

REFERENCES

California Department of Transportation. 2002. Statewide Transit Oriented Development Study: Factors for Success in California. September. www.dot.ca.gov.

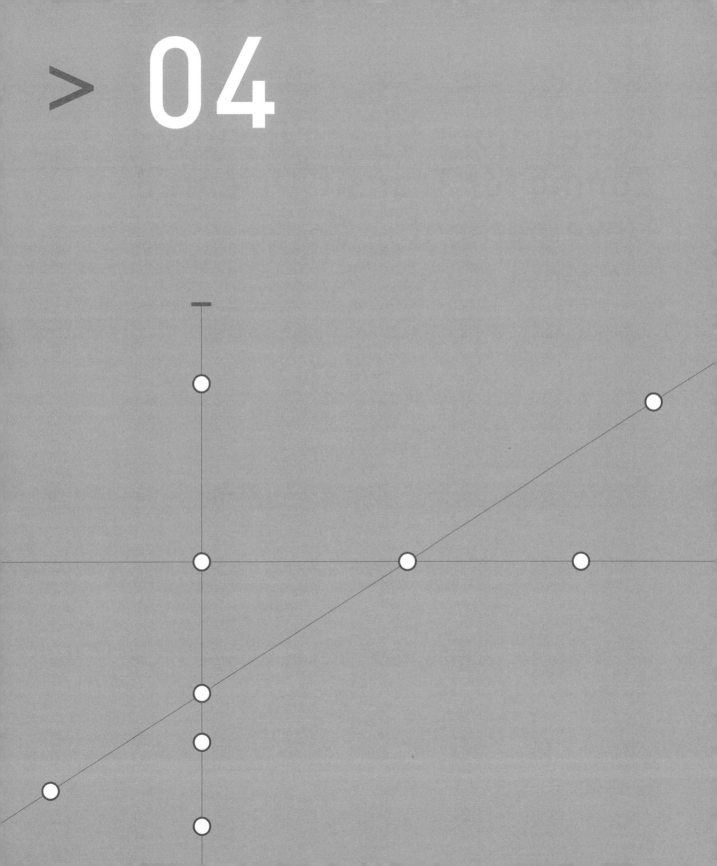

> 04

Regulations Shape Reality: Zoning for Transit-Oriented Development

Ellen Greenberg

Successful transit-oriented development (TOD) projects have many makers. Transit agencies, developers, architects, neighborhood activists, and residential and commercial tenants all help bring projects from concept to concrete. This chapter focuses on one player, the municipal government, and one set of its many functions, planning and zoning for TOD. Transit agencies such as the Santa Clara Valley Transportation Authority (VTA), the Metropolitan Atlanta Rapid Transit Authority (MARTA), and the Washington Metropolitan Area Transit Authority (WMATA) have all undertaken major efforts to stimulate TOD and to advocate local and even federal regulations that support it. But only local governments have direct authority for regulating and approving development.[1] All development projects are influenced to a greater or lesser degree by the zoning regulations under which they were approved, and TOD projects are no exception. Transit-oriented development advocates, project proponents, and local government representatives who see successful projects elsewhere and want to replicate them need an understanding of the planning and regulatory framework that supported their creation.

ABCs of TOD

From coast to coast in places large and small, three dimensions of successful TOD receive the lion's share of attention in planning documents and land development regulations. These are the ABCs of TOD zoning. Each is discussed at greater length later in this chapter.

Active, walkable streets: Places where people take transit are places where people walk. Every transit trip starts and ends with a walking trip, and places where walking is comfortable and appealing have a larger catchment area for transit patrons. Increasingly, zoning provisions are used to create walkable, active streets, although this extends the scope of regulations beyond what is customary in many localities by addressing the design of building, site, and street as well as the mix of land uses.

Building intensity and scale: The regulation of building intensity through standards for floor area ratio, minimum lot area per unit, and height and/or massing is a well-established function of zoning regulations. Assigning and locating density and scale so that it supports transit ridership and walkable streets is less familiar to planners and zoning administrators. A concentration of activity that correlates with both the scale of individual buildings and the extent of the transit-oriented district is a key factor supporting both transit and active uses such as restaurants and shops that contribute to a vibrant street life.

Careful transit integration: Where train tracks, stations, or routes are part of the site, zoning must address how they will be successfully integrated into the project. Where transit is in the right-of-way adjoining the project, regulations should consider the relationship between the project and the facility. Both of these conditions, the former in particular, create special demands on TOD projects because they perform as both private land uses and points of public interface with the transit system.

> This chapter reports on the findings of an investigation into planning and zoning for TOD. The research strategy was to identify successful—though perhaps imperfect—projects, and to learn about the planning and regulatory framework under which they were conceived and approved. Put simply, we asked what the public agency did in terms of planning and regulation to support, facilitate, or stimulate successful TOD. TOD can be encouraged in many ways: we found that states with strong local planning traditions and mandatory consistency between local comprehensive plans and development regulations used policy documents as well as more focused development regulations to foster transit-oriented projects.

Practices in TOD Zoning

Much of what makes a project is idiosyncratic, stemming from the particulars of location, ownership, and surroundings. Because so much of project design is necessarily customized, any aspect of TOD that can be approached systematically should be in the interests of economy, efficiency, and predictability. The research reported on in this chapter revealed a number of consistent practices that appear to be significant contributors to successful projects. When these are tailored to individual jurisdictions, they can take at least some of the idiosyncrasy—and uncertainty—out of the process of creating TOD. These practices are of two types:

Planning and Policy Approach: "Approach" is a catch-all term for the choices about which policy and regulatory mechanisms to use, how they are managed, which partnering organizations participate, and so on. In some cases, the local government's approach may be specific to TOD; in others, the locality may use the same approach for TOD that it employs in planning other types of desirable development. The most common example is the planned development, which is a common tool for allowing creativity in site planning and design.

Regulatory Provisions: Whatever the approach to planning and policy for TOD, the details must be addressed through specific provisions unique to the project under consideration or applicable to TOD generally. The ABCs of TOD, listed earlier, provide an outline of the types of TOD provisions considered in greater detail later in this chapter.

Types of TOD

A total of eleven case study projects, listed in table 4.1, were investigated. Five are case studies from this book. The other projects were selected in part because they reflect many of the characteristics of good TOD as defined in chapter 2. The projects were intentionally selected to vary with respect to the following:

- *Location:* The case study locations are in nine regions and eight states.
- *Size:* The case studies are at various scales, from the smallest—16 Market Square in Denver, Colorado, which is on a downtown site of 0.8 acres—to the largest—Orenco Station in Hillsboro, Oregon, which occupies 200 acres.
- *Transit integration:* Relationships to transit facilities and services are varied. They range from the Central Park Market project at Del Mar Station in Pasadena, California, where apartments will span a light-rail line that crosses the project site, to the Boulder, Colorado, infill project that is within walking distance of three high-frequency bus lines, to projects located on what were transit district parking lots in Atlanta and San Jose.
- *Transit agency participation:* Joint development projects on transit agency–owned property such as Ohlone-Chynoweth in San Jose and Lindbergh Station in Atlanta are included. Other projects, like Mercado Apartments in San Diego and Clarendon Market Common in Arlington County, Virginia, had no direct transit agency participation. Transit agency cooperation has been instrumental in the realization of some ambitious projects; for example, the Chicago area's Metra relocated a station platform and agreed to construct a station as part of the new Willow Springs Village Center.
- *Transit mode:* Projects in Renton, Denver, and Boulder relate to bus transit; Mountain View's projects capitalize on intermodal connections between bus, automobile, and light-rail; and in Atlanta the focus is on heavy-rail with supplementary bus services. At present, projects in Addison, Texas, and Willow Springs, Illinois, both rely on a single mode (bus in Addison and heavy-rail in Willow Springs), but long-term plans call for both bus and rail service.

· *Legal framework for planning and regulation:* In each of the eight states where case study projects are located, state enabling laws for planning and zoning establish different structures for land-use regulation. While local governments have crafted many creative responses to the possibilities provided by their state statutes, these approaches are not always transferable because of the constraints of enabling law. For example, Arlington County uses a negotiated site plan review process to allow rezonings for significantly higher density. In California, this approach might be called into question because of the state's requirements for so-called vertical consistency between local comprehensive plans and zoning.

> Information on each of the projects was collected through telephone interviews and correspondence during 2002 and early 2003 as well as through review of planning and regulatory documents. In some cases these sources were supplemented with materials such as site plans or project descriptions by project architects or developers, and by newspaper articles or website materials. For the projects described in the case studies in this book, information gathered by the authors was also consulted.

TABLE 4.1—PROFILES OF PROJECTS EXAMINED IN CHAPTER 4

PROJECT	LOCATION	DESCRIPTION	SITE	USES	DENSITY AND COVERAGE	HEIGHT	PARKING	TRANSIT PROXIMITY
Ohlone-Chynoweth Commons	San Jose, CA	Mixed-use project built on light-rail station parking lot	7.3 acre former park-and-ride lot	195 affordable townhouses, 4,400 sq.ft. of retail, 3,000 sq.ft. day care, 4,000 sq.ft. community room	27 units/acre	2 stories	366 spaces for the TOD, 200 park-and-ride spaces	2,000 feet to bus and light-rail station
Del Mar Station	Pasadena, CA	Retail and apartment project integrating planned station	4.16 acre urban infill site includes 0.64 acres of track, 0.13 for street widening, net acreage of 3.39 acres	347 apartment units in four buildings, 11,000 sq.ft. retail, 1 acre plaza	10.1 du/acre net	4–7 stories	1,200 below-grade (600 for apt. residents and 600 for rail patrons)	On Gold Line light rail line connecting Pasadena to downtown Los Angeles, to become major intermodal transit center for Pasadena
16 Market Square	Denver, CO	Office, residential, and retail building fronting on downtown Denver's transit mall	8 acre infill site	23 condos 25,000 sq.ft. retail, 180,000 sq.ft. office	7.0 FAR	5 stories above grade 3 levels underground parking	120,000 sq.ft. garage	On 16th Street Transit Mall served by bus and light-rail
The Steelyards	Boulder, CO	Small-scale urban redevelopment project with housing and commercial uses	10.6 acre greyfield site	90 dwelling units (including 18 affordable), 221,000 commercial space	8.6 units/acre (gross), 0.67 FAR, residential 10.6 FAR, commercial	2–4 stories	426 spaces surface and underground	Within 1,000 feet of bus line

CONTINUED ON NEXT PAGE

TABLE 4.1—PROFILES OF PROJECTS EXAMINED IN CHAPTER 4 (CONTINUED)

PROJECT	LOCATION	DESCRIPTION	SITE	USES	DENSITY AND COVERAGE	HEIGHT	PARKING	TRANSIT PROXIMITY
Metropolitan Place	Renton (Seattle region)	Small-scale urban redevelopment integrating structured parking owned by transit district, affordable housing and retail	30,000 sq.ft. infill site in suburban downtown	90 apartments, 4,000 sq.ft. retail	120 units/acre	5 stories (3 res. levels above 2 levels of parking and ground floor retail)	240 total, 90 for apartments and 150 park-and-ride leased by county	Bus transit center across the street
Lindbergh City Center	Atlanta, GA	Major employment center (BellSouth) with Main Street retail and housing at MARTA station	80 acre infill site within existing neighborhoods	566 apartments; 259 condos; 1 million sq.ft. office plus 1.2 million sq.ft. in second phase; 330,000 sq.ft. retail	21.5 units/acre	Ranges from 3 stories to high-rise towers	2.3 spaces/ 1,000 sq.ft. of commercial, less than one space per residential unit (10,000 space garage)	Located at MARTA (heavy-rail) station
Addison Circle	Addison, TX	Mixed-use infill project creating new activity center for community, adjoining major bus transfer center	80 acre suburban site	1,500 housing units to date (4,000 at full build-out), mostly rental and live-work; later phases have for-sale condos and townhomes. 115,000 sq.ft. of retail and 342,000 sq.ft. of office. Parks and public spaces	100 units/acre, 1.86 FAR for commercial uses	Residential is up to 5 stories, office up to 10 stories	1/bedroom 3.2/1,000 sq.ft. office 3.7/1,000 sq.ft. retail	Adjacent to proposed light-rail line. Bus service existing at 15–30 min. peak and 30–60 min. nonpeak
Market Common at Clarendon	Arlington, VA (DC Region)	Mixed-use redevelopment introducing urban development types to WMATA's Clarendon station area	13 acre former retail center	300 luxury apartments, 87 townhomes, 240,000 sq.ft. retail, 31,000 sq.ft. office	30 units/acre (3.0 FAR with 1.0 additional FAR permitted as bonus), 1.5 FAR for commercial uses	75 feet in C-3 zone and 45 feet in C-2 zone	900 spaces structured above retail	Site between two Metro stops, first within 900 feet of development
Willow Springs Village Center	Willow Springs, IL	Mixed-use redevelopment creating a new village center	40 acres of former industrial properties	138 townhomes, 136 condos, 52,000 sq.ft. retail and office, new Village Hall	1.16 FAR, townhomes at 16 du/acre	3-story mixed use and office buildings, 6-story condo buildings	Surface parking and 104-car structure	Metra Station located adjacent to project behind City Hall
Orenco Station	Hillsboro Oregon (Portland region)	New mixed-use neighborhood	190 acre suburban greenfield	300 single-family homes and townhomes, 350 condos, 600 apartments, 27,000 sq.ft. retail, 30,000 sq.ft. Class A office (adjacent to site is a 50 acre regional shopping center).	10.5 units/acre (gross)	Ranges from 2-story detached res. units to 4-story mixed-use buildings in commercial center	Requirement ranges from 0.9 spaces/ unit to 0.75 spaces/senior or student housing unit	1/4 mile to light-rail station
The Crossings	Mountain View, CA (San Francisco Bay Area)	Mixed-housing residential redevelopment on 18 acre shopping center; includes affordable housing	18 acre suburban greyfield site	630 units, including single- and multi-family and townhomes, 5,000 sq.ft. retail parks	30 du/acre (net)	2 stories	36 surface park-and-ride spaces	Heavy commuter rail (Caltrain) stops at site

A FUNDAMENTAL DISTINCTION

The case study projects can be sorted according to a number of different scales, but two of these—project size and transit integration—stand out as most significant in relation to planning and regulation. It is evident from the case studies that those developments integrating a transit station, whether they are small or large, require extraordinary effort if they are to succeed at creating value in their own right as well as functioning as part of the regional land-use and transportation system. These projects must perform as gateways into the transit system. Their design can either encourage or discourage people from using the system. The fact that the number of people using the development to access the transit system will in many cases exceed the number of people who take advantage of whatever uses the buildings contain highlights the importance of transit integration as a factor in overall project success.

>   The demands on projects that integrate transit stops or stations have been recognized either explicitly or by default by most of the localities that host them. The planning and policy approaches for these projects have been characterized by detailed, lengthy planning, usually involving many agencies. The time, money, and effort invested in projects that fit this profile have been extraordinary, as is reflected in the case studies of Lindbergh Station and Ohlone-Chynoweth in chapters 9 and 10. The record suggests that this effort may well be warranted, given the importance of many aspects of both the site design and the development program in achieving TOD objectives. In some cases, a prolonged time frame is unavoidable, as conflicts about the project can take protracted effort to resolve.

>   The effort required to bring different types of TOD projects into being ranges along a continuum. At one end are projects that required substantial investments of time, money, and energy. It is not unusual for them to be cultivated for a decade or more, with conditions carefully controlled to maximize the chance of success. For the purpose of this discussion, we will call these "customized" projects. Customized projects are those of any size that integrate transit facilities on site, as well as larger TOD projects that do not include a transit facility. At the opposite end of the continuum are those projects that are produced as the result of systematic planning efforts combined with effective implementing regulations. These are "standardized" projects, not because they are mass-produced, but because they are a result of routine production activity. All of the standardized projects are small- to midsize projects that are in a transit district but do not incorporate a transit station.

>   A fundamental distinction can be drawn between large, high-value station projects and small projects incorporating stations or stops. High-value projects—whether or not they integrate a transit facility—are typically initiated with the expectation of high soft costs, including planning, design, and engineering efforts. In these cases, the marginal cost associated with integrating a transit station may be easily absorbed into the overall project budget. In contrast, the design effort required on even a small site with a transit station, such as the 3.4-acre Central Park

Market at Del Mar Station, might well overwhelm a project budget and schedule. All customized projects share the need for a high level of customized planning and design. Separating them into two categories by size reflects their varying abilities to carry the relatively high costs associated with bringing a customized project to fruition. Many smaller projects, combining as they do small size and big effort, will warrant a high level of financial participation in project development from transit agencies and/or local governments.

> Standardized projects represent a systematizing of TOD, with the potential for a concomitant reduction in cost, effort, and risk. The case studies suggest that while a standardized level of planning and design effort is the right goal for those small- to medium-sized projects that create or reinforce the transit-supportive nature of a district, it is not a suitable goal for projects of any size that incorporate a transit station, or for high-value projects that will comprise major segments of transit districts. These projects demand the high level of site-specific planning, regulatory and design effort that characterizes customized projects generally.

Planning and Policy Approach: The Skeleton

Six recommendations for the planning and policy approach emerge from the case studies and are discussed in this section. Together, these help to establish a framework for the regulations themselves, which are discussed in the following section on regulatory provisions.

CREATE CUSTOMIZED ZONING FOR PROJECTS INTEGRATING TRANSIT FACILITIES

The largest and most ambitious TOD projects require intensive investments of time and effort during the planning and development phases—in this they differ little from projects of comparable size and complexity that are not transit-oriented. In fact, smaller projects that actively integrate transit facilities share the essential characteristics of customized projects, due to a combination of operational, technical, and place-making challenges. Ideally, a project incorporating a transit station or major stop will have a unique identity that will draw transit users and—depending on the mix of uses—business patrons, residents, and visitors. In developing and redeveloping are as, investment in customized zoning for these sites should pay off not only in terms of the quality of on-site development, but also in setting the stage for transit supportive development on adjoining and nearby properties.

> Common approaches for planning customized projects are the use of specific plans, as in Mountain View, Atlanta, and Arlington County, and the use of the planned unit development (PUD) process, illustrated by the Ohlone-Chynoweth and Willow Springs Village Center projects. The specific plans focus on a small area, sometimes with multiple ownerships, and both express policy and establish development regulations uniquely tailored to the location. The specific plans are generally prepared by local government, and often require a detailed master plan to be submitted by the developer in order to demonstrate compliance with the specific plan's provisions.

The PUD process is generally established in local zoning, with specific districts adopted subsequently to promulgate standards that apply to a specific development project or suite of associated projects, as with the Willow Springs example. The advantage to both of these approaches is that they are often familiar to local governments, which have used them in many locations. Experience with the regulatory structure, though, has to be matched by expertise in incorporating the ABCs of TOD into the specific plan or PUD. For example, the Pasadena General Plan Land Use Element states: "The City will use specific plans to encourage transit-oriented and pedestrian-oriented developments. Specific plans determine precise land-use patterns, zoning, setbacks, and design within defined boundaries. Within the specific plans, the principles of transit-oriented and pedestrian-oriented developments can be applied."

MINIMIZE CUSTOMIZED PLANNING AND DISCRETIONARY REVIEW FOR STANDARDIZED PROJECTS

The importance of establishing and maintaining a concentration of buildings and public spaces that support pedestrian activity and transit use cannot be overstated. The density and intensity recognized as one of the ABCs of TOD is not the result of any single project but is a product of an urban fabric that extends throughout a transit-oriented district.

> In the transit-oriented district, zoning provisions should encourage the ABCs: active, walkable streets, building density and intensity, and careful integration of transit. Uses that will strengthen these characteristics should be permitted as of right, and discretionary review of development proposals incorporating them should be minimized or eliminated.

> The mixed-use zoning district of Boulder, Colorado, takes this approach by minimizing discretionary review for projects conforming to design and development standards. Most of the city's mixed-use zoning districts provide incentives for housing by allowing projects by-right if they have at least 50 percent of the floor area devoted to residential uses. This "by-right" approach has reduced the planning approval time for mixed-use projects from three to four years to four to six months. Designers of projects subject to these regulations report that the advance knowledge that well-designed projects will be approved without discretionary review operates as a significant stimulator of development activity in the city's core transit area.

> In Denver, the 16 Market Square project is the largest building in the Lower Downtown (LODO) district since the historic district was established in 1987. While mandatory design review is required, the eight-story, 380,000-square-foot building was approved by right under the city's B-7 zoning district supplemented by the design and street regulations for the LODO district. No customized regulations were needed to approve this project, which made a very significant contribution to the fabric of the transit-oriented district. Denver's downtown B-5 zoning, which applies to most of the downtown core, similarly establishes both design standards and guidelines that supplement the zoning district regulations. The city offers two procedures

for design review and allows the project applicant to choose. Under the design standards review option, described as the faster and most objective process, all aspects of a project that meet standards are approved through a staff review to be completed in no more than fifteen calendar days. The alternative is a design guidelines review that allows approval of any aspect of project design that does not conform to the design standards through a negotiated process that is completed in not more than forty-five calendar days.

PROVIDE AN EXPLICIT FOUNDATION IN POLICY AND POLITICS

Given the long time frames and substantial investments in planning and design required for TOD projects, clear and sustained public policy favoring transit-oriented development is enormously important. Decades of commitment by Arlington County in the Rosslyn-Ballston Corridor, described in detail in chapter 7, is a valuable example of the impact of an agency's long-term policy commitment to using the rail system as an integral part of economic and community development.

> Successful projects all along the continuum are founded in clearly stated political and policy guidance for local officials, public agency staff, and project proponents. Formal policies as well as funding and program priorities help establish shared expectations among community members, transit agencies, and developers and smooth the way for development projects. In King County, Washington, county executive Ron Sims introduced a smart growth initiative— "Shaping Tomorrow"—in 1998 to better manage the county's growth through strategies such as TOD and supporting local efforts like those in the City of Renton to redevelop the downtown and build affordable housing. In the Portland, Oregon, region, Hillsboro's Orenco Station was one of several TOD projects that resulted from the 2040 regional plan prepared and adopted by Portland Metro, the regional planning authority. Metro also facilitated the light-rail station area planning process, working with local jurisdictions. As the regional planning authority, Metro coordinates land-use and transportation planning and together with the transit authority, TriMet, made funding for the light-rail station contingent on local planning and zoning policies to promote ridership through compact, mixed-use development.

> In other locations, the policy foundation has consistently been at the municipal level, as demonstrated by the City of Mountain View, California. There, planners crafted multiple specific plans that collectively displayed a solid vision of a transit-oriented community. Ideally, the policy and political foundation is expressed both in planning documents and in the words and actions of public officials and staff who champion TOD. The "purpose" statement from Mountain View's San Antonio Station Precise Plan does a good job of linking regional issues to city goals and tying both to plans for a specific property: "Since 1985, the extent of the imbalance between jobs and housing located in Mountain View has grown substantially and the availability of moderately priced housing has declined significantly. To address these issues, the City Council and

Environmental Planning Commission have established a goal of facilitating development of appropriately situated and planned residential communities, especially those integrated with existing transit networks. Area D offers a unique opportunity to combine housing, transit, and proximity to shopping services that makes it ideal for a higher-density residential development."

> A clear and consistent policy framework frequently contributes to a focused and effective public involvement process. Arlington County, with its long history of working within a framework supporting TOD in the Rosslyn-Ballston Corridor, provides a valuable example of structured community input. Because the broad policy parameters are well established, the focus of community involvement in the project review process is on specific planning and design issues. Similarly, in Pasadena, California, policies supporting walkable, active streets and high-quality design are well established. The design review process provides an opportunity for scrutiny of a project's design characteristics, all the while sustaining a clear commitment to transit-oriented development. Like Pasadena, Denver has a design review process focused on each project's contributions to meeting specific objectives for the district rather than allowing debate on the broad themes of walkability, building intensity, and careful transit integration.

ENGAGE TRANSIT ORGANIZATION POLICY LEADERSHIP

Projects have benefited from activist transit agencies that have a comprehensive view of their goals and mission rather than one that focuses exclusively on conventional notions of transit productivity. An indirect outcome of the Lindbergh City Center project in Atlanta was a change in federal rules that made it possible for transit agencies to support transit-oriented development on property that had been bought for right-of-way with federal funding. Prior to the rule change any excess land was to be sold in order to reimburse the Federal Transit Agency. But MARTA as well as other transit agencies lobbied FTA to allow TOD and to permit agencies to keep revenues from ground leases. Interestingly, MARTA lobbied for the rule change not because of an interest in TOD per se, but mostly because, with no Georgia state funding for transit, it needed new sources of revenue.

> Transit agency leadership has stimulated TOD on private property and assisted with careful transit integration at a number of the case study projects. A high impact example is the requirement by the Portland region's TriMet that local governments adopt transit-supportive land development regulations as a condition of regional investment in light-rail. In San Jose, Santa Clara Valley Transportation Authority (VTA) works with cities to plan and develop higher density, mixed-use projects around transit stations. VTA identifies existing and planned station areas that would benefit from TOD and creates urban design plans for these properties. Local governments have jurisdiction over the actual land-use decisions.

> In several cases, project designers and city planners have had to work with transit agency requirements for areas including or immediately adjoining transit agency right-of-way. Pasadena's

Del Mar Station project incorporates track and platform areas owned by the Los Angeles County Metropolitan Transportation Authority and subject to their design specifications. Denver's Regional Transportation District participated in review of the plans for 16 Market Square, assuring that buildings directly fronting on the 16th Street transit mall met with or exceeded special transit mall standards. The agency concerned itself with all aspects of the public right-of-way, including sidewalk materials, street planting, and outdoor furniture.

MEET MULTIPLE OBJECTIVES

TOD projects can be judged as successful only when measured against multiple yardsticks. The best TOD projects integrate diverse elements to serve multiple public and private objectives, thereby expanding the constituent base in support of the project and justifying public and private investment. For example, at Metropolitan Place in Renton, Washington, affordable housing is part of a major downtown revitalization program that provides commuter parking and supports a new bus transfer station; and at Del Mar Station in Pasadena, the preservation of the historic Santa Fe depot, restored for retail use, is an integral element of TOD project design.

> Boulder's TOD approach has a more regional perspective and is integrated with the city's overall efforts to contain urban sprawl. The comprehensive plan designates focus areas for development and areas planned for annexation. An urban growth boundary, agreed to by the city and county, limits growth and dedicates the remaining land to rural uses. Inside the urban growth boundary, the city has created subcommunity plans for areas expected to see the bulk of growth. There is a plan for the business main street (village center) and four other mixed-use zoning districts. These areas were selected for their proximity to transit, available land, and appropriateness for development, particularly the need for a transition between two disparate types of district (e.g., industrial to residential). The Denver Regional Council of Government's Metro Vision 2020 Plan sees compact mixed-use transit-serviced centers in existing urbanized areas as the solution to overcoming traffic and environmental problems. The plan calls for cities to designate urban centers, envisioned as compact urban villages that are pedestrian friendly with a range of retail, business, civic, and cultural uses, as well as diverse residential opportunities. These should serve as transit origins and destinations that are friendly to all travel modes.

> Diverse objectives sometimes dovetail readily, but in other cases conflicts emerge that are not easily resolved. The chapters focusing on Atlanta and San Jose both detail cases where project development moved forward without the clear resolution of conflicts. In Atlanta, the desire to accommodate a major employer in 1 million square feet of office space so increased the scale of the Lindbergh project and the amount of parking required that it precipitated a lawsuit and will likely exacerbate traffic congestion. The experience of this and other projects shows that it may be necessary for projects to mature before it is possible to determine whether varied objectives have indeed been satisfied successfully.

ANTICIPATE A LENGTHY TIMELINE FOR CUSTOMIZED PROJECTS

Customized projects and major developments in transit districts take a long time to plan, design, and build. Establishment of the planning and policy foundation needed to support them may start many years in advance of development. Arlington County began developing sector plans for station areas in 1972. In 1982, revisions targeted the Clarendon Metro Station for high density mixed-use development and required a special planning process when property owners wanted to redevelop. The process was not used until 1994. In Atlanta, the city collaborated with MARTA on transit station area development studies in 1971, and revised its zoning to conform to those policies in 1977, but the first of the customized transit station area districts was not adopted until 2000.

Recommendations for Regulatory Provisions: Meat on the Bones

The case study projects in this chapter are located in all kinds of places—from the small town of Willow Springs, Illinois, to downtown Denver. Despite the wide variation in their settings and features, all demonstrate application of the ABCs of TOD zoning. Each does so in the context of a unique regulatory structure, as is shown later in the chapter in table 4.2. The findings of the case studies with respect to regulatory provisions are developed below with regard to four topics:

- ACTIVE, WALKABLE STREETS
- BUILDING DENSITY AND INTENSITY
- CAREFUL INTEGRATION OF TRANSIT
- WHEN THE ZONING DOESN'T FIT

> A general issue confronted by anyone drafting development regulations is the degree to which regulations should prescribe specific development characteristics, as opposed to offering project designers greater flexibility. The regulations reviewed offer a range of approaches, with some, such as Denver's B-5 district, offering project proponents a choice of more or less flexibility, with greater flexibility requiring more time in the review process. In Addison, Texas, design standards and zoning for the initial phases of Addison Circle were very prescriptive in order to control the quality of the product; they were later modified to add flexibility because municipal planners felt that the look of the project was too uniform. In Denver, the developer of 16 Market Street praised the LODO design guidelines as both very effective for preserving historic buildings and encouraging context-sensitive modern design. The challenge is to identify those elements that are essential for success and feasible from a market perspective. Mandates should focus on these, without sacrificing opportunities for creative and original design.

ACTIVE, WALKABLE STREETS

Active, walkable streets are a function of many urban elements working together, as is well expressed in the City of Denver's "Design Guidelines for Denver Landmarks and Landmark Districts":

> "Pedestrian friendly" is a measure of the quality of an environment from the perspective of a person on foot. A pedestrian friendly environment is a place where people can enjoy public life in a comfortable setting. The Lower Downtown Neighborhood Plan seeks to foster this kind of an environment by recommending several community development strategies, including approaches to land use, building design, historic preservation, streetscape design, transportation, mobility, traffic management, parking, and economic development. For example, the Plan's design guidelines advance pedestrian friendliness through such things as built-to-property-line requirements, minimum and maximum heights, and human scale development, all of which serve to enclose and define public space and to create a pedestrian environment people understand and to which they can relate. ...

Some of the elements of active, walkable streets are elaborated upon in more detail below.

Land Use

Active streets are supported fundamentally by a mix of land uses. Location efficiency, expanded mobility, and shopping and housing choices are additional favorable outcomes that are dependent on a mix of uses in the transit district. Not all TODs should have the same mix of uses, but a desired mix needs to be determined and articulated in local policy, then incorporated into development regulations.

> Regulation for mixed use should allow the full range of desired uses as of right, and specify clearly that permitted uses may be (or in some cases must be) mixed on single properties and buildings. Regulations may limit some activities to ground level or to upper floors, typically locating retail on the ground floor with office or residential above. Uses that will not generate pedestrian activity are often prohibited from ground floor locations on major streets in walkable districts.

> An option in markets that may not have immediate demand for storefront retail is to require buildings to be designed with spaces that are suitable for ground-floor retail, but to allow other uses. This will create the opportunity for transformation at a later time. Planning at the district level should identify those blocks where ground floor retail is most important for place making and TOD success.

> Addison, Texas regulates building type, while other cities, including Willow Springs, regulate tenancies on their most important pedestrian streets. Addison's Urban Center District requires that "Buildings fronting on the special events parkway/retail street (category E/F) must be designed to accommodate ground level retail. The ground level floor area may be used for office, civic or special uses." Willow Springs Village Center Planned Unit Development Ordinance 99-0-6 establishes that "One hundred percent (100%) of the total of all block frontages within the mixed use commercial portion of the Village Center should be occupied by pedestrian oriented businesses on the ground floor, preferably retail stores and shops."

4.1
The Crossings in Mountain View, California, was an early effort to bring transit-based housing into an area with a severe jobs–housing imbalance. (Photo: Calthorpe and Associates.)

4.2
Peter Calthorpe's plan for the Crossings incorporated a mix of housing types, including town-houses (shown here) and bungalows. (Photo: Calthorpe and Associates.)

> In addition to addressing residential and commercial uses, many ordinances also address the inclusion of civic and open space uses in the TOD. In many cases, the transit-oriented district is a community or even a regional downtown, where civic uses are an important part of the urban scene. In highly urbanized environments like Pasadena and Denver, formal open spaces adjoining the case study projects serve project users and others. In Mountain View, the focus is on open space to serve residents of the Crossings. In Addison, open spaces help form the community's identity.

> The mix of uses is not formulaic and reflects both existing patterns and objectives for the future. Boulder's IMS-X zone, which applies to a portion of the Steelyards site, is unusual in that it promotes mixed use with industrial predominating. At least 50 percent of the floor area must be industrial, and residential uses are intended to be secondary. This zone is planned to be located near to a full-service retail/office center, so by-right retail uses are limited to neighborhood-serving restaurants. Office uses are limited to technical offices (e.g., surveyors, engineers, graphic designers) that are accessory to the primary industrial use.

Sidewalks

Sidewalks are consistently required on all public streets in transit-oriented districts. Many localities delineate different sidewalk zones to allocate space for plantings and street furniture, sidewalk dining or vendors, and a clear walkway for pedestrians. Some ordinances or design guidelines establish standards for special paving or other distinctive treatments.

Building Placement and Orientation

Buildings should be oriented to the street with small or zero setbacks, depending on established patterns and on the level of urbanism. Corner buildings are particularly important and are generally required to "hold the corner" with facades on both streets. Arlington County's Urban Design Redevelopment Guidelines for East Clarendon establish the following for main street and pedestrian/open space linkages:

1. Maintain a recognizable enclosure of space along main street, and primary and secondary connectors by placing buildings, walls, and other features at the edge of the sidewalk, respecting the "build-to" line.

2. Along main street the retail base on buildings should come out to the edge of the sidewalk helping to create an active pedestrian environment and clearly defining the streetscape.

> Establishing a "build-to" line or zone as recommended in the East Clarendon guidelines is a technique for creating a street wall with building frontages consistently set at the property line. This is an alternative to the conventional approach, which specifies minimum distances from the property line, resulting in buildings behind the property line and allowing considerable variation in building placement.

Entrances

Zoning provisions consistently require that primary entrances open onto public streets. Boulder requires "primary building entrance location facing street." Renton's design guidelines state that "The minimum standard requires buildings to be oriented to the street with clear connections to the sidewalk. A primary entrance of each building shall be located on the facade facing the street." This orientation ensures pleasant and simple access for pedestrians.

Fenestration

Windows are frequently required at ground level, and a certain percentage of glass is often specified. The intent is to "enliven" the street by providing visual interest that encourages people to walk and take transit. Requiring fenestration goes hand in hand with avoiding blank walls on pedestrian streets. Atlanta's Lindbergh SPI-15 district establishes the following specific regulations for storefront streets:

Properties which front Piedmont Road north of Lindbergh Drive, Sydney Marcus Boulevard and Morosgo Drive shall be deemed to constitute storefront streets within the meaning of this chapter and shall meet the following detailed regulations for fenestration: . . .

- Fenestration shall be provided for a minimum of 65 percent of the length of the frontage:
    - Beginning at a point not more than three feet above the sidewalk, to a height no less than ten feet above the sidewalk, or
    - Beginning at the finished floor elevation to a height no less than ten feet above the finished floor elevation when the finished floor elevation is three or more feet above the sidewalk, or
    - Beginning at a point not more than sidewalk level, to a height no less than ten feet above the finished floor elevation when the finished floor elevation is below the sidewalk.
- Properties with ground floor residential uses on Morosgo Drive and greater than 350 feet east of Piedmont Road shall be permitted to substitute the fenestration requirements of section 16-180.027(1)(c) with the fenestration requirements of section 16-180.014(5)(c).
- Fenestration shall not utilize painted glass, reflective glass or other similarly treated or opaque windows. Entrances may be counted towards fenestration requirements. (Ord. No. 2001-91, § 1, 7-11-01)

Block Size

For projects involving land subdivision, small blocks are generally required in order to create a high level of connectivity that provides a choice of routes for travelers, active walking environments, and the opportunity for diversity in design. Addison, Texas, mandates blocks with between 200 and 600 feet per side. Mountain View's San Antonio Station Specific Plan requires that "The site plan shall lay out city blocks. The size of the blocks within the area shall be minimized to create a neighborhood of buildings oriented to streets. The length of any block face should generally be 200 to 250 feet long, and never longer than 350 feet. Blocks shall be delineated by either streets or major pedestrian separations."

Placement and Supply of Parking

Zoning generally addresses both the placement and supply of parking, topics discussed in greater detail in chapter 6. Prominent surface parking is consistently and correctly prohibited in transit districts. Especially in core districts, there should be no parking between buildings and the street. Renton's provisions specify "No parking shall be located between a building and front property line or street side corner of a lot. Parking entries should not subordinate pedestrian entries and should not dominate the streetscape. The street side of parking garages in the CD zone should incorporate retail or service commercial facilities." Renton also eliminates parking requirements in the downtown core area, where the Metropolitan Place TOD project is located.

>   In Mountain View, parking requirements are not eliminated, but the specific plan notes "Because of the plan's focus on the improvement and utilization of transit facilities, and because of the mix of uses required, ordinance requirements for residential or commercial parking ratios may be reduced if warranted. A parking study prepared by an independent traffic engineering professional will be necessary to determine what, if any, reduction of parking requirements is warranted. Any such study shall be supervised by the city and paid for by the applicant."

>   Denver's zoning ordinance recognizes that shared parking and transit use reduce parking demand in mixed-use districts:

ARTICLE III. DIVISION 25. MIXED-USE DISTRICTS, Sec. 59-430.14. Off-street parking requirements.
Reduction of parking spaces. In all mixed-use zones with the exception of the T-MU-30 zone district, the number of off-street parking spaces for uses and structures located within one-fourth (1/4) mile of the outer boundary of a rail transit station, a regional or urban ten-minute bus corridor or within one-half (1/2) mile of the B-5 or B-7 zone districts may be reduced where, in the opinion of the zoning administrator, residents, employees, customers or visitors will use the transit system or will walk to their destinations. The zoning administrator shall not reduce the number of required off-street parking spaces by more than twenty-five (25) percent.

Street Standards

Many regulations include standards for public streets. Streets that are comfortable for walking are essential to transit-oriented districts, and all elements of the street design are frequently addressed. For larger projects, regulations may address the need for connectivity between the project and the local road network. The original Lindbergh Station plan included a street grid that would connect with existing streets. But when the scale of the project was increased, neighborhood groups protested this plan, fearing the impact of traffic. The developers agreed to make several traffic calming improvements, including pedestrian crossings, medians, and bulb-outs.

>   The use of an historic street pattern is also emphasized in Hillsboro's Orenco Community Townsite Conservation District: "Any new development is contingent on, where necessary,

rededication of previously vacated alleys and/or expansion of the grid of streets and alleys in order to reestablish and, as appropriate, expand the original network of streets, alleys and block perimeters."

BUILDING DENSITY AND INTENSITY

Though density and concentration of activity sufficient to support transit operations are TOD essentials, there is no absolute density standard for TOD. Given the variety of urban forms and settings in the case studies, it is not surprising that project densities vary from under ten to one hundred units per acre. What is consistent is that TOD density matches or exceeds the highest densities found elsewhere in the community. Hillsboro, Oregon, Arlington, Virginia, and other communities vary basic development standards depending on the distance from the site to the light-rail station, thus formalizing the density gradient that is an outcome of the design process in many TOD projects.

> While conventional ordinances often establish density maximums, TOD ordinances are more likely to establish minimums in order to ensure density adequate to support transit orientation. On mid- and large-sized sites there is generally a density gradient, with lower densities (and heights) at the perimeter of the property and higher density at the center, reflecting the fact that the TOD is generally the highest density development in the neighborhood.

> There are a variety of ways to regulate density, two of which are described here:

- *Specifying minimum densities.* San Jose, California, specifies in its General Plan density minimums for areas within 2,000 feet of transit stations (twenty units per acre for suburban locations, forty-five units per acre for urban ones). Hillsboro, Oregon, mandates minimum residential and nonresidential density, floor area ratio, and height based on the proximity to light-rail stations. Minimum height may also be regulated, as in Denver, where buildings facing the 16th Street Mall are required to be at least four stories tall.
- *Establishing an average density.* The City of Mountain View establishes an average density within the specific plan area, without specifying minimums or maximums for individual parcels. This has resulted in a mix of housing types with highest densities closest to the transit stations. The Whisman Station precise plan required an average density of 12–14.5 units per acre.

> To ensure the livability of TOD districts, many localities balance requirements for higher density with detailed requirements for open space. Mountain View requires that not less than 50 percent of net site area be open green space in the residential portions of the specific plan area. Density bonuses are often offered as incentives, most frequently for the inclusion of housing. Density and/or height bonuses for the provision of residential units at specified affordability

levels are incorporated in Atlanta's special public interest (SPI) zoning, in Arlington, and in a number of Denver's downtown and mixed-use districts. The SPI zoning provides density bonuses of 20 percent additional residential floor area ratio (FAR) for affordable housing. Outside of the San Antonio station area, Mountain View uses a transit overlay zone that allows an increase in office/R&D floor area from a 0.35 FAR to 0.50 FAR in exchange for transit-oriented improvements. A number of the case study projects are in localities that also offer expedited project review as an incentive. In Boulder's mixed-use zones, for example, incentives are offered for the inclusion of housing. When housing is part of a proposed mixed-use project, the requirement for discretionary review is lifted and the project's parking requirement is substantially reduced.

CAREFUL INTEGRATION OF TRANSIT

While the integration of transit is only infrequently addressed explicitly through standard zoning provisions, it emerges in the case studies as an essential element in successful TOD. In customized projects incorporating transit stops or stations—such as Lindbergh Station, Central Park Market at Del Mar Station, Willow Springs Village Center, and the Crossings—the design for the station area is detailed in the applicable customized planning and zoning documents. Circulation and parking are, not surprisingly, central issues, as project designers and agency staff seek designs that will enhance the project while providing access to transit patrons who may never take advantage of land uses within the project. In some cases, such as the L.A. County Metropolitan Transportation Authority in Pasadena and Denver RTD, transit agencies have specific regulations for the treatment not only of their right-of-way but also adjoining public space.

>   The specific plan for Mountain View's San Antonio station area offers a good example of regulatory language that addresses transit as an integral part of the project, requiring that " . . . Site planning and building design shall emphasize a pedestrian-oriented medium/high-density neighborhood character, with convenient pedestrian access to on-site retail/service

4.3
The Del Mar Station project in Pasadena, California, incorporates the new Gold Line track and platform area directly into the project. (Rendering: Moule & Polyzoides.)

4.4
Del Mar Station is a dense urban transit-oriented development, incorporating housing, office, and retail and preserving a historic depot. (Rendering: Moule & Polyzoides.)

4.5
The 1600 Market Square
project was built in accordance
with the City of Denver's
design guidelines for the
16th Street Mall. (Photo: Congress
for the New Urbanism.)

establishments, to office and retail uses in Area B, to adjacent transit connections, and to the San Antonio Center. The design of the project should create a strong neighborhood identity and image to distinguish the project from surrounding commercial uses. This character should be created by development of attractive, memorable public spaces, including streets; provision of high-quality open space amenities; distinctive architecture; and establishment of a landmark/ focal activity area. Sidewalk and plaza areas shall be provided across from the train station to create room for kiosks, coffee stands and similar light commercial uses."

> Denver's T-MU-30 transit mixed-use district specifically addresses urban development proximate to a mass transit railway system station to promote a mix, arrangement, and intensity of uses that support transit ridership and walking (this did not apply to the 16 Market Square Project, which was approved under B-7 zoning, discussed elsewhere): "The arrangement of uses allows residents, workers, and shoppers to walk to transit and other destinations within the district. The T-MU-30 district allows the broadest range of uses and most development intensity. The T-MU-30 district is intended for station areas with adequate land to create a viable transit-oriented development (TOD) and to transition to the surrounding community. A T-MU-30 district must be proximate to a mass transit railway system station and have a direct pedestrian connection to that station. That point of a T-MU-30 district that is nearest to a mass transit railway system station shall be located no more than 1500 feet from the intersecting center lines of the tracks and adjacent passenger loading platforms."

WHEN THE ZONING DOESN'T FIT

As table 4.2 illustrates, many different approaches have been used to customize zoning. Some cities, though, have chosen not to prepare unique documents or plans for customized projects, but to apply established zoning regulations and approve variances for desired characteristics. Sometimes, as with the Ohlone-Chynoweth project, both rezoning and a variance were required. The rezoning allowed increased residential density, and the variance exempted the project from standard parking requirements.

TABLE 4.2—PLANNING AND REGULATIONS FOR CASE STUDY PROJECTS

PROJECT	APPLICABLE PLANS AND POLICIES	APPLICABLE DEVELOPMENT REGULATIONS, GUIDELINES, AND PROCEDURES
Ohlone-Chynoweth San Jose, CA	San Jose General Plan Transit Corridor Residential	Planned Development Ordinance
Central Park Market at Del Mar Station Pasadena, CA	Pasadena General Plan, Pasadena Central District Specific Plan	Design Guidelines for the Central District, Central District sub-district 9 regulations, design review, 8 variances relating to height, setbacks, parking
16 Market Square Denver, CO	Denver Comprehensive Plan, Lower Downtown Neighborhood Plan	B-7 District, Design Guidelines for Lower Downtown, Design Guidelines for Lower Downtown Streetscape
The Steelyards Boulder, CO	City of Boulder Comprehensive and Subcommunity Plans	Industrial Mixed-use zoning (IMS-X) with site plan review and Main Street Mixed-use Zoning (BMS-X)
Metropolitan Place Renton, WA	City of Renton Comprehensive Plan	Center Downtown Zoning District with exceptions due to location in the "Downtown Core area." Design review under Urban Center Design Overlay Regulations
Lindbergh City Center Atlanta, GA	Atlanta Comprehensive Development Plan, Lindbergh Transportation Area Development Study	C-3-C zoning with implementing urban design provisions from Lindbergh Special Public Interest District (SPI-15)
Willow Springs Village Center	Village Comprehensive Plan	Village Center Planned Development (VC-PD) District
Addison Circle Addison, TX	1991 Comprehensive Plan	Urban Center and Special Events District with required concept plan, development plan and final development plan
Market Common at Clarendon Arlington County, VA	Clarendon Sector Plan, East Clarendon Special Coordinated Mixed-use District Plan	Site plan review; zoning districts: low office-apartment-hotel (up to 1.5 FAR for office and up to 72 units/acre for apartments) and low residential (11–15 units/acre on block facing established low density residential at 1–10 units/acre
Orenco Station Hillsboro, OR	Portland Metro 2040 Plan, Hillsboro Comprehensive Plan	General Development Standards for Station Community Planning Areas, General Design Standards for Station Community Planning Areas, Orenco Station Area Standards
The Crossings Mountain View, CA	Mountain View General Plan	San Antonio Station Precise Plan

> In approving the Del Mar Station project, the City of Pasadena, California, granted eight different variances based on the rationale that the unique project met the objectives of the city's General Plan. In Pasadena and some other communities, variances, rezonings, and incentives were readily granted when a project met community goals—especially if the goals were clearly articulated in established policy.

Outlook

In the second generation of TOD, both customized and standardized projects should emerge that feature the following:

4.6
Metropolitan Place in Renton, Washington, is a bus-oriented development aimed at revitalizing the community's downtown area. (Photo: Courtesy of King County.)

· Clearly articulated and consistent policy support for transit-oriented development that is characterized by density, mixed-use, and high-quality design.
· For all customized projects, procedures that allow site-specific design and zoning within a framework of principles for walkability, building density, and integration of transit.
· For smaller customized projects, public support for design and construction to achieve optimal integration of the transit stop or station.
· For standardized projects—each of which in turn can stimulate additional projects and collectively contribute to the making of a transit-supportive place—zoning districts that incorporate the ABCs of TOD zoning into requirements for by-right projects.

THE CHALLENGE OF PLACE MAKING

Place making is where many first-generation TOD projects fail to realize their potential. Stations in Arlington County's Rosslyn-Ballston Corridor outside Washington, D.C., have had considerable success in attracting development and creating density, but little success in creating interesting places. The Arlington County Board initiated a midcourse review of development in 1989, bringing in an urban design team to conduct a three-day charrette with professionals, developers, staff, and citizens. Their key findings included: "The vision for the different Metro station areas alludes to the development of urban villages, small town centers, and a new downtown. However, community design traditions after which current development is modeled relate more to suburban rather than to urban development." The shortcomings of the first generation projects inspired the county to use a focused planning process to control outcomes of the second generation, including a project called Market Common. Both the retail and residential portions of Market Common incorporate many more design features associated with successful places; the sale of the project in 2002 for $166 million—reportedly the highest price in the country for many years—suggests the midcourse correction was on target.

> In a number of the case study locations, regional and historical architectural and landscape traditions contribute to successful place making. Regulations in Denver's LODO District and

Pasadena's downtown explicitly refer to historic styles and patterns, thereby building on the existing urban fabric. Pasadena's General Plan supports imaginative and creative design; the guidelines discourage imitations of earlier architectural styles, and suggest that anyone relying on that approach reinterpret historical architecture in a contemporary manner. The Village Center in Willow Springs draws on regional historical influences as evidenced in the design of many towns along the Illinois & Michigan Canal.

> The extent to which zoning regulations address place making is varied. The Hillsboro, Oregon, general design standards for station community planning areas (section 138) provide a good list of place-making elements, including:

- Improvements between streets and buildings
- Building entries and orientation
- Ground floor windows and building facades
- Building step-backs
- Location and design of off-street parking
- Drive-through uses (seriously restricted)
- Outdoor display, storage, and signs
- Alleys
- Streetscape design standards and guidelines
- Standards for protection within historic and cultural conservation districts

> Defining place-making objectives is challenging, since a successful place seems to always have something intangible about it. In Mountain View, public spaces are emphasized as a way to create a neighborhood "feel": "A primary goal for Area D [site of former Old Mill Shopping Center, to become The Crossings] shall be to establish a strong sense of neighborhood. The project shall be organized around public streets, with streets as public open space, buildings oriented to streets, and a neighborhood-serving retail center. The physical design of the project shall include: physical elements that provide places for casual interaction between neighbors; recreational facilities that give opportunities for residents to interact; and a quality of design that fosters pride of ownership." The challenge of place making is present in all development projects. It is heightened in TOD projects because of the importance of "getting it right" in a way that benefits the project itself, its immediate surroundings, and the broader community of transit users.

> Planning and zoning offer tremendous opportunity to advance TOD. While some municipalities create financial incentives for desirable projects, they may not appreciate the value of providing incentives by laying out a clear policy framework and effective zoning. The real incentive is in laying out a clear policy framework; we cannot stress enough how important it is that public agencies take on this responsibility. If public agencies are doing a good job with zoning,

planning, and predevelopment work, then they are creating workable projects for developers—and thus creating value for both the developer and the community.

NOTES

1   There are a small number of exceptions when state or federal legislatures grant special agencies independence from local government regulations, as is the case with the Pasadena Blue Line Construction Authority, which built the rail line to the Del Mar station in Pasadena and then turned the line over to the L.A. County Metropolitan Transportation Authority to operate.

REFERENCES

Ohlone-Chynoweth

California Department of Transportation. 2002. Statewide TOD Study Appendix, Vol. 2, "Profile of Ohlone-Chynoweth."

City of San Jose. 2001. Chapter 20 Municipal Code, Zoning Ordinance. Effective 11/29/01.

Marketing Information on City of San Jose's Affordable Housing Program. At www.ci.san-jose.ca.us.

Central Park Market at Del Mar Station

City of Pasadena. 2002. Citywide Design Principles. Adopted Oct. 21, 2002.

City of Pasadena. Central District Specific Plan (online version). At www.ci.pasadena.ca.us.

City of Pasadena. Land Use Element of Pasadena General Plan. At www.ci.pasadena.ca.us.

City of Pasadena. Website information on project development. At www.ci.pasadena.ca.us.

City of Pasadena. 2001. Zoning Hearing Officer Staff Report on Variance #11386 for Del Mar Station project. December 19, 2001.

Cronin, Jeff (City of Pasadena Design Commission Staff). 2003. Phone interview with the author. January 9.

Miller, Denver (Zoning Administrator, City of Pasadena). 2003. Phone interview with the author. January 9.

16 Market Square

City and County of Denver Community Planning and Development Agency. 1995. Design Review for B5 Downtown Zoning. Spring.

City and County of Denver Landmark Preservation Commission. B-7 Zone District Ordinance, as amended. At www.denvergov.org.

City and County of Denver Landmark Preservation Commission. Design Guidelines for Denver Landmarks and Landmark Districts. At www.denvergov.org.

City and County of Denver Landmark Preservation Commission and Community Planning and Development Agency. 1991. Design Guidelines for Lower Downtown Streetscape.

Fleissig, Will (Director of Development, Continuum Partners). 2003. Phone interview with the author. January 16.

City of Denver. Denver B-5 Zone, Chapter 59 Zoning, Article III District Regulations, Division 21, B-5 District, Sec. 59-368. At www.denvergov.org.

City of Denver. Lower Downtown Neighborhood Plan. At www.denvergov.org.

The Steelyards

City of Boulder. N.d. Project information sheet on The Steelyards.

City of Boulder. Title 9 Municipal Code Land Use Regulation, Chapters 3.1, Uses of Land 3.2, Bulk and Density Standards. Chapter 4, Land Development Review. Adopted by Ordinance No. 5562. Amended by Ordinance No. 5894. Standards for Industrial Mixed-use zoning (IMS-X) with site plan review and Main Street Mixed-use Zoning (BMS-X), Business Main Street (BMS-X) zone. Industrial Main Street (IMS-X) zone.

Denver Regional Council of Governments. Metro Vision 2020. At www.drcog.org.

McHeyser, Ruth (City of Boulder). 2002. Phone interview by Sarah Pulleyblank. May 8.

Metropolitan Place

Carlson, Susan (Director of Economic Development, City of Renton). 2002. Phone interview with the author. May 10. City of Renton. Comprehensive Plan. At www.ci.renton.wa.us.

City of Renton, Department of Planning/Building/Public Works. 1999. Administrative Site Plan Approval & Environmental Review Committee Staff Report for Sheridan Mixed Use Development. LUA-099-141. December 14.

City of Renton. 2001. Land Use Districts. Chapter 2 of Renton Zoning Ordinance Last amended by Ordinance 4917, September 17.

City of Renton. 2000. Ordinance #4821, Urban Center Design Overlay District Guidelines. January 3.

Lindbergh Station

City of Atlanta, Department of Planning, Development and Neighborhood Conservation. An Ordinance to Amend the 1982 Zoning Ordinance of the City of Atlanta, 01-0-0544, Z-01-23 SPI-15 Lindbergh Transit Station Area District Regulations.

City of Atlanta, Department of Planning, Development and Neighborhood Conservation, Bureau of Planning. 2001. 2001 Lindbergh Transit Station Area Development Study. Draft of Executive Summary. January.

Tunnell-Spangler & Associates. N.d. Project Information. At www.tunspan.com.

Willow Springs Village Center

Skrodzki, Rick (Willow Springs Village attorney). 2003. Phone interview with the author. January 9.

Teska, Robert (Consultant to Village of Willow Springs). 2003. Phone interview with the author. January 7.

Village Board of Willow Springs. 1998. Comprehensive Plan Amendment for the Village Center. Prepared by Teska Associates, Inc. Ordinance #98-0-26. November 24.

Village of Willow Springs, Cook County, Illinois. 1983. Village Center Planned Unit Development Ordinance (No. 99-0-6) 3/1/99, amendment to Title 9A (Zoning Regulations) of the Village of Willow Springs Village Code.

Addison Circle

Appendix A Zoning, Article XIX. UC Urban Center District Regulations.

Gosling, John R. 1996. Addison Circle: Beyond New Urbanism. *Urban Land* March.

Moran, Carmen (City of Addison, Texas). 2002. Phone interview by Sarah Pulleyblank. April 30.

Town of Addison, Texas. Marketing Materials distributed by the Town of Addison. At www.ci.addison.tx.us.

Town of Addison, Texas. Ordinance No. 095-019 5/3/95 establishing the UC Urban Center District. At www.ci.addison.tx.us.

Market Common Clarendon

Arlington County, Virginia. 1994. Department of Community Affairs, Planning, Housing, and Community Development Division. Planning Section, Clarendon Sector Plan. May.

Arlington County, Virginia. 1994. East Clarendon Special Coordinated Mixed-use District Plan, September 20.

Arlington County, Virginia. 1999. PLA-1917, Amendment to General Land Use Plan, and rezoning request for a change in land classification. Approved November 13.

Arlington County, Virginia. PLA-2098, SP #339 Site Plan Amendment for Market Common Clarendon.

Arlington County, Virginia. 2002. PLA-2723, Carry-over amendment to Market Common Clarendon Site Plan. January 31. 1990. Clarendon Sector Plan Addendum A. May 19.

Orenco Station

City of Hillsboro, Zoning Ordinance No. 1945, as amended. Volume II: Sections 136 through 142, Station Community Planning Areas. Passed 9/3/63, amended through April, 1997.

Parsons, Brinckerhoff, Quade & Douglas et al. 1996. Public Policy and Transit Oriented Development: Six International Case Studies. TCRP Project HI, Transit Cooperative Research Program, Transportation Research Board. March.

The Crossings

American Planning Association. 2002. Mountain View Transit Vision Wins APA Award. January 25. At www.planning.org.

City of Mountain View. 1997. San Antonio Station Precise Plan. Approved June 29 At www.ci.mtnview.ca.us.

Calthorpe Associates. N.d. The Crossings Transit-Oriented Neighborhood Project information. At www.calthorpe.com.

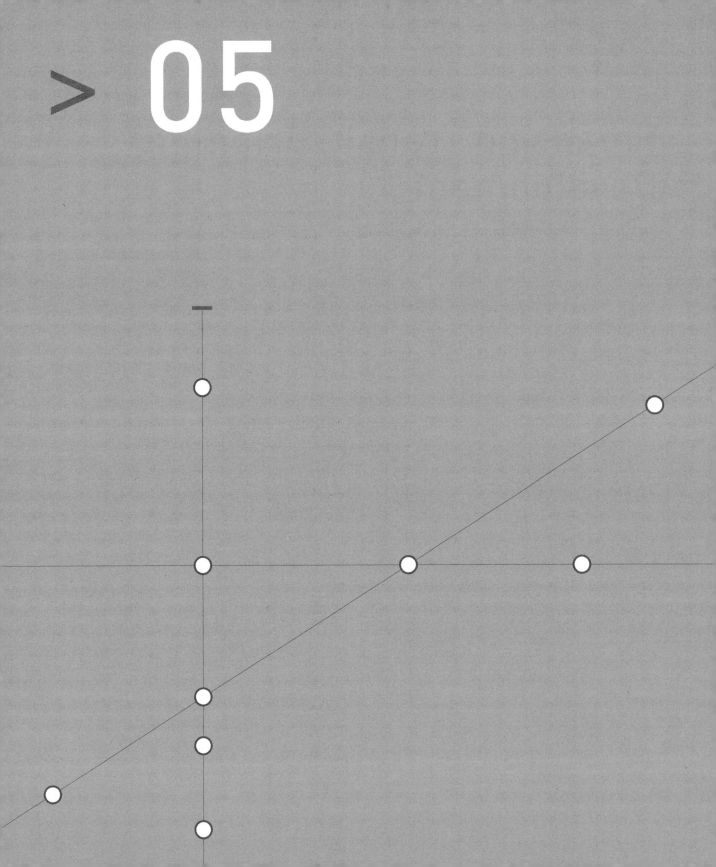

Financing Transit-Oriented Development

Julia Parzen and Abby Jo Sigal

Financing complex mixed-use transit-oriented development (TOD) projects is easier than it was a decade ago. This is the case not only in the 24-hour cities, such as New York, Chicago, and San Francisco, but also in Dallas (both city and suburbs), Houston, Denver, Pasadena, Tampa, midtown Atlanta, Pentagon City, and an array of other cities and suburbs. Many more investors in both debt and equity understand mixed use, live-work, and ground floor retail and are willing to provide capital, including long-term debt. Loan officers across the nation are willing and able to do deals, as are a growing number of insurance companies, pension funds, and established real estate industry players such as Trammell Crow and Millennium Partners. Creative developers have tapped a myriad of public funds and public interest funds for housing, community development, brownfields, and other purposes. Many special funds are looking for good projects and would appreciate the benefits of TODs.

> Still, there are continuing challenges to financing these complex and less familiar projects. In many cases where TOD, and mixed-use infill projects in general, have been successfully financed, there has been a public role. Developers say that for higher density, mixed-use projects to be attractive to private capital markets, they need strong community planning and support, local champions willing to streamline the process, and, often, public financial support to fill gaps. In addition, developers who have financed these projects have had to do everything possible to make them recognizable to investors and to minimize uncertainty. It is no surprise that financing has been easier to attract when the developer has a track record, can produce comparables, provides a detailed business plan, has prior relationships with lenders, and simplifies the financial structure as much as possible.

> This chapter describes the challenges to financing TOD, the strategies people are using to succeed in spite of the challenges, and ideas people have about how to make it easier to finance TODs in the future.[1] Many of the strategies described are replicable, especially where there is strong public and private leadership. The chapter is organized into four sections:

·   *Increasing certainty.* In this discussion, we describe how the handling of the very early stages of TOD projects impacts the actual as well as perceived risk and thus can either help or hinder the ability to secure financing.

·   *Enabling public investors to capture the value of public investment.* Here the focus is on public leadership and investment in TODs, which private investors often consider essential, and how it can be expanded to enable public investors to earn fair returns on their investment.

·   *Structuring the Deal.* This section highlights the importance of thinking comprehensively about TOD projects, while deconstructing them to secure both equity and debt from a wide variety of sources, including cultivating new capital sources.

·   *Addressing place and node: financing TOD's distinctive components.* The final section presents strategies for addressing the financing issues related to creating a main street feel, providing mixed-income housing, establishing community services, getting parking right, reusing contaminated land, reusing historical buildings, and developing on transit agency land.

>   The illustrative examples throughout the chapter come from not only transit-oriented developments (TODs) but also, where they are relevant, New Urbanist projects, infill developments, mixed-use developments, brownfield redevelopments, and other projects. While these examples are relevant in addressing financing issues related to aspects of TOD, TODs are often more complex than any of them because of the transit agency involvement, which also is described and illustrated in this chapter.

THE REAL ESTATE DEVELOPMENT AND FINANCING PROCESS
To understand the financing issues related to TOD, it is helpful to be familiar with the steps involved in the real estate development process. This sidebar provides an introduction for those new to real estate development.

> A real estate development project begins with an idea for a project. Typically, the developer is the entity that pursues the idea. The developer can be a for-profit or not-for-profit organization or, in some cases, a government agency. Developers fill gaps in their expertise by adding partners to create a development team.

> A successful development team will have the range of skills needed to mitigate four risks associated with a real estate development project: entitlement risk, construction risk, financial risk, and market risk.[1]

·   Entitlement risk is the risk associated with securing the approvals, zoning, and permits critical for the project to be built and occupied. The savvy required to navigate through the entitlement process is essential for any development project, unless the developer comes in

after the project has its entitlements, or if the project can be built without any zoning changes or variances. Such as-of-right development is very rare for TOD projects.

·   Construction risk is the technical risk related to actually building the project, including unknown site conditions, any environmental issues that may arise, the physical engineering of the project, the dangers of a construction site, and time delays. Real estate development skills that mitigate this risk are due diligence, good project management, and working with skilled contractors.

·   Financial risk is the risk related to securing funds for the project. The first tier of this risk is whether the project can get financing at all. Is the project attractive to market rate equity and debt investors? Does it need below-market-rate financing? What are the financing terms? Organizations with real estate development acumen manage this risk with strong underwriting and deal structuring skills and relationships with financing sources such as banks, pension funds, high-net-worth individuals, foundations, and government agencies. The second tier of risk, assuming a project can secure the needed financing, is interest rate risk. This aspect of financial risk can be managed with sophisticated use of financial tools such as derivatives and bridge loans.

· Market risk is the risk associated with insuring that the project meets its pro forma projections, that is, whether or not it will lease up or sell at the anticipated rents or prices and within the projected time frame. To mitigate this risk, developers make sure they have experience in positioning and marketing similar types of projects, understand the nuances of the project's market, pre-lease or pre-sell, and plan ways to mitigate overall real estate market cycles.

> Once an experienced development team is in place and the project is conceptualized, the next step in the real estate development process is gaining control of the site. A variety of legal arrangements can give the development team site control, including fee-simple purchase,[2] option to purchase, a ground lease, joint venture with the property owner, or some other legally binding document. Often, the development team creates a limited liability corporation or partnership to sign the contracts that give them site control and to incur the project costs going forward.

> The next step is to translate the idea into a set of buildable drawings and plans. Plans with an increasing level of detail need to be prepared and presented to the agencies, planning committees, and other entities that will enable the project to go forward by giving it the necessary approvals and permits. The development team will use a final set of these drawings and plans to determine how much the project will cost. The team will either have the expertise in-house to act as general contractor or select a general contractor through a bid process or a negotiated bid with a selected contractor.

> As the plans become more detailed, the development team typically begins seeking financing commitments for the project. If the team itself does not have sufficient equity, it looks for equity from other sources such as real estate equity funds, high-net-worth individuals, foundations, and public agencies. The team must also identify debt sources for the construction loan and the permanent financing, also known as the "take-out," when construction is complete. The construction loan is a short-term loan that takes on the construction risk of the project and the permanent financing is a long-term loan, from five to thirty years, that takes on primarily the market risk of the project. A construction lender is very concerned that a permanent loan commitment be secured so that it can be taken out; whereas the permanent lender focuses on the project's cash flow and whether or not it will cover the loan's debt service.

> A development team may decide to have a short-term take-out, known as a mezzanine or bridge loan, between the construction and permanent loans. Mezzanine debt or bridge loans have a shorter term than permanent loans. A project that is perceived as very risky is a likely candidate for mezzanine debt, using the mezzanine financing until it can prove its value and secure a long-term loan at a reasonable rate.

> Once the design of a project is complete, the entitlements secured, and the financing in place, the construction loan closing takes place and the construction begins. As the construction proceeds, the limited liability corporation or partnership draws down on the construction loan and equity to pay the bills. A good development team closely monitors the construction to ensure that it comes in on time and on budget, because time delays and changes can greatly increase the total development cost of the project.

> During construction, the development team begins to position and market the project with the goal of pre-leasing as much space and selling as many units as possible. Once the project is built and reaches stabilization—that is, a previously agreed to percentage of units leased or sold—the construction loan is taken out by the permanent or mezzanine debt. In some projects, additional equity may also come in at this point. Project reserves are often funded when the construction loan is taken out. Reserves may be required if the financial projections indicate an operating deficit any time during the duration of the loan, or, in the case of low-income housing tax credit projects, during the compliance period for the equity. Some developers may sell the project at this point, while others decide to keep it for the long term in their portfolio.

1   Abby Jo Sigal thanks Steve Chamberlin for identifying these four risks in his class on Real Estate Development at UC Berkeley.

2   A fee simple buyer acquires ownership of the entire property, including both the land and the buildings. The fee simple owner does not pay ground rent, but does pay maintenance fees and real property taxes.

Increasing Certainty: Laying the Groundwork

The early stages of a real estate project, like any new business, are highly uncertain. As a result, the cost of capital is high. The complexity of TOD projects can magnify the uncertainty and result in capital that is not only expensive, but also often very difficult to find. Often developers of these complex projects seek early stage capital from "patient" sources such as public coffers, foundations, special funds with social missions, friends, and sympathetic investors. The alternative is to reduce the uncertainty. There is much that can be done early on to create greater certainty and make it easier to leverage more financing sources to complete a TOD project.

PUT ZONING AND PERMITTING IN PLACE

Local planning and zoning rules that set up roadblocks and require special variances for TOD scare off developers and investors. Cities that have proactively addressed zoning and permitting barriers, as described in chapter 4, have helped developers of higher density mixed-use projects attract investors. Creating a streamlined process with supportive codes and other incentives is even better. The success in attracting private investment to the new light-rail line between Portland and Hillsboro in Oregon has been attributed to a public vision for transit-oriented development, adoption of plans and regulations to allow TOD, and public incentives that made structured parking feasible. Developers across the nation who are experienced in TOD choose to do projects in localities that they know are supportive of TOD projects.

PARTNER WITH EXPERIENCED DEVELOPERS

Many of the developers who have tackled TOD most aggressively have been smaller firms with strong community ties that are stretching to make the deals work. They have had a harder time attracting capital for complex and innovative TOD projects than have larger, better-capitalized firms.[2] Investment partners prefer not only well-capitalized but also experienced developers that understand the many details of making mixed-use development work. Developer incentives and streamlined processes can attract more and larger developers and help smaller and less-experienced developers break new ground.

CREATE A BROAD VISION AND GET COMMUNITY SUPPORT

Projects that have had an inclusive planning process often encounter fewer objections along the way and have an easier time with financing because of their broad support. In places such as Portland, Oregon, Boulder, Colorado, and Seattle, Washington, a factor in the successful creation of transit-oriented communities has been broad citizen involvement and the adoption of master development plans. At Swan's Market, a mixed-income development in Oakland, California, a broad coalition, consisting of not only city and county leaders, but also historic preservation organizations, local merchants, residents, a church, and potential tenants drove the project forward. Charrettes can be a good way to build both shared a vision and close deals with investors. Potential retail investors in a new downtown Albuquerque development realized the potential of the development site after they participated in a charrette. While planning processes take time, the cost of the time spent planning can be mitigated if cities preapprove projects that are formulated through rigorous processes.

BUILD A DETAILED BUSINESS PLAN WITH STRONG MARKET ANALYSIS

The traditional preparation for funding—pro forma financial statements, a back-of-the-envelope market study, comparables and existing relationships—is often not enough for a TOD project. More complex projects, in particular, need a business plan that provides a detailed analysis of the market and costs for each use, a strategy to capitalize on the mix of uses and phasing to enhance value, an analysis of key stakeholders and their motivations, and a description of potential sources of funding for each period of the project's life. The business plan must be a tool for exploring how to best finance the deal and position it to secure financing.

> Demonstrating the market for each of the uses in a mixed-use project is a continuing challenge. It helps to show that there is a market by preleasing space or enlisting support from potential public and private tenants in approaching investors. Another strategy is to provide stories of successful mixed-use, infill, and transit-oriented projects that have been built in comparable locations, as well as to share data on the impact of these developments on property values.

PUBLIC INVESTMENT IN PREDEVELOPMENT CAN JUMP-START PRIVATE INVESTMENT

There are few sources of capital for zoning work, architectural work, or land acquisition. Often a developer has to use its own money to carry land until construction starts, which for TOD projects can be three years or longer. For this reason, public sector investment in predevelopment has jump-started private investment in many TOD projects.

> Communities, transit agencies, and foundations often help developers by funding the early planning for TOD projects. At the Pleasant Hill Bay Area Rapid Transit (BART) Station in the San Francisco Bay Area, the county paid for the charrette process, which helped invigorate the project. (The county will be paid back once the project is under way.) BART provided funds for planning projects near stations in West Oakland and Pittsburg/Bay Point. New Jersey Transit and the Geraldine R. Dodge Foundation split the costs of planning studies for a station renewal program targeting a number of stations.

> Some public agencies help developers by acquiring land, accepting less than market value for land, and delaying payment on land to improve the economics of TODs. TriMet, the Portland regional transit authority, has purchased several sites for resale to transit-supportive projects, as has the Santa Clara Valley Transit Agency (VTA). For the Pleasant Hill BART station in the Bay Area, the Contra Costa County Redevelopment Agency assembled land parcels and invested in infrastructure improvements valued at $20 million through tax increment financing, which is a commonly used mechanism that funds infrastructure up front with expected future increases in tax revenues.

> Nonprofit TOD developers have gotten help from the Local Initiatives Support Corporation (LISC) and the Enterprise Foundation for predevelopment and site acquisition funding. For example, Enterprise made a $260,000 loan for acquisition and predevelopment financing to

Human Solutions for the Ankney Arms, a higher density infill affordable housing project a block from light-rail. The Enterprise Foundation's $20 million Smart Growth Fund, or Metropolitan Regional Acquisition Fund, was created to bank land in Portland, Oregon, including land for housing development along transit corridors. There are plans to replicate the fund in Seattle and Salt Lake City with the Federal Home Loan Bank of Seattle providing the capital.

> There is growing interest in creating new investment funds to assist with land acquisition for projects, especially mixed-use transit-oriented developments that will benefit low- and moderate-income people. The Collins Center has formed a Community Land Trust Fund to encourage investment in older urban areas in South Florida. The Bay Area Smart Growth Fund, which was created to invest in mixed-use development projects, will be used to finance land acquisition.

Enabling Public Investors to Capture the Value of TOD Investment

Many of the strategies to increase certainty for TOD projects include a role for the public. TODs often need a champion in the public realm in order to obtain capital from the private sector. Private investors look for signs that local governments will facilitate the public review process. Investors also look for signs of transit agency commitment, recognizing the uncertainty and complexity associated with transit access, offset parking, and zoning changes. Local government and transit agency champions can clarify and simplify the steps, substantially reducing risk and lowering financing costs. At Swan's Market, the combination of community and city support, along with good operating economic projections and regulatory encouragement, convinced lenders to invest in a project they otherwise would not have considered.

> The majority of first-generation TOD projects has needed a boost of public investment. Joseph Freed & Associates was able to finance mixed-use transit-oriented developments in Arlington Heights and Palatine, suburbs of Chicago, because the two towns had concrete development plans for the area and were willing to pay for structured parking lots, use tax increment financing, and float bonds. In addition to lowering costs and increasing certainty, public investment is a tangible demonstration of the local government's commitment.

> Enabling public investors to "capture the value" of public investment in TODs is key to obtaining local government and transit agency support for these projects. The public should benefit when private land values increase as the result of public investment in a TOD. Successful TODs can produce substantial financial and social returns, especially in the medium and long terms. At a time when competition for public money is intense, TOD value capture can provide a way to help fund transit projects, rebuild communities, and create vibrant urban centers.

> It takes skill to structure a fair deal for value capture. Strategies need to maximize the capture from the increase in land value without diminishing the incentive for private investment in improvements to the land. Past experience suggests transit agencies and local governments need to work together to create the most attractive investment package for all participants. Still,

because local governments and transit agencies have different tools and opportunities, each merits its own discussion.

VALUE CAPTURE FOR LOCAL GOVERNMENTS

Local governments have many tried-and-true tools they can use to invest in TODs. A housing authority may agree to contribute funds so that some share of housing is affordable. A district may pay for shared parking to attract commercial development. For example, as an equity partner for the TOD at the Pleasant Hill Bart Station in the Bay Area, the Contra Costa Redevelopment Agency assembled the land for the private developers; helped finance the infrastructure, BART replacement parking, and community amenities; and helped finance affordable housing on the site.

> Local government investment can produce solid public returns, including more livable communities, property taxes, sales tax increment, special assessments, parking fees, utility user fees, business license fees, and the "multiplier effect" generated by the new jobs and businesses. KPMG Peat Marwick estimated in a northern Virginia study that the Commonwealth of Virginia is receiving an annual rate of return of 19 percent on its investment in Metrorail through additional development attracted by Metrorail. The Village of Arlington Heights in Chicago has seen its much smaller project also produce large early returns. For example, the village invested $9.9 million dollars in a garage and another $4 million in infrastructure and land acquisition in one early mixed-use project. Before development, the site produced approximately $65,000 per year in property taxes, and it was projected that by 2003, when the development would be fully assessed, it would produce $1.5 million in property and sales taxes. Prior to the recent wave of development, downtown restaurant gross sales receipts were $7 million, and were projected to increase soon to $16–17 million.

> Public agencies need staff skilled in real estate finance and deal structuring to negotiate TOD deals that avoid wasting subsidies and maximize public benefits. To ensure that it was successful at value capture under its long-term plan for downtown redevelopment, Arlington Heights studied likely gaps in private financing and produced projections of what tax increment could be generated and its potential return on investment for each project. The village then developed a redevelopment agreement that includes a provision for reducing the subsidy if the developer received more than the target rate of return.

VALUE CAPTURE FOR TRANSIT AGENCIES

The 1997 Federal Transit Administration's revised "Policy on Transit Joint Development" removed many federal obstacles to partnerships between transit systems and private developers. The policy made it clear that property acquired with federal funds could be used to support transit-oriented joint development and that development project income could be used by the transit agency for eligible transit purposes. In addition, transit agencies could place income from the sale of surplus property or air rights development into revolving funds to support additional transit-oriented development activities.

> Transit agency investment in TOD can take the form of station investments, sale or lease of land, or investment in amenities and parking near the station. Sometimes transit agency investments are below the market rate to make a project work. For example, the Metropolitan Transit Development Board in San Diego actively encourages lenders to fund mixed-use projects that are part of joint developments, sometimes providing a modest reduction on rent to make the financing work.

> While the initial transit agency approach to value capture has been to focus on lease or sale revenues, transit agencies are increasingly interested in the potential to improve ridership. For example, the Washington Metropolitan Area Transit Authority (WMATA) began a program in 1991 to encourage the establishment of child care centers at Metro stations based upon the finding that commuter side trips for child care are a major barrier to the use of public transit by working parents. The Santa Clara Valley Transportation Authority invests in high density residential joint development to generate revenue to defray operating and other expenses and to increase ridership, both by increasing density and by enhancing the environment at and around its park-and-ride lots.

> Transit agencies also benefit from TOD by reducing parking requirements, attracting partners to fund station renovations, and broadening the constituency for transit service. According to the senior director of planning at Metra in the Chicago area, TOD will help it save millions in parking construction costs by increasing the number of transit users who walk to its stations. New Jersey Transit was able to complete station renovations in spite of budget cuts because of its partnership with local governments and other entities, which added resources to the projects and improved New Jersey Transit's ability to access special federal transportation funds. Finally, transit agency involvement in the extensive community process that produces good TOD can create a broader constituency for funding to expand and improve transit service.

> A handful of transit agencies have taken the lead on development around transit stations and have been pleased with the returns on their investment. For example, WMATA has undertaken fifty-six revenue-producing joint development projects at a value of more than $3.5 billion on land it owns. These projects have generated more than $129 million annually in revenue for WMATA, an amount that is expected to double to $214 million between 2002 and 2007.[3] At Lindbergh Station in Atlanta, the Metropolitan Atlanta Rapid Transit Authority (MARTA) is investing $81 million in infrastructure, parking structures, utilities, landscaping, and amenities. In return MARTA expects to receive lease revenues, increased ridership, and a positive community response to its support of the project. MARTA's Paul Vespermann projects that the

combined revenues from ground leases and increased ridership should add up to a 22 percent return on MARTA's investment in Lindbergh Station.

> To be effective at TOD joint development, transit agencies need to see themselves as developers and investors and hire people with real estate expertise. Increasingly, transit agencies are hiring staff to work with local governments on land-use planning and on funding partnerships. For example, TriMet in Portland subcontracted for this expertise by bringing in the Portland Development Commission.

> It is important that transit agencies understand the impact that their choices will have on value capture for potential investors. In particular, the common transit agency preference for ground leases over sales can adversely impact financing. A ground lease is a long-term lease of unimproved land. The developer constructs and operates the improvements on the property and pays the lessor rent on a net basis. Ground leases are becoming more prevalent in the United States, especially for infill parcel developments.[4] Ground leases can be less attractive to equity investors than simple ownership because it is more difficult to establish a clear exit strategy. It can also be more difficult to offer equity investors market rate returns, as the resale value of property on leased land can be diminished by as much as 10 percent depending on the term remaining on the lease. Also, research suggests that developers will not redevelop already leased property to the highest and best use because they must amortize improvements over the remaining life of the lease.

> To improve the attractiveness of TOD to private investors, transit agencies are finding ways to sell land that allow them to maintain some control over land use. For example, they may require that the land continue to be used for transit-compatible uses. Transit agencies that sell land also are finding ways to share in the upside potential. For example, in Ballston, Virginia, WMATA agreed to a percentage share of gross proceeds from condominium sales rather than rent payments on land leases, realizing a 50 percent price premium (over appraised value) on the land sales.

> Transit agencies are experimenting with equity participation, both as a way to improve private investor appeal and to share in upside returns on successful projects. When a transit agency contributes land to a project in exchange for an equity stake, its interest in the property is subordinate to the lenders. Lenders prefer this arrangement to a ground lease because it reduces the lender's risk. Although the returns are less certain than for a ground lease, a well-structured equity investment can allow a transit agency to enjoy the benefits of upside potential in the property. The City of Albuquerque is an equity investor in a 500,000-square-foot commercial and residential development in downtown Albuquerque. In return for contributing the land, building a 635-space public parking garage, and providing the project with tax abatements, the city will receive 25 percent of the cash flow after expenses and debt service in years six to twelve and 50 percent

in years twelve to twenty or until 125 percent of its investment is returned, in addition to any other public revenues the project generates for the city.

> Not yet satisfied with the tools transit agencies have for value capture, some people are advocating for taxing mechanisms to collect revenues generated by increases to real estate values that occur following transit improvements. Bay Area developers for the Pleasant Hill BART Station joint development participate in an assessment district that pays for TOD improvements. The BART developers prepaid annual assessments for twenty years to provide $20 million in infrastructure improvements. The assessment can be passed through to the tenants if the market is strong, thus not impacting the net operating income. However, in a softer real estate market tenants may demand rents that are too low to cover the assessment.

Structuring the Deal

How TOD projects are structured impacts access to equity and debt financing. Developers have found they can position projects for financing by thinking about the projects comprehensively, while deconstructing them to meet the needs of a wide variety of investors. They have carefully phased projects to produce early cash flows for impatient equity investors. They have cultivated new special interest equity investors that are more patient. Finally, they have simplified the projects to produce familiar-looking deals for debt investors.

PHASE THE PROJECT TO PRODUCE EARLY CASH FLOWS

Unlike shopping malls, which have their highest returns when they are shiny and new, TODs tend to have a value gap. A value gap exists when the initial value of a project is lower than its long-term value. A project that either creates a neighborhood or transforms it, attracting new investment and people, will tend to have a much lower value—and lower returns—in the beginning than it will several years down the road. TODs often test new markets, either through design or through location. Design innovations include the development of higher density housing in areas that traditionally have had only single-family homes; untested locations include underutilized areas in suburban downtown and industrial brownfield sites.[5] Either way, early revenues do not reflect the future value of the place.[6] The cost of the place-making and transportation features that are important to TOD can compound the value gap by adding extra costs to the project.

> Financiers will finance TODs that have a value gap if experienced developers carefully phase the projects. Phasing mitigates risks by reducing the initial financial outlay until a track record is established. For example, a developer may wait to add high density market rate housing to a project until after commercial office and retail is established adjacent to a transit station. Phasing allows developers to focus on aspects of the project that can produce early returns. It also allows developers with differing types of expertise to come on board when it makes the most sense for them to do so.

CULTIVATE NEW AND SPECIAL INTEREST EQUITY INVESTORS

Even with thoughtful project phasing, many TOD projects may not be attractive to traditional real estate equity investors. For example, the real estate equity market includes privately held and publicly owned real estate companies, such as real estate investment trusts (REITs). Many REITs, as well as other equity investors, are not willing to accept the different appearance or slower returns that can come from creating or redeveloping a place through a TOD. Publicly traded REITs are under great pressure to show quarter-by-quarter growth. Also, TOD developments can be more difficult for these intermediaries to sell, especially if they are encumbered with a ground lease or with less parking than the norm. In 2002, Federal Realty Investment Trust ended its eight-year-old program targeting the acquisition and development of mixed-use town center properties, such as the Lindbergh City Center TOD in Atlanta. It said that mixed-use urban-style projects require too much investment up front, but pay off only gradually, which does not align well with the objectives of most REIT shareholders for steady earnings and a growing dividend.

> Still, many TODs attract equity investors. Some developers are able to self-finance. Some, especially larger, more experienced developers, have found that their usual equity partners are willing TOD investors. Some developers have identified investors with a special interest in a location, such as a local family with a sense of civic responsibility. And some developers have attracted public equity. In Ballston, Virginia, for example, WMATA became an equity partner in one condominium project. Even with the exit of Federal Realty Investment Trust, a few REITs remain active investors in mixed-use developments. For example, Madison Park REIT in Oakland, California, specializes in the adaptive reuse of large industrial buildings into live-work lofts and mixed-use projects with live-work lofts as a component, using the sale of historical tax credits to obtain low-cost equity capital.

> Some TOD developers are cultivating insurance companies, pension funds, and endowments funds, which have longer-term liabilities that they need to match with cash flow from assets. Jacoby Development has put up a substantial amount of its own capital and has identified a joint venture partner in AIG Global Real Estate Investment Corporation, the largest insurer in the nation. Arcadia Land Company is pursuing multiple partnerships with local, place-based foundations, as it has done in downtown Albuquerque, New Mexico, with the McCune Foundation. The largest pension funds are increasingly involved in urban infill development. The California Public Employees Retirement System (CalPERS), the nation's largest public pension fund, has invested $405 million into CIM California Urban Real Estate Fund LP to invest in commercial and residential real estate projects in urban areas and work with community redevelopment agencies and developers on redevelopment projects. Another CalPERS partnership between Bridge Housing, the largest provider of affordable housing in the Bay Area, and RREEF, a major real estate investment advisor, is running a $200 million Northern California urban infill

program. As of late 2001, Post Properties had undertaken three joint ventures with the New York State Common Retirement Fund, the nation's second largest public pension fund. Another active pension fund investor in urban projects is AFL-CIO Investment Trusts, which is already an experienced investor in affordable, mixed-income, and market-rate housing and commercial development.

> Some developers believe new financial products are needed to attract broader pension fund and foundation investment. Christopher Leinberger, the founding partner of Arcadia Land Company, urges pension funds to consider investments in time tranches, an idea borrowed from the concept of commercial mortgage-backed securities, where pieces of debt called tranches are divided according to the risk associated with each of them. Rather than tranching solely based on risk, his strategy is to tranche equity based on time. The first position, which has the lowest yield, is paid off first. First tranche investors are typical equity investors. Then the mezzanine piece is paid off at a higher yield in years six through twelve. Leinberger has been urging pension funds and insurance companies to invest in the second tranche. The third time tranche is paid off in years thirteen through twenty. The third time tranche investors would include municipalities, churches, or transit agencies that provide land for new development. While foundations in two cities have invested in the second tranche of Leinberger projects, in 2003 pension funds were waiting to see the track record on these deals.

> Proponents of TOD also are looking to new smart growth funds to broaden the equity market. A variety of civic-minded investors have been receptive to regional equity funds created to fill a piece of the equity gap in low-income communities, although these funds also have a relatively short time horizon. The Bay Area Smart Growth Fund's purpose is to find transit-oriented, mixed-use projects where the numbers don't quite work by stepping in with equity for a three- to five-year horizon. Pacific Coast Capital Partners, LLC is the fund manager and investors include Wells Fargo, Bank of America, and the PMI Group, a mortgage insurance company. The $40 million Nehemiah Sacramento Valley Fund will primarily invest in mixed-use projects in low- to moderate-income neighborhoods in the six contiguous counties of the Sacramento region. The Collins Center has been working for some time on a series of funds to support mixed-use, mixed-income projects that are pedestrian-oriented in South Florida. One fund would be an equity real estate fund for projects in inner-city neighborhoods. Fund-raising efforts would target pension funds, banks, and private foundations.

> It is too soon to say whether the new smart growth funds will fill a part of the perceived equity gap. They will have the greatest impact if they help demonstrate that there are viable investment opportunities in particular markets and show how deals can be structured to appeal to the broadest number of real estate equity investors, including pension funds. To do so, the funds will need to be carefully structured to respond to specific local capital gaps; the deals will need to be structured to eventually attract mainstream market-rate investors; and performance data

demonstrating that the risk profile or returns are better than assumed will need to be tracked and broadly shared.

KEEP IT SIMPLE TO ATTRACT DEBT FINANCING—HORIZONTAL MIXED USE

Lenders prefer the familiar and the straightforward. For the most part, they focus on a specific product type, such as apartments, for-sale housing, commercial office, retail, or industrial. Each layer of complication, each additional use—vertical as opposed to horizontal mixed uses, additional developers, ground leases, and so on—makes the project more complicated and less standard, which results in a higher cost of capital.

> To make it easier and cheaper to finance their projects, TOD developers simplify their projects, breaking them into familiar-looking pieces. This might mean establishing blocks by use to capitalize on efficiencies in the marketplace, keeping a secondary use to below 15 percent of the project, planning for horizontal rather than vertical mixed use; segmenting the commercial part of a project so that it can get a conventional mortgage and take advantage of the commercial mortgage-backed securities market, or segmenting the affordable housing piece so that it can fit into the standard underwriting for low-income housing tax credits or bond financing. A project that is able to fit into conventional pieces allows investors to price the risk efficiently, and thus lower its financing costs.

5.1
The Historic District Improvement Company's project to revitalize downtown Albuquerque around its rail hub employed an innovative "three tranche" financing strategy to meet the needs of typical equity investors, more patient capital, and municipal partners. (Photo: Moule and Polyzoides.)

> Most TOD developers who simplify their TOD projects find that both construction and permanent loans are available. Some developers find it easiest to deal with the bigger national banks that have headquarters in Chicago, San Francisco, and Manhattan. Because of their location in 24-hour cities, these banks are familiar with the live-work type product and will be likely to provide financing if it is well articulated in the business plan. In contrast, some developers find smaller community banks more approachable and open to these projects, especially where there are prior relationships.

> For projects that take a little longer to demonstrate a market, some TOD developers have used mezzanine debt financing to improve their ability to secure permanent financing at attractive rates. Peak Development in Oregon has used three-phase financing arranged by Central Source Financial Services, including a construction loan and mezzanine financing between construction and a final phase of permanent financing. Having the intermediate mezzanine financing provides time to achieve market-rate rents before locking in long-term rates.

> The most common approach to simplifying a TOD project is to build separate buildings for each use in a mixed-use project. A goal for mixed-use is that mutually supporting activities will have a synergistic effect, but this does not always have to occur in one building. If the land allows for different uses in close proximity and is designed in a way that is walkable, horizontal mixed-use can work very well. Ridenour Development planned to create a 45-acre pedestrian-friendly live-work-play project with vertical integration in Atlanta. When it could not finance the project for four years, the developer chose to separate the uses horizontally, relying on sidewalks and green space to create a pedestrian-friendly environment.

> Horizontal mixed use with multiple developers has advantages beyond the fact that this creates a recognizable product for investors. As long as the smaller projects are guided by a larger vision, each developer can focus on his or her own expertise. There will be a diversity of designs, which will enhance the place, and there will be a broader base of support by the time the project is ready to be built. As each developer finances its own piece, there are more financing relationships to tap. The overall project will not fail if one small project falls off the table. Horizontal mixed use allows developers to build pieces at different times for different market cycles. The strongest components will get better financing deals because they will not be compromised by weaker components. Finally, public investment can be better targeted to the project components that really need it.

SEPARATE THE USES IN MIXED-USE BUILDINGS TO SECURE FINANCING

When achieving TOD project goals requires one or more mixed-use buildings, developers face several challenges. Mixed-use buildings raise concerns for lenders about whether developers have the capacity to develop multiple uses, as each one requires different skills. In addition, mixed-use, multi-story developments often require specialized skills in engineering, design, and construction. Lenders have seen empty retail space on the bottom of mixed-use buildings, even in very transit-oriented cities such as San Francisco, Seattle, and Portland, which has made them wary. Finally, many commercial banks underwrite their mortgages so that they can sell them in secondary markets. Both Fannie Mae and Freddie Mac, and many private mortgage conduits, limit the fraction of space and rents that can arise from nonresidential property types in their projects. For example, Fannie Mae places a 20 percent limit on nonresidential square footage for all product types and restrictions on the fraction of project income from nonresidential rents. To stay within Fannie Mae standards, a building with 15,000 square feet of retail would need to have about seventy-five residential units.

> Developers have gotten past these barriers in markets where mixed-use buildings have a toehold. In the San Francisco Bay Area, banks such as Washington Mutual or Cal Fed are used to financing commercial space with residential space above it. Lenders can point to streets where such buildings have been occupied for more than thirty years. The same is true in New York, Boston, and other densely populated cities where mortgage brokers easily find lenders for construction and permanent financing, particularly for high-end projects, among banks, insurance companies, pension funds, government sponsored enterprises (GSEs), and various other companies.

> Experienced, well-capitalized, and flexible developers with thoughtful plans can finance mixed-use buildings in many more markets and without any risk premium. At Addison Circle, outside of Dallas, four hundred units of multifamily rental with 30,000 square feet of ground floor retail were completely funded with private debt and equity. The developer provided 35 percent equity raised with partners. Bank United provided the construction financing. Wells Fargo Bank provided take-out financing, based on the developer credentials, size, and project location. There was no preleasing, but the retail was a small share of the total project and the developer provided very conservative rent projections and demonstrated that this was a well-trafficked area with adequate demand. In addition, the first floor retail was designed as flexible space that could be used as office, retail, or live-work space.

> The funding environment for retail as part of mixed-use development probably will continue to improve. Moody's, a New York–based global credit rating, research, and risk analysis firm, anticipates that more real estate investors will explore urban retail. According to Moody's, the retail sectors offering the most promising growth potential include mixed-use town centers and urban mixed-use properties.

> In the meantime, developers have found many ways to negotiate financing for mixed-use buildings from lenders that are less receptive. Keeping the share of retail in a building small is one approach used to make mixed-use building loans attractive in primary and secondary markets. Banks also are reassured if there are strong tenants for the retail portion of buildings. Many banks want to see 35 to 50 percent preleasing of first floor commercial space.

5.2-A, B
The Fruitvale Transit Village employs a mix of community development strategies, transportation funding sources, and private investment to revitalize a community long impacted by BART. (Photo: McLarand Vasquez Emsiek & Partners, Inc.)

> Some developers attract financing by cross-subsidizing mixed uses. To obtain retail financing for a mixed-use building, they may load the building envelope, systems, foundation, and fixed costs onto the housing or commercial office space. For larger developments, they may subsidize Class B commercial space above retail with Class A office buildings. While it can play an important role in place making because it serves small professional firms, including doctors, lawyers, and architects, Class B office space can be hard to finance and build.

> Designing flexible spaces, such as live-work units and multifamily flex buildings, sometimes solves the mixed-use financing problem by allowing lenders to assume all the space is residential. Projects with flexible spaces, such as Orenco Station in Hillsboro, Oregon, generally are selling well. Creating flexible spaces also makes it possible to phase in additional retail as the market for it grows.

> When the retail component is large or there are more than two uses in a building, developers find it easier to finance separately each piece of their mixed-use buildings. This is especially true when there is one less attractive component that can impose a penalty on the financing for the whole project. In this case, developers often condominiumize the project or sell air-rights for certain floors. Jonathan Rose & Companies often creates an office condominium, retail condominium, and housing condominium for one building. Segmenting in these ways can provide a pathway into REITs and other equity investors who may be willing to invest in particular parts of a TOD project, such as the office or residential piece that can stand alone. However, while it is a workable solution, it is imperfect. The synergy of the mixed use can be lost if lenders ignore the other uses and the possibility that the uses enhance each other. Also, it is more complex for the developer to divide and manage the project.

> Segmenting a mixed-use building can address restrictions on public financing by legally separating uses. East Bay Asian Local Development Corporation (EBALDC), an experienced nonprofit mixed-use developer, prefers air-rights deals because there is no condominium association. Lenders on the commercial piece of a mixed-use building do not want to have to worry about a lawsuit from the condominium association. At Frank G. Mar, a mixed-use building that EBALDC developed, there are three parcels top to bottom. The top parcel is affordable housing, funded by affordable housing sources. The middle parcel is commercial, funded by a $500,000 grant from Health and Human Services for job creation for small retailers. Ground level and underground parking is the third parcel, with parking funded by an Urban Development Action Grant (UDAG). A downside to this approach of air-rights deals is that they limit the developer's exit strategy.

> New funding programs are being created to address the unique problems that nonprofit affordable housing developers have financing the retail component of their mixed-use buildings. While they often have enough money to build the shell for commercial space, there is no funding available for outreach to potential tenants or tenant improvements. Bay Area LISC has taken a

5.3
Swans Market in downtown
Oakland incorporated a variety
of unusual funding sources,
including historic preservation
tax credits and EDA funds.
(Photo: Michael Pyatok.)

strong role in supporting ground floor retail in buildings, creating a special loan product specifically for build out and tenant improvements. The New Markets Tax Credit, if used in conjunction
with housing credits, also may address this need. Various approaches to providing subsidies for
retail are described in the discussion on amenity retail in the next section of this chapter.

>   Still, it would be easier to finance mixed-use buildings if special techniques, such as condo-
miniumization and air-rights deals, were not necessary. One step in this direction is expanding
access for mixed-use loans to secondary markets. As there is more seasoned mixed-use product,
private secondary markets may become more open to buying these loans. The experience of the
Community Preservation Corporation (CPC) suggests one approach for expanding secondary
markets for mixed-use loans. CPC is a nonprofit mortgage lending consortium established by
New York City banks and insurance companies to finance affordable housing through a one-stop
intermediary. CPC has provided both construction and permanent financing for mixed-use redevelopment. New York City and state pension funds buy the whole mortgages of $250,000 or
more when the properties are leased up. The State of New York Mortgage Agency provides 75 to
100 percent insurance for each mortgage, which is what makes it possible to sell the mortgages
to the New York City and state pension funds. Some argue that there is a need for an insurance
product, available across the country, to broaden the secondary market for mixed-use projects.

Addressing Place and Node: Financing TOD's Distinctive Components

To create the great TOD projects where people want to be, there must be a main street or town square feel with parks and gathering places, a variety of housing types and costs, community uses such as day care, offices above shops, and structured or underground parking. Alongside these principal objectives, there are often additional challenges such as the adaptive reuse of buildings, redevelopment of contaminated land, and the location of new buildings on leased land. Making all of this happen requires both financial acumen and, often, financial subsidy. This section of the chapter describes financing approaches to securing these place-making components.

FINANCING THE MAIN STREET OR TOWN SQUARE

TOD projects tend to have more streets, sidewalks, and parks than other developments to create a main street or town square feel. Investment in this kind of place making in a real estate project is comparable to building a brand in the consumer marketplace. It can add value to the real estate project and extend its life. With the exception of very strong markets, it is difficult to provide this level of infrastructure unless the public helps fund it. In many downtown redevelopment projects in small cities, parks and infrastructure are contributed by local governments, which tap a variety of local, state, and federal programs. Developers with expertise in TOD gravitate toward municipalities and states that provide this kind of support to TOD projects.

> One of the most common approaches to public funding for infrastructure and amenities is tax increment financing. For example, at Atlantic Station in Atlanta, tax increment financing (called a "tax allocation district" in Georgia) is financing $150 million in water and sewer infrastructure, sidewalks, and other improvements. The bonds will be repaid out of future property tax revenues generated by Atlantic Station. The Town of Addison, Texas, funded pocket parks, benches, streets, and trees for its TOD using a hotel/motel tax. In Los Angeles, special assessment districts apply a higher property tax rate within designated areas around transit stations with the proceeds used to fund the infrastructure costs for redevelopment.

> Some local governments prefer to provide incentives for developers to take on the higher infrastructure costs of TODs. Arlington County granted the developers of Ballston Metro Center density bonuses partly in recognition of the public plaza and housing component that were included.

> Redevelopment agencies are an important source of infrastructure funds. For the Swans Market project in Oakland, California, EBALDC separated out all of the public space development, including the parking, and received an Economic Development Administration grant of $1.7 million through the Oakland Redevelopment Agency, with a 40 percent match from the city. Wells Fargo Bank also provided a $30,000 grant for the central courtyard of this three-building development.

> Local transit agencies also contribute funds for place-making infrastructure. More than $2 million from BART plus funds from several other sources, including the San Francisco County Transportation Authority (SFCTA), funded the final design and reconstruction of the 16th Street

Bart Station Plaza. Also in the Bay Area, the Metropolitan Transportation Commission's (MTC) Transportation for Livable Communities (TLC) program has funded planning and infrastructure for TODs at many locations. MTC set aside more than $50 million in federal and regional transportation funds through 2003 for TLC projects, with annual awards of approximately $9.5 million. Grants of up to $10,000 are awarded for technical assistance, up to $50,000 for planning, and up to $2 million for capital projects. The program has played an important role in well-known projects, such as the Ohlone-Chynoweth Commons and Fruitvale BART Station.

>   Federal programs play an important role in funding TOD place making. In El Paso, Texas, the Federal Transit Administration's Livable Communities Initiative funded the Union Plaza Streetscape Project's streets and sidewalks. Using a Transportation and Communities and System Preservation grant from the U.S. Department of Transportation, New Jersey Transit created the "Transit-Friendly Communities" program in 2000 to allow four to six selected communities to receive technical and financial assistance to better link stations to their surrounding districts.

>   State funding for infrastructure is also an important resource for TOD. Maryland, under its Smart Growth and Neighborhood Conservation Initiative, provides targeted funding for infrastructure and other community improvements. California Treasurer Phil Angelides has incorporated smart growth and community reinvestment into the investment criteria used by the California Infrastructure and Economic Development Bank. Florida also provides developers with a financial incentive to build infill projects and other developments that promote use of transit.

PROVIDING A VARIETY OF HOUSING TYPES AND COSTS

Mixed-income housing helps to create more vibrant TODs, with people coming and going at various times of the day and more people living and working near the transit hub. In turn, mixed-use transit-oriented development can improve housing affordability for people with lower incomes because it can lower their transportation costs. Nonprofit affordable housing developers are starting to focus on TOD as the next step toward comprehensive and lasting revitalization of neighborhoods.

>   Still, many TOD projects do not include affordable housing. One reason is resistance from developers who do not see how to make the numbers work. Another challenge is local land-use regulations and controls that work against mixed-income and mixed-use development. There also can be community resistance. Finally, the demand for housing subsidy far exceeds the supply from the Home Investment Partnership Program, Community Development Block Grants, tax credits, and other programs. The challenge is how to create mixed-income projects without taking away from the poor.

>   Some developers have found ways to include affordable housing in their TOD projects. Art Lomenick, a leading TOD developer, includes affordable housing in many of the projects he develops. In Austin or Phoenix, a minimum percentage of moderate-income units is required to

get public support. The units, identical to other units in appearance, are funded as part of the negotiation with the city for the overall development. The developer demonstrates the impact of the housing on its pro formas. The city helps fill the gap with parking, infrastructure, or some other kind of assistance to help make the project work.

> Nonprofit developers have shown that it is possible to use current affordable housing financing programs for TODs. There are many such programs, including federal and state tax credits, tax credit investment pools, redevelopment tax increment funds, housing trust funds, inclusionary housing fees, bond financing, the Federal Home Loan Bank's Affordable Housing Program, Fannie Mae grants and program related investments (PRIs), private foundation grants and PRIs, community land trusts, and affordable housing tax abatements. The Federal Home Loan Bank of San Francisco added smart growth to its scoring procedures for the Affordable Housing Program, as part of its community stability category. CDBG funds also have been a source of gap financing in some localities. It has been demonstrated that affordable housing programs can be used for affordable housing sited on leased parking lots and on leased air-rights over buildings, which are not uncommon for TODs. For example, Ohlone-Chynoweth Commons was built by Eden Housing, Inc. of Hayward on an underutilized parking lot leased from the Santa Clara Valley Transportation Authority.

> Various state and local authorities are beginning to reward efforts to place affordable housing near transit. California, Minnesota, and Maryland have such criteria in their state rules for the low-income housing tax credit. The State of California's Debt Limit Allocation Committee has incorporated not only smart growth but also community reinvestment into its investment criteria, prioritizing investment in low-income urban-core communities. Some local agencies encourage affordable housing as part of TODs through special incentives such as density bonuses and streamlining regulatory processing and permitting requirements.[7] Portland, Oregon, is one of a number of cities that have written down land costs (taken less than market value for land) and provided low-interest loans to projects that include affordable housing.

> Transit agencies also can play a role in ensuring affordable housing is built as part of TOD. Transit agencies in several cases have exchanged discounts on land costs for commitments to affordable housing based upon anticipated higher transit usage. Santa Clara Valley Transportation Authority has been successful in partnering with nonprofit affordable housing providers to produce more than one thousand units of affordable housing constructed at VTA stations. BART has even more. One model program is the Bay Area Metropolitan Transportation Commission's Housing Incentive Program (HIP). HIP offers financial awards in the form of transportation funding to local jurisdictions that locate compact housing within one-third of a mile of transit. Affordable units earn an additional $500 per bedroom over the $1,000 per bedroom base award, or $2,000 per bedroom for higher density. MTC's program was modeled after a HIP program in nearby San Mateo County.

> Although it is possible to use affordable housing funds for TOD projects, there is simply not enough money to go around. The only way to solve the problem is to increase the availability of subsidy for affordable housing and, hopefully, reduce the need to spend years constructing a patchwork of funding sources to produce a small number of units.

> More effort also is needed to figure out how to ensure that affordable for-sale housing in TOD stays affordable. Land banking could be an important tool. The Rosemont Commons is a 7.6-acre mixed-income community within the Piedmont neighborhood in North Portland, Oregon. The Portland Development Commission purchased the property for the development for $1.5 million. It transferred the land underneath the development—which includes a senior housing project, rental townhomes, a Head Start facility, and seventeen homeownership units—to the Portland Community Land Trust (PCLT). PCLT will help ensure permanent affordability of the housing units.

FUNDING AMENITY RETAIL WHEN LENDERS DON'T BELIEVE THE NUMBERS WORK

While local-serving retail plays an important role in TOD, it can be difficult to convince both major retailers and lenders that the market exists for this retail. Credit tenants, who promise to continue paying rent even if the business closes its doors, reduce lender fears about slow lease-out and tenant turnover. They also improve the potential to sell commercial loans in secondary markets. However, it has been hard to attract these tenants, usually chain stores, to TOD projects in revitalizing inner-city areas because of their requirements for minimum area median income as well as design issues such as store size and number of dedicated parking spots.

> Many advocates for inner-city communities believe that both banks and retailers greatly underestimate the buying power of inner-city neighborhoods. The Initiative for a Competitive Inner City has made the case for businesses to expand into distressed urban areas through studies that suggest that retail establishments have traditionally underserved inner-city households. Taking the analysis several steps further, the Shorebank Corporation created a Web-based information system to allow national retailers to quickly and cost-effectively assess urban markets where typical trade area characteristics and customer profiles are not easily found. Its forecasting models take into account the greater spending and density of urban markets.

> In projects where ground floor amenity retail plays an important role in place making (or the zoning requires it), but the numbers do not work for banks, public agencies have stepped in to subsidize the retail component. The redevelopment authority of the City of El Cerrito, California, for example, became an equity partner in Del Norte Place, a rental housing project with ground floor retail, leasing land to the developer for $1 per year and 15 to 20 percent of cash flow. The retail space did lease up slowly, demonstrating that a subsidy was necessary. Sometimes a transit agency is willing to give a developer a discount on its ground lease in exchange for building retail where there is the expectation that market rents will not support the retail. At Addison

Circle, near Dallas, Columbus Realty's funding arrangement with the transit agency subsidized some of the retail.

> Increasingly, special loan funds are supporting retail that is part of mixed-use developments and will take time to build a market. The Downcity Partnership, Incorporated, in Providence, Rhode Island, is a lender of gap financing for mixed-use rehabilitation projects where there is a lag time for ground floor rents to catch up to the rents that can be generated by upper floor housing and office uses. The source of the Revitalization Loan Fund is a $9 million program-related investment from the Rhode Island Foundation. The City of Oakland has a retail-financing program, under which the city provides all the up-front cost and takes the construction risk on ground floor retail. Enterprise Foundation's New Communities Fund is another new source, although it requires credit tenants. The New LISC Retail Initiative is likely to be more receptive to urban mixed-use projects. Mixed-use properties also can look to Fannie Mae's American Communities Fund, a community development investment fund that provides debt and equity to support neighborhood housing and community revitalization efforts.

> Foundations are playing an increasing role in supporting small retail in low-income communities. For example, the Heron Foundation made a seven-year senior loan to EBALDC to finance the development of commercial real estate to create and preserve jobs for low-income residents of Oakland. The California Community Foundation fostered a $10 million program-related loan fund called the Los Angeles Emerging Markets Fund, which has already lent $1 million to a new food market.

> Nonprofit developers are piecing together financing for retail and commercial from all of these sources. For example, the commercial space at the Swans Market development includes food vendors, restaurants, and gallery space. Loans included conventional construction loans from Wells Fargo and StanCorp Mortgage Lenders (a subsidiary of Standard Insurance Corporation, which also provided the permanent loan); grants from the U.S. Department of Health and Human Services and U.S. Economic Development Administration; low-interest loans from the Oakland Redevelopment Agency and the Heron Foundation PRI program; and equity investments from historic tax credits, the nonprofit developer's capital campaign, and tenant improvement funds (relocation payments to tenants and prepaid rents).

> In spite of all the new programs, developers in primarily low-income communities are still finding it difficult to include commercial uses in their developments. Most housing agencies have not recognized the benefit of small retail in improving affordability by reducing transportation costs. The low-income housing tax credit cannot be used for commercial purposes. There still is not enough patient, long-term money and guarantees to mitigate the risk of commercial uses in low-income communities.

> The New Markets Tax Credit, a new federal financing program, may help finance more retail in low-income neighborhoods. Although the New Markets Tax Credit was initially intended to

focus on small business finance, the expectation is that it will be used heavily for commercial real estate development, where the risk profile is better than for small business finance. This seven-year, 39-percent credit is available to lenders and can be used for loans to any commercial development in older neighborhoods across the nation. It could be used for the nonhousing portion of a mixed-use affordable housing deal, as long as the loan is not repaid from residential income. The New Markets Tax Credit Program will not solve the entire problem, as the credit is for seven years and the projects often need twenty-year financing.

> Some developers believe that what is needed is a mixed-use credit enhancement or loan guarantee fund to guarantee rental income for important retail projects within uncertain markets. A foundation could create a small guarantee fund to test the concept. Shorebank Advisory Services has floated the idea of a guaranty fund to provide 15 percent guarantees to help lenders deal with the perceived risk of nonresidential space in residential buildings. Guarantees would gradually reduce as the projects reach agreed-upon debt coverage ratios. The purpose of the loan guarantee fund would be to change market perceptions.

MAKING ROOM FOR COMMUNITY USES

Day care and other community facilities in close proximity make it easier for working parents to use transit and those uses help make great places, but they often need some sort of subsidy. A few transit agencies have actively supported community facilities at transit stations. In 1995, the Santa Clara Valley Transportation Authority (VTA) sought to jump-start the Tamien TOD by building a day care center that accommodates 140 children on the station site. In 1999, BART was awarded a $2.3 million grant through the FTA's Livable Communities Initiative for construction of the Fruitvale Transit Village's child care center, which will be developed by the Unity Council. Since the Unity Council was not an eligible recipient for FTA grant funds, BART agreed to accept the funds and allocate them to the Unity Council. Cities also have played a supporting role in making child care a part of TODs. For example, the City of San Diego provides density bonuses for developments that include child care centers near light-rail stops.

> Several nonprofit lenders have developed effective loan programs for child care center financing, but these programs are not large enough to meet the need. Funding is available from the Low Income Housing Fund, the Illinois Facilities Fund, the Enterprise Foundation, and the Reinvestment Fund. To fill the gap, Shorebank Advisory Services has proposed the creation of state facilities funds, which would use a combination of state, foundation, and local monies to provide a revolving loan fund for small loans for nonprofit facilities, such as child care and social services in low-income neighborhoods.

REDEVELOPING ON CONTAMINATED LAND

Some TODs are built on infill sites that are contaminated because of prior commercial or industrial uses. These sites are called brownfields. Concerns about environmental liability have deter-
red potential debt and equity investors, but this is beginning to change. Changes in the federal
brownfield law reduced liability for voluntary cleanup projects, as long as liable parties have prepared a cleanup plan that meets state requirements. Memorandums of agreement between the
states and the U.S. EPA assure all parties that they are free of further liability. Owners can get further guarantees of safety through a growing number of environmental insurance programs.

FITTING INTO THE NEIGHBORHOOD THROUGH REUSE

The reuse of old buildings can play an important role in creating places where people want to be
and in linking TOD projects to the surrounding neighborhood. What has made the redevelopment of many historic buildings possible is the federal historic-preservation tax credits (HPTC).
Current law allows a 20 percent investment tax credit for the rehabilitation of income-producing
properties, which investors can deduct against their federal income tax liability. There is no bias
against mixed-use projects in the HPTC. In fact, twenty to thirty of the HPTC projects in the past
few years were in the mixed-use/other category. The National Trust for Historic Preservation
offers extensive technical support for historic property restoration and the financing of projects,
including the application of tax credits through its Community Partners Program.

>   Some states also offer historic-preservation tax credits. States and local governments also
provide additional incentives. For example, the City of Dallas abates city, county, and school
property taxes for historic-preservation projects where at least 50 percent of the structure is converted to residential use. Many developers have become adept at using the credits. At Swans
Market, the nonprofit developer came up with a creative way to increase the historic tax credit.
Several tenants prepaid their leases fifteen years in advance in exchange for slightly lower rents,
which allowed the developer to use lease prepayments for tenant improvements. The project was
able to receive the 20 percent tax credit on top of their improvements, which the developer put
back into project. Other tenants had relocation funds that were used in the same way. It has been
hard to do historic tax credit deals on smaller buildings, but now the Bank of America Historic
Tax Credit Fund provides equity to developers of projects that qualify for as little as $500,000 in
historic tax credit equity. The National Trust Community Investment Corporation, a for-profit
subsidiary of the National Trust for Historic Preservation, manages the fund. The fund's first
investment was for approximately $1 million in the Dalton Building in Rock Hill, South Carolina,
a mixed-use housing and office property on the town's main street. There is still a need to educate lenders about the tax credits, how they are structured, and why they require a limited liability corporation (LLC) and partnership.

LOWERING PARKING RATIOS AND DEALING WITH THE EXPENSE OF STRUCTURED PARKING

Because of the importance of place making and walkability, TOD needs well-designed parking garages: they need to be well placed, cleverly managed, and tucked behind other uses. Parking spaces in parking garages, either structured or underground, cost about three to five times more to build than surface lots. Typically, the cost of building and operating parking is bundled with the transit, commercial, or residential uses of a project. Few markets have rents high enough to support this more expensive parking. A financing strategy for parking needs to include both convincing lenders to accept fewer parking spaces in a project and developing ways to fund expensive structured parking.

> Lenders often will accept lower than standard parking ratios if the developer can show that local parking requirements are met, there is no community opposition to the lower ratios, there will be sufficient spaces for each use when needed, transit will decrease demand, and that there is a backup plan if transit does not decrease demand. Ray Gindroz of Urban Design Associates has been successful in reducing parking ratios in about half of his projects by producing market studies showing buyer or rental profiles for the developments and providing case studies and comparables from other regions. For Albina Corner, a mixed-use project outside of downtown Portland, Oregon, the developer convinced lenders to accept lower parking ratios based upon photos showing that apartment parking lots are almost empty during the day.

> Public agencies have a crucial role to play in reassuring lenders. The City of Reston, Virginia, showed its support for mixed-use development by changing codes and design guidelines, as well as parking ratios and standards. Urban Design Strategies completed a project in Norfolk where the parking authority funded a free electric bus through downtown to use existing parking lots more effectively and avoid building another lot. Lenders more readily accept lower parking ratios when the change is modest and when housing is in the low and middle range of costs. An incremental approach will not only reassure lenders but also help developers avoid costly mistakes. In the early years, as a new place is getting established, required parking is likely to be closer to accepted standards and then decline over time. Lenders from Bank of America say they are more open to reduced parking for affordable housing than for higher end projects because the housing demand is so strong. The bank knows there will be renters even with fewer parking spaces.

> Developers often make the case for reduced parking by incorporating shared parking into their development. Sharing parking can allow 20–40 percent more users than if each motorist is assigned a space.[8] Joseph Freed & Associates was able to reduce parking at mixed-use transit-oriented developments in Arlington Heights and Palatine, suburbs of Chicago, by not assigning parking spaces to specific uses, such as retail or commercial. Atlantic Station in Atlanta is making extensive use of shared parking to lower the cost of parking. Because the lender for the

office space is concerned about whether parking will be sufficient, Atlantic Station has provided legal commitments that commercial users will have access to the shared parking during specified hours.

> The parking structures and underground parking still required to meet real parking needs often require public investment. In Virginia, the county agreed to cofinance a 3,200-car garage for Ballston Common by issuing industrial development bonds. Maryland passed legislation recently to create a parking authority to finance parking for TOD. Arlington Heights, near Chicago, which has championed the development of mixed-use, transit-oriented projects throughout its downtown, has used tax increment financing to fund four structured parking lots. The Unity Council helped BART secure a $7.3 million grant from the FTA to construct a parking facility near the Fruitvale Station.

> Another approach to addressing the costs of structured parking is to unbundle the costs of parking from other uses by relying on paid parking. At Pleasant Hill Bart Station, almost six hundred temporary spaces are to be replaced by fee parking that will fund its construction. This approach diminishes the negative economic impact parking has on uses that do not need it and allows parking to become a profit center over time rather than a cost burden. However, this is not yet an accepted approach in most markets.

CREATING A FINANCEABLE GROUND LEASE

Although a growing number of lenders are financing properties with ground leases, market acceptance still depends on the economics of the deal and the structure of the lease contract. Lenders prefer to finance buildings on leased property when the term of the lease is longer than the term of the debt, usually by ten years. This is a relatively easy condition to meet for the initial development on leased land. However, redevelopment on leased land with a lease term below thirty years can be difficult to finance, particularly for residential units that often have thirty-year mortgages. Lenders are more likely to make these loans if the transit agency extends the lease or sells the land to lessees. Lenders also prefer fixed rent on leases. Certainty about the rent payments improves the certainty of loan repayment. Rent adjustments over time, especially participation clauses, can discourage lenders.

> Lenders strongly prefer deals where the landowner subordinates its fee interest in the land to the lien of the lender's mortgage because this vastly reduces the risk of default. Santa Clara VTA's board agreed to subordinate the lease payments for the Almaden Lake Village project to bank loans for this reason. Lenders find unsubordinated ground leases more palatable if the landlord agrees to give them copies of any notice of default by the tenant, the opportunity and time to fix it before the landlord can terminate the ground lease, and a chance to obtain a new ground lease on the same terms if the landlord terminates the ground lease.

Conclusion

The examples from this chapter suggest that it is getting easier to attract private financing for TODs, but, at least for now, public partners are making these projects work by championing them and filling funding gaps. This is why it is so important to perfect value capture strategies for public investors. Only TOD projects in the strongest markets are relying solely on private, market-rate financing without any subsidy. Still, there is a great deal that developers can do to increase acceptance in private financial markets by reducing uncertainty for potential investors and appealing to a broad range of investors.

> More still could be done to make it easier to fund TODs. First and foremost, the many special programs that are being tapped to finance TODs could more formally target transit-oriented development and they could be replicated in additional regions. Second, the amount of money available for the place-making components of TODs—site assembly, infrastructure, affordable housing, parks, and other public purposes—needs to be expanded. Third, investor experience with the growing stable of TODs should be documented in order to pave the way for expanded private investment. These are among the objectives of the new Center for Transit-Oriented Development, initiated to bring TOD to scale as a viable real estate project. Continuing resources on TOD financing will be provided by the Center at its website: www.transittown.org.

NOTES

1   This chapter is based on a review of much of the TOD literature as well as relevant articles in the fields of real estate finance, mixed-use development, housing, secondary markets, community and economic development, transit funding, and parking markets. Additionally, the authors interviewed more than forty people experienced with TOD and complex real estate projects, including developers; representatives from public and transit agencies; identified experts in TOD, housing, and community development; lenders at banks as well as government sponsored entities such as Fannie Mae; people in the foundation community; and real estate advisors to institutions such as pension funds. Rather than footnoting each interview, we will list the persons interviewed and thank them for their insight and generosity here. Interviews were conducted during 2002. Those interviewed included Art Lomenick, Jonathan Rose, Don Chen, Jeff Rader, Brian Leary, John Stainback, Jim Mather, G. B. Arrington, Robyn Mosle, Bill Mohr, Paul Vespermann, Harold A. Dawson, Jr., Christopher Leinberger, Christine Faust, Mary Henthorn, Adam Zoger, Al Escoval, Jim Kennedy, Mike Andrews, Bill Lieberman, Jim Whittington, David Leland, Dennis Harder, Charles Perkins, Alvin McNeil, Ray Kuniansky, David Lowenfeld, Dena Belzer, Kathleen McSherry, Mark A. Willis, Shelley Poticha, Helen Dunlap, John Leith-Tetrault, Rick Jacobs, Frank Altman, Warren McLean, and Raymond Gindroz.

2   Starkie, Edward and Bonnie Gee Yosick. 1996. Overcoming Obstacles to Smart Development. *Lincoln Institute of Land Policy*. Volume 8. Number 4. July. Leland Consulting Group, Smart Development Program, and Financing Capital Sources.

3   WMATA, press release, June 20, 2002, "Metro Transit-Oriented Development Program marks a 26-year history of success."

4   Rent Kickers in Ground Lease Deals. Lease Agreement Reference Guide. At www.leasingprofessional.com.

5   Juan Onesimo Sandoval, John Landis, Lan Deng, and Heather Koch. Estimating the Housing Infill Capacity in the Bay Area. 2000. Working Paper 2000-06. Published by Institute for Urban and Regional Development, University of California at Berkeley, October 2000. An empirical study of land supply in the Bay Area highlights the broad reach of the value gap, suggesting that it applies to many infill sites.

6   This discussion of the value gap is adapted from an as yet unpublished paper for 2003 written by Strategic Economics and the Congress for New Urbanism for the Smart Growth Funder's Network. The authors of the paper are Abby Jo Sigal, Steven Bodzin, Shelley Poticha, and Dena Belzer.

7   Roger K. Lewis. 2002. A Sense of Mission for Affordable Housing. *Washington Post Online* March 9, page H05. Summary of the discussion at the eleventh annual Affordable Housing Conference in Montgomery County, Maryland.

8   Victoria Transport Policy Institute. 2002. TDM Encyclopedia, Parking Management, Strategies for More Efficient Use of Parking Resources. At www.vtpi.org/tdm/.

REFERENCES

Bernick, Michael and Robert Cervero. 1997. *Transit Villages in the Twenty-First Century.* New York: McGraw-Hill.

Brinckerhoff, Parsons. 2001. CalTRANS Statewide Transit-Oriented Development Study: TOD in America Working Paper. January 21.

Center For Transportation Excellence. N.d. At http://www.cfte.org/washington_dc.asp.

Chen, Donald D.T. 2000. The Science of Smart Growth. *Scientific American* December.

Christman, Raymond R. 2001. Testimony before the Millennial Housing Commission: Models for Mixed Income/Mixed Finance Communities, March 12.

Collins, Mary and James McDaniel. 1999. Report on Innovative Financing Techniques for Transit Agencies. Transit Cooperative Research Administration, *Legal Research Digest* 13:11–163.

Dale-Johnson, David. 2000. Evaluating Alternative Ground Lease Contracts Using Real-Option Techniques. *Real Estate Newsline* Spring. E & Y Kenneth Leventhal Real Estate Group.

Deakin, Elizabeth A., Christopher Ferrell, Jonathan Mason, and John Thomas. 2002. Policies and Practices for Cost-Effective Transit Investments: Recent Experiences in the United States. Department of City and Regional Planning and University of California Transportation Center, University of California–Berkeley.

Dekle, Carolyn and Phyllis Mofson, editors. 1997. Barriers to Infill Development, eDesign, posted April 30. At http://sustainable.state.fl.us/fdi/edesign/news/9704/barrier.htm.

Dyhrkopp, Erik (Bell, Boyd & Lloyd LLC, Antitrust and Trade Regulation Department). Winter 2000. Prospecting the Last Frontier: Legal Considerations for Franchisors Expanding into Inner Cities. Available from Bell, Boyd & Lloyd LLC.

Erickson, Scott. Financing Mixed-Use. *NW Builder Online.* June 2001. www.nwbuilder.org.

Federal Reserve Bank of Minneapolis. 1998–1999. Mixed-use development: Through the Lenders' Looking Glass. *Community Dividend* Winter.

Federal Transit Administration, U.S. Department of Transportation. 1998. Innovative Financing Techniques for America's Transit Systems. April. At http://www.fta.dot.gov/library/policy/IFT/ift3.htm.

———. Case Studies, Fruitvale Transit Village Project. At http://www.fhwa.dot.gov/environment/ejustice/case/case6.htm.

Frankel, Merrie S. 2001. Urban Retail, Implications for Retail REITs and REOCs. *Urban Land Archives* February.

Gihring, Tom. 2001. Financing Community Redevelopment through Value Capture. Working Paper. Seattle, Washington, February.

Gyourko, Joseph and Witold Rybczynski. 2000. Financing New Urbanism Projects: Obstacles and Solutions. *Housing Policy Debate* (Fannie Mae Foundation) 11,3.

Haughey, Richard M. 2001. Urban Infill Housing: Myth and Fact. Washington, DC: The Urban Land Institute.

Hernandez, Daniel (President of the Red-Tail Group). 2001. Speech. At Building Stronger Communities: Making Transit-Oriented Development Work for You, Norman Y. Mineta International Institute for Surface Transportation Policies, San Jose State University.

Hilkevitch, Jon. 2002. Metra Plans to Bolster Parking. *Chicago Tribune.* April 14. Metro Section, page c.

Irwin, Neil. 2002. Federal Realty to Shift From 'Main Street.' *Washington Post Online* March 12, Page E01.

Johnson, Mark. 2002. Brownfields Are Looking Greener. *APA Planning Magazine* June.

Johnson, Spencer A. 2000. Changing the Grid. *Urban Land Archives* July.

Leinberger, Christopher. 2001. Arcadia Land Company, Financing Progressive Development. *Capital Xchange Journal* (The Brookings Institution, Center on Urban and Metropolitan Policy) May.

Listokin, David and Barbara Listokin. 2001. Historic Preservation and Affordable Housing: Leveraging Old Resources for New Opportunities. *Fannie Mae Foundation, Housing Facts & Findings* 3,2.

Local Initiatives Support Corporation. N.d. Smart Growth. At www.liscnet.org/resources/smartgrowth/best_practices/transpo_primer.shtml.

Markus, Henry S. 2000. What's TOD Got To Do With It? American Institute of Certified Planners (AICP), Seattle, Washington, January 3.

Marx, Paul (Office of Policy Development, Federal Transit Administration). December 1, 1999. Financing Innovations in Transit: Methods and Issues, a Resource Paper.

Northeast-Midwest Institute and Congress for the New Urbanism. 2001. Strategies for Successful Infill Development. Washington, DC.

Ohland, Gloria. 2000. Transit-Oriented-Development Projects To Watch: Barrio Logan, Natural-Born Transit Village. San Diego, California, 2000. At www.stationfoundation.org.

———. 2001. Transit-Oriented Development in Four Cities. For the Great American Station Foundation, Presented to the Partnership to Regional Livability, Chicago, Illinois.

Rosenberg, Sharon Harvey. 2001. Collins Center Hopes Investment Funds Will Help Kick-Start Redevelopment in Inner-City Neighborhoods. *Floridabiz.Com* April 6.

Sigal, Abby Jo. 2001. Foundation Investment in Smart Growth, Early Draft, December 18.

Simon, Joshua (East Bay Asian Local Development Corporation). 2001. Speech. TOD Financing Tools and Techniques for Assuring Affordability. At Building Stronger Communities: Making Transit-Oriented Development Work for You, Norman Y. Mineta International Institute for Surface Transportation Policies, San Jose State University, October 17.

South Florida Regional Planning Council. Existing Infill and Redevelopment in the Study Area: Challenges and Opportunities. At www.sfrpc.com.

Stainback, John and Renata Simri. September 2001. Public/Private Partnerships Are Key to Sucessful Transit-Oriented Development. LCOR Incorporated.

TLC. 1999. 16th Street BART Community Design Plan. San Francisco, July/August. At www.mtc.ca.gov/projects.livable_communities/lcindex.htm.

University of California. 2000. Third Party Development of Housing via Ground Leasing. *Campus Land* June.

Willis, Mark A. (J.P. Morgan Chase and head of JP Morgan Chase Community Development Group). 2001. Testimony before the Millennial Housing Commission, July 23.

Zilvay, David. 2001. New Urbanism: Changing the rules for Northwest Builders. NW Builder online. February.

Zweifler, Adam F. 2000. Understanding the Basics of Ground Lease Financing. *Commercial Mortgage Insight* November.

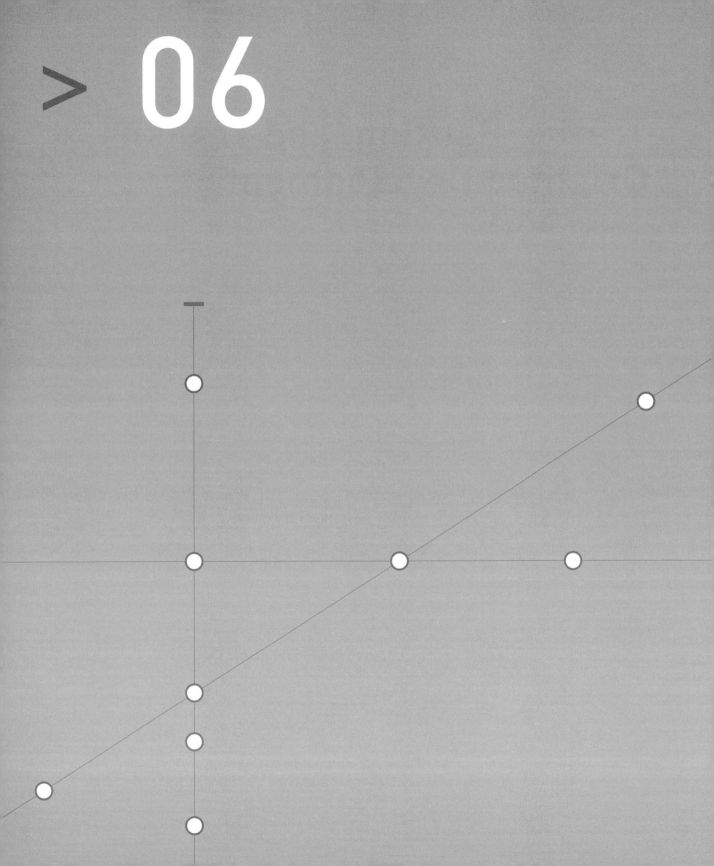

Traffic, Parking, and Transit-Oriented Development

James M. Daisa

Transit agencies invest billions of dollars of public money on transit systems that capture only a fraction of the trips Americans make each day. While there are a multitude of reasons why people do not use transit, the primary reason is that it is hard to serve sprawling suburban development effectively with transit. The nation's metropolitan areas have extensive rail, light-rail, and bus transit systems, but development continues unchecked into the surrounding suburban and exurban areas where transit stations remain isolated from people and surrounded by parking. Many of these stations serve mostly as park-and-ride lots for increasingly distant low density development. It seems obvious that in order to maximize the return on the tremendous public investment in transit we need not only to bring transit to communities but also to bring people and jobs to transit by building transit-oriented development (TOD) that makes transit use a convenient and attractive travel and lifestyle choice. Yet regulatory obstacles and lack of understanding continuously impede these projects.

> Transit-oriented development is a key strategy being used by planning and transportation professionals to curb growth, reduce traffic congestion, provide transportation choice, and improve quality of life. TOD will not solve our transportation problems, but is an important contributor toward this end. This chapter explores transit-oriented development from a transportation planner's perspective.

> As a "land-use type," transit-oriented development is infinitely more complex than single-use land uses, such as residential, office, or retail. Planning and evaluating traffic and parking for isolated land uses is relatively straightforward because there is a great collection of trip generation and parking demand data available. One simply goes to the published trip and parking generation manuals to find hundreds of surveys from across the nation. Of course there are local and regional variations even in isolated land uses, but the traffic and parking characteristics of a suburban office park or big box retail center in Raleigh, North Carolina, is pretty similar to one in San Jose, California. National averages and prototypes work well for these kinds of land use because there usually is no transportation choice other than the automobile, and no complex relationship between a mix of uses, so it becomes a simple exercise in single-mode planning.

> In contrast the traffic and parking characteristics of TOD are dependent on a multitude of factors and interrelationships between land uses. Because modern transit-oriented development

in the United States is a relatively new land-use type, there is little empirical data from which to build transportation planning prototypes. Additionally, because of the lack of data, there is no definitive answer as to the effectiveness of TOD in reducing traffic and parking demand at the local and regional level. Developing transportation planning prototypes to address these issues could begin with defining a continuum, and then breaking it into discrete typologies.

> Two primary components define the traffic and parking demand characteristics of transit-oriented development:

- The demand generated by the transit facility independent of the adjacent land uses; and
- The demand generated by the land uses themselves.

Additionally, there are a number of secondary factors that help define TOD characteristics and interrelationships, including the following:

- Whether land uses are conducive to transit ridership.
- Whether the mix of land uses promotes an internalization of trips.
- The land-use emphasis (e.g., primarily residential or employment) that influences travel patterns.
- The type, scale, interconnectivity, and coverage of the transit system.
- The location of the TOD in relation to the region.

> Some argue that TOD has negligible impacts on travel. While an individual TOD, at any scale, may seem to provide only a modest benefit when compared to the magnitude of total travel in a metropolitan region, collectively many transit-oriented developments distributed throughout a region can have substantial benefit. For a simple illustration, ten thousand workers who live and work in areas not served by transit and who drive alone during the peak hour for an average fifteen-mile trip on freeways would require seventy-five lane miles of capacity. At about $1.5 million per mile to construct a lane of freeway, this demand would cost over $112 million. Shifting those workers to TOD where they can live or work and use transit would result in a dramatic fiscal benefit. The real benefit is so subtle as to be almost invisible at the local level, but it is at the aggregated regional level that TOD provides its greatest benefit.

Traffic and Parking Attributes of TOD

The traffic and parking attributes of TOD include location efficiency, which results when higher density mixed use is located in proximity to transit, resulting in decreased auto use. The synergy that occurs with an appropriate mix of land use has the potential to further reduce travel by internalizing trips.

LOCATION EFFICIENCY AND AUTO TRAVEL

Location efficiency is a pattern of development that improves accessibility between a variety of land uses and transportation. Higher density, mixed-use development in proximity to transit increases location efficiency. Suburban sprawl, in contrast, decreases accessibility because of an intentional separation of land uses over vast areas poorly served by transit and with few pedestrian connections. This pattern of development ensures increased automobile travel because there are no reasonable alternative transportation choices. If sprawl is uncontrolled, an estimated $927 billion of new roads will be needed to accommodate growth in the United States over the next twenty-five years. In a scenario where growth is controlled and concentrated in existing metropolitan areas this cost can be reduced by $110 billion.[1] Location-efficient development provides an opportunity, at all scales, to curb the growth and impacts of sprawl.

Synergy between Land Uses

If TOD has an appropriate mix of land uses it provides an opportunity to reduce travel by internalizing trips. Internal trip capture is the ability of a mix of land uses to retain trips internal to the development in contrast to external travel that occurs with a single type of land use. There have been a number of studies on the effects of mixed use on travel demand. The research consistently finds that a mix of uses, combined with other factors such as pedestrian-friendly form and design, can reduce the magnitude and length of local nonwork trips, particularly for midday and afternoon trips.

> The internalization of trips requires complementary land uses that allow people to walk where they need to go to take care of everyday needs, including shops and restaurants, and personal and business services. The broader the mix and diversity of land uses, the higher the probability that trips can be captured.

Transit Supportive Land Uses for Employment Centers

When asked why they do not use transit, many commuters say they need their cars for midday trips. When a place of employment is in a single-use environment, even one that is well served by transit, an automobile may be needed in order to conduct everyday business. But if there are appropriate retail services within walking distance, people can be encouraged to use transit. Employer-sponsored transportation services, such as subsidized transit fares, guaranteed ride home programs, company vehicles for personal use, or membership in a car-sharing program can greatly increase transit use. The uses that best support employee transit use include the following:

· Banking services
· A wide variety of eating establishments
· Convenience retail such as drug stores and food marts
· Child care

- Personal retail such as dry cleaners, hair styling, bookstores, and health clubs
- Business retail such as office supply, copy and print shops, overnight delivery
- Recreational opportunities, parks, plazas

Transit-Supportive Land Uses for Residential Development

Residents of TOD have many of the same needs as employees but also have their own distinct needs, particularly for retail and services they would patronize on their way to or from work. These are primary transit-supportive uses for residents:

- Neighborhood-serving grocery stores
- A wide variety of eating establishments
- Drug stores and pharmacies
- Banking services
- Personal retail, including dry cleaners, hair styling, bookstores, and health clubs

The Role of Housing Density in Successful TOD

There is general agreement that transit use increases, and single-occupant driving decreases, as residential density increases. However, the research shows that while there is a correlation between residential density and transit use, it is complicated by a multitude of demographic and socioeconomic factors.

> Just what level of density results in a dramatic shift toward transit use is a subject of debate. Transit agencies typically use planning criteria that recommend a minimum of seven dwelling units per acre to support basic bus service. Research has indicated that a substantial increase in transit use occurs at a minimum of ten dwelling units per acre.[2] One study found that transit and walking dramatically increase for shopping trips when residential densities reach six to twenty units per acre.[3] These minimums are significantly lower than many TOD residential densities, which can range from forty to one hundred units per acre. Robert Cervero's research on rail transit–focused development in California concluded that proximity to transit and density were the two strongest predictors of transit use. Cervero concluded that rail station area residents are five times as likely to commute by transit as the average resident in the same city.

Traffic and Parking Characteristics Defined by Transit Service

From a traffic and parking perspective, TOD is composed of two components: the transit facility and the land uses surrounding the facility, each with its own traffic and parking generation characteristics. The characteristics of transit facilities vary by the type and location of the station or stop and the frequency and coverage of transit service. One of the issues surrounding transit-oriented development is that while the land uses surrounding transit facilities can reduce travel and parking demand, the transit facilities themselves generate demand independent of the land uses. The characteristics of the two primary types of transit facilities are discussed below.

BUS TRANSIT FACILITIES

Bus-oriented development can be a place or a node along a major transit route or bus rapid transit corridor, or it can be centered on a transit center or timed transfer station. Bus stops themselves generate very little automobile traffic and parking demand. Rather, they attract pedestrians from surrounding land uses. Transit centers or transfer stations may have limited parking available, and often have kiss-'n-ride areas for the loading and unloading of passengers from automobiles. Transit centers do generate traffic and parking demand independent of the surrounding land uses. The magnitude of the demand depends on the size of the center, the number of lines, and the destinations served.

RAIL TRANSIT FACILITIES

Rail-oriented development can be a place or a node centered around a light-rail or commuter rail station. Rail stations generate substantial traffic and parking demand independent of surrounding land uses as they serve as transportation hubs for the greater region. Rail stations are often intermodal transfer centers as well. Many rail stations, particularly for commuter rail and light-rail located in suburban areas, have large amounts of parking as well as kiss-'n-ride areas. Urban rail stations have limited or no parking, but still generate traffic demand as passengers are dropped off or picked up. When rail station property is developed, transit agencies usually require that all the parking that is lost be replaced; sometimes it is integrated with new parking built for the development. This presents an opportunity for shared parking.

Planning and Design Principles for Minimizing Traffic and Parking

As more transit-oriented development is built, lessons are learned about which practices work best for creating great places and minimizing automobile use. These best practices combine transportation planning, context-sensitive street design, architecture, and urban design, and changes in conventional policy. Successful TOD requires an interdisciplinary approach because in order to encourage people to walk, take transit, and otherwise achieve the fundamental transportation benefits of the internalization of trips, TOD planners must rely on attractive, well-designed, dense, mixed-use development. Without the three "Ds"—density, diversity, and design—development around transit is simply "transit adjacent." The following are key planning and design principles.

CONNECTIVITY, STREET DESIGN, AND TRIP REDUCTION

It is important that TOD and the network of streets that support it remain friendly to the pedestrian as well as accommodate other users. Transportation demand management can help

Left to right, top to bottom

6.1

Attractive street furniture and a
sheltered place to wait are key
to bus service.
(Photo: Steve Price/Urban Advantage.)

6.2

Neighborhood transit service in
Alexandria, Virginia, features
"colonial" bus shelters.
(Photo: Steve Price/Urban Advantage.)

6.3

Portland's light-rail operates in
mixed traffic in the downtown
area, using sidewalks as platforms.
(Photo: Steve Price/Urban Advantage.)

6.4

Light-rail can also serve station
areas situated in the median of
transit boulevards.
(Photo: Steve Price/Urban Advantage.)

6.5

The collapse of the San Francisco
Embarcadero Freeway during the
Loma Prieta earthquake allowed
the city to redevelop the
Embarcadero as a waterfront
transit boulevard, with these
distinctive platforms.
(Photo: Steve Price/Urban Advantage.)

encourage the changes in travel behavior that will minimize traffic. The following guidelines can help create TOD-friendly neighborhoods:

- Locate development close to transit. Effective TOD places residential and office space as close to transit as possible. The optimal walking distance between a transit station or stop and a place of employment is 500 to 1,000 feet. Residents are willing to walk slightly longer distances to get to transit, between a quarter- and a half-mile.

- Provide a pedestrian-scale street network. A dense grid of streets with short, direct connections between land uses and transit encourages walking. A grid also disperses traffic, minimizing pedestrian exposure to high traffic volumes; creates multiple alternative routes, which shorten walking distances and are more interesting; and increases pedestrian exposure to ground floor retail and services on the way to transit, which makes the walk interesting and shopping and errands convenient. Pedestrian-scaled blocks are typically 200 to 400 feet wide and/or long. In smaller TOD projects, an internal system of walkways can replace streets.

- Provide connections to local and regional multiuse paths and trails that encourage longer walking and bicycle trips and improve accessibility for the greater community.

- Use multimodal street design. Conventional street design standards intended to facilitate automobile travel may not be appropriate for TOD. Developing a hierarchy of street designs that vary in modal emphasis provides a balanced transportation system. Some larger region-serving streets may emphasize auto and transit vehicles, whereas other streets within the development must emphasize pedestrians and bicycles. All of the streets in the hierarchy must safely accommodate pedestrians.

- Revise level-of-service standards. Local and regional agencies establish level of service requirements to maintain traffic flow at "acceptable" levels. When intersections and roadways fail to meet the standards, the solution is usually building larger streets and adding lanes to intersections. Although this temporarily relieves traffic congestion, it impacts other modes of travel, discouraging walking and bicycling. This is particularly problematic around transit-oriented development. Many agencies recognize this dilemma and are revising level-of-service policies and traffic-impact analysis methods to reflect the multimodal nature of transit-oriented development. Here are some strategies being used:

  - Requiring multimodal assessment and mitigation of transportation systems to balance the needs of all users.
  - Relaxing or eliminating automobile level-of-service standards near transit- and pedestrian-oriented districts.
  - Using the environmental review process to override traffic impacts.

- Developing multimodal level-of-service methods and establishing new standards that reflect the unique characteristics of transit-oriented development.
- Replacing vehicle mitigation measures with a general impact fee used for multimodal improvements.

- Plan for local and regional travel routes. The continuum of transit-oriented development types range from very local serving nodes at bus stops to major intermodal transit stations. Each type along the continuum plays varying local and regional transportation roles. Differentiating street design between local and regional routes is a way to balance regional accessibility to the transit station with local circulation and access.
- Integrate transportation demand management. Proximity and accessibility to transit is no guarantee that residents and employees will change travel behavior. Transportation demand management (TDM) is a set of strategies, measures, and incentives that result in more efficient use of transportation resources. A broad range of TDM strategies exist with various levels of effectiveness. Strategies range from improving transportation options to changing when and where people travel and reducing the need for travel through more efficient land use or transportation substitutes. Measures have different levels of effectiveness in reducing automobile travel when viewed individually. For example, land-use patterns, density, and mix of uses are more effective than improved transit service alone. Combining land use, TDM, transit, and infrastructure strategies together offers the greatest potential to reduce single-occupant vehicle travel.

PARKING

Parking must be treated carefully so as not to become an impediment to pedestrians, and because the provision of ample free parking can help generate traffic. In addition to charging for parking—one of the most effective ways to change travel behavior—there are many other strategies that can be employed.

- Configure parking so that it does not dominate. A sea of surface parking surrounding development is one of the greatest barriers to walking. It impresses upon the pedestrian the domination of the automobile. It also uses valuable land that could be used to create a great place. Parking should be oriented away from the pedestrian realm, behind buildings, or preferably in structures or underground. Increasing the amount of developable land and density in transit-oriented development may offset the cost of structured parking.
- Charge for parking. Charging for parking is one of the most effective ways to change travel behavior. Whether workers realize it or not, employers who provide free and ample parking are subsidizing their employees' transportation costs and encouraging them to drive.

Parking pricing can be direct (charging a fee to park) or indirect (parking cash-out or transportation allowances). Appropriately priced parking can reduce parking demand between 10 and 30 percent. Depending on the land use or type of transit facility, pricing can be structured to achieve specific objectives. For example, in development with a strong retail component, charges can favor short-term parking for shoppers and discourage long-term parking by commuters.

- Reduce off-street parking requirements. Zoning code parking requirements do not reflect the characteristics of transit-oriented development and can result in excessive parking that encourages driving because they are based on demand studies of isolated suburban uses with free parking. Parking requirements in transit-oriented development can be reduced for a number of legitimate reasons, including shared parking between complementary uses, internal trips, use of on-street parking, TDM programs, and the trip reduction benefits of transit-orientation. After factoring for these efficiencies, off-street parking supply can often be reduced by up to 30 percent. Reductions should not be arbitrary but based on an understanding of a development's specific land-use relationships, efficiencies, and trip-generation attributes. Innovative parking strategies include establishing maximum parking requirements in lieu of minimums, requiring landscaped reserves that can be converted to parking in the future, and formation of a transportation management association that can act as a "broker" of underutilized parking facilities.

- Protect neighborhoods. Those opposed to reduced parking requirements and parking pricing often use spillover impacts in adjacent neighborhoods to validate the need for free and ample parking. While a legitimate concern, neighborhood parking impacts can be mitigated with time restrictions, enforcement, and residential parking permit programs. Some places have priced on-street parking in neighborhoods (using meters) exempting residents from charges or time restrictions. Larger transit-oriented development projects, especially those with concentrations of retail and entertainment uses, should have overflow contingency plans to accommodate occasional special events and peak seasons.

- Utilize on-street parking. With a denser grid of pedestrian-oriented streets in development projects, on-street parking can be used to reduce off-street parking requirements and provide parking supply for adjacent retail and service uses. On-street parking should always be time restricted, and can be metered, to minimize employee parking.

- Use remote parking facilities with shuttle and express connections to major intermodal transit stations. One of the challenges of developing the property around transit stations is the replacement of existing commuter parking. A solution is to build or lease remote park-and-ride facilities and provide frequent express bus service to the transit station.

- Unbundle parking. Private parking is usually included in the sale or lease of residential units and commercial buildings. By separating the cost of the parking from the sale or lease of the

6.6
Rail stations are hubs for both transit and for development, as at King Street station in Alexandria, Virginia.
(Photo: Steve Price/Urban Advantage.)

6.7
Structured parking offers transit agencies the opportunity to free up land adjacent to stations for development.
(Photo: Steve Price/Urban Advantage.)

home or building, tenants pay only for what they need and any excess parking can be sold or leased to others, reducing the overall parking requirements of the development.

- Create parking districts. Larger areas adjacent to transit-oriented development can benefit from the creation of parking districts with municipal parking facilities funded by in-lieu fees and annual maintenance fees. When considering shared parking efficiencies, transit-orientation, and internal trips, the cost of funding municipal parking facilities can be less than providing on-site parking for individual buildings.

Performance Measures

From the perspective of traffic and parking, the true measure of the performance of transit-oriented development is not form but function. The form of transit-oriented development—such as density, mix, connectivity, and pedestrian orientation—is an important factor in its function, but the actual measure of TOD transportation performance is the share of people traveling by means other than the single-occupant automobile, and the reduction of travel altogether by keeping trips internal to the development. A primary objective, and a key promotion, of transit-oriented development is its ability to reduce auto traffic by increasing walking, bicycling, and transit use and by keeping trips internal. Therefore, performance is primarily measured by mode split and trip internalization.

MODE SPLIT

Mode split is the proportion of people who travel by a specific mode. At the simplest level, modes generally include drive-alone, carpool/vanpool, walk, bike, and transit. From a transportation and parking perspective the paramount objective of transit-oriented development is to reduce dramatically the drive-alone mode of travel, particularly in the peak commute periods, because this one mode has the greatest impact on the transportation system and community livability. As a performance measure, mode split is a measure of external impacts: how transit-oriented development reduces traffic congestion, how it moves people more efficiently on transit, or how it reduces automobile travel altogether by encouraging walking and biking.

INTERNAL TRIP CAPTURE AND LAND-USE DIVERSITY

An important performance measure of transit-oriented development, or any mixed-use development, is the extent to which trips can remain internal to the development or surrounding neighborhoods, reducing the need to travel by car and thus reducing traffic and the need for parking. Criteria for evaluating transit-oriented development, therefore, include the percentage of trips that potentially remain internal and a measure, or index, reflecting the mix of land uses.

> There is a vast need for more information for transportation professionals on the travel relationships between a mix of uses and the ability to internalize trips. The Institute of Transportation

Engineers has published a methodology for calculating trip internalization of mixed-use developments. Although widely used and one of the only good sources of data, the methodology is limited to isolated single-development projects and three broad categories of uses: office, residential, and retail. This method, for example, is not appropriate for evaluating mixed use in dense urban areas such as a central business district.

>	Another measure used to assess the effectiveness of transit-oriented development is the mix and diversity of land uses. Researchers are attempting to develop various methods and indices for quantitatively measuring land-use mix. However, these indices only represent the magnitude of land-use diversity, and do not reflect the optimal synergy between specific uses.

Factors Impeding the Effectiveness of TOD

Free and excessive parking. The availability and price of parking is a significant determinate in a person's choice of transportation. Free and ample parking at the workplace encourages single-occupant driving. In urban areas where parking is a commodity and charged at market prices, transit ridership is dramatically higher than in the suburbs where there are large amounts of free parking. In one study, employees who paid for parking drove alone 33 percent less and used transit 25 percent more than those who did not pay for parking or whose parking was subsidized.

>	Parking charges and a limited parking supply are already part of the urban environment, but the suburban population is used to free and available parking at their destinations, even at transit centers. However, this is changing. As suburban populations expand, land values rise, and infill development increases, the land now used for expansive parking lots at transit stations provides an opportunity for transit-oriented development. In the San Francisco Bay Area, BART has introduced fee parking and begun developing parking lots at suburban stations. Managing parking by controlling the amount of parking and its cost will be a gradual but necessary process if TOD is to be effective in suburban areas.

Poor pedestrian environment. The effectiveness of transit-oriented development is highly influenced by the quality of the pedestrian environment. The internal and external system of walkways must be direct, well connected, safe, and visually interesting. Streetscape, urban design, building orientation, and public places all influence the decision to walk. It is particularly important that surrounding neighborhoods have quality pedestrian connections to the development without gaps or major barriers. Additionally, auto-oriented street design standards create barriers to walking. The streets within the TOD and those providing access to the TOD need to be multi-modal, emphasizing pedestrian travel.

Poor-quality transit service. Poor-quality transit service will reduce the effectiveness of the transit-oriented development, especially TOD located along bus routes. Frequency, reliability, and amenities are important factors for sustaining transit ridership. Maintaining high-quality transit continues to be a challenge as transit agencies struggle with higher costs, shrinking funding sources, and the need to cut back on services.

Incorrect mix of land uses. Effective transit-oriented development has a mix of uses that internalizes trips and provides the types of services residents and employees need so that they can use transit without worrying about needing a car to run errands. When land uses lack synergy, they function as isolated uses and compound traffic and parking demands.

Lack of transit link between housing and jobs. An important determinant in whether the residents of a TOD will commute by transit is whether their workplace is served by the transit system. Similarly, workers' residences need to be reasonably accessible to the transit system serving their place of employment. Having a destination served by transit is, of course, a prerequisite of all types of trips to maximize the effectiveness of transit-oriented development. This fact supports the need to develop transit-oriented development at a regional scale.

Current zoning practice. In many places zoning standards are a barrier to transit-oriented development. Traditional zoning emphasizes single-use zones originally established to protect neighborhoods from incompatible uses or to limit housing density. These inflexible regulations have become an obstacle for developing mixed-use sites. Additionally, zoning requirements for parking are designed to accommodate the demand of conventional development, do not provide for shared parking opportunities, and often result in an oversupply of parking. Zoning codes need to be redesigned to address specifically the opportunities and efficiencies of transit-oriented mixed uses and provide flexibility in parking requirements.

Challenges

While transit-oriented development has been in existence in the nation's urban areas for decades, it is a relatively recent land-use phenomena in the suburbs. With the growth of suburban development patterns in the 1950s, '60s, and '70s, the art of planning and designing development around transit had been slowly replaced with the science of planning and designing shopping centers, subdivisions, and business parks. The newer generation of transportation planners and engineers have come to rely on data and techniques developed around isolated auto-oriented land uses. Zoning codes and engineering standards have evolved around the development patterns of the past fifty years to the point where now little is known about the traffic and parking characteristics of transit-oriented development. This presents tremendous challenges not only to planning and designing TOD, but also to gaining professional, public, and political acceptance of the benefits of TOD and instituting change in the standards and regulations that govern TOD. Some of the critical challenges for transportation professionals are discussed below.

A lack of data on traffic and parking characteristics. Unlike conventional isolated suburban land uses for which there is a tremendous amount of traffic and parking information, there is very limited information on this aspect of TOD. This is partly due to the relative newness of transit-oriented development, and partly due to the unique interrelationship between land uses and transit. Isolated land uses are easy to study—just count the cars. Mixed-use development requires quantifying trip internalization, transit use associated with the development's land uses, and mode of travel used to access the development. The best mechanism for arriving at this information is comprehensive surveys, and there has yet to be a systematic approach and national clearinghouse to compile and disseminate transit-oriented development information.

No systematic and widely accepted method exists for modeling and evaluating TOD. Another challenge for the transportation professional is developing an approach to evaluate TOD's benefits and impacts and measure performance and effectiveness. This is particularly important at the local level when conducting traffic impact analysis or environmental assessment. Because of the lack of data on TOD, estimating traffic generation and parking demand requires a customized model based on an assortment of local, national, or assumed parameters. Often the assumptions and methods are challenged because of the lack of widely accepted data. This results in the use of conservative, and most likely inaccurate, traffic and parking estimates.

Standards reduce transit-oriented development effectiveness. Street design standards that emphasize the movement of automobiles are incompatible with the principles that create effective transit-oriented development. Transit-oriented development requires street designs that balance all modes of travel, and even emphasize pedestrian travel over automobiles. Auto and transit vehicle access to transit-oriented development is important, but not to the level where the pedestrian environment is compromised. Differentiating design standards between region-serving streets and local-serving streets can provide a multimodal balance, but all streets serving transit-oriented development must enhance pedestrian accessibility. While geometric design standards may remain the same, how they are applied is undergoing an evolution. Flexible street design or "context-sensitive design" recognizes the need to balance multiple objectives and reflect community values in an interdisciplinary approach. It encourages engineers to use the latitude inherent in the design process. Context-sensitive design has become a popular topic and many local agencies, state departments of transportation, federal transportation agencies, and national organizations are developing guidelines for its applications.

> Another type of standard, the level-of-service, also adversely affects the effectiveness of TOD. Level-of-service standards, which are qualitative measures of traffic congestion, focus entirely on the efficient movement of traffic. When level-of-service standards are not met, the solutions—typically to provide additional vehicular capacity—impact other modes of travel. These secondary impacts are often ignored and their consideration even conflicts with mandated environmental and congestion management procedures in some states.[4] One solution to this dilemma is the adoption of multimodal level-of-service methods and standards that measure performance and gauge impacts on all modes of travel. While a few agencies across the country are using multimodal level-of-service methods, there is no widely accepted practice. The proposal to use a multimodal method is often opposed by public agencies on the grounds that it impacts the development review process by adding yet another layer of technical analysis, has elements based on subjective criteria such as the quality of the pedestrian environment, and lacks the quantitative nexus required as leverage for developers to fund transportation projects, among other reasons. Certainly, multimodal assessment can be complex and somewhat subjective, but when the time is taken to comprehensively examine and provide for the transportation needs of all users, the results are exceptional.

Agency reluctance to reduce parking standards. It always seems that transit-oriented development and smart growth principles are popular until it comes to parking. Proposals to reduce parking ratios at transit-oriented developments are often denied by local agencies for the reasons stated earlier: a lack of experience with TOD, lack of parking data from other similar developments, and concern that there won't be enough parking. For this reason there is a tendency to want to provide ample parking, employing the standards developed for isolated auto-oriented land uses, instead of using parking management as a vital tool to ensure the success of TOD. Lenders have propagated the reluctance to reduce parking standards with their formulaic requirements for meeting outdated zoning code regulations. This issue will gradually be resolved as transportation professionals learn more about the parking characteristics of TOD and how to apply this information under a variety of development types.

Recommended Actions

The following recommended actions are a starting point for addressing the challenges. These actions emphasize the importance of a nationwide and industrywide effort to conduct research and develop a database of empirical information, promote collaborative interdisciplinary planning and design, and eventually establish widely accepted methods and standards for evaluation and development of transit-oriented development.

Improve TOD definitions for transportation planning. Transit-oriented development cannot be effectively discussed among a broad spectrum of interest groups until there are uniform and accepted definitions. Much like the transportation profession's functional classification system, transit-oriented development definitions should have subclassifications and define TOD by land use, transit service, and regional, subregional, and local function. Development and acceptance of these definitions should be a joint effort involving national professional organizations such as the American Planning Association, the Congress for the New Urbanism, and the Institute of Transportation Engineers.

Conduct extensive traffic and parking surveys. Transportation planners and traffic engineers thrive on empirical data because it offers a statistical justification and scientific basis for their analyses. In order for planners and engineers to accept TOD, they must have confidence in the assessment of benefits and impacts, and empirical data is the foundation of a sound evaluation. Collecting traffic and parking data on TOD is much more complex than collecting data from isolated single-use development. Traffic, transit, and parking counts should be augmented with comprehensive resident, employee, and user surveys to distinguish the interrelationship between land uses, internal trips, transit-generated versus land use–generated traffic, and socioeconomic and demographic characteristics.

Establish systematic methods for transportation analysis. Conventional transportation analysis of land use without the use of computerized forecasting models relies on the three-step modeling process: trip generation, trip distribution, and trip assignment. This long-established method works well for analyzing individual land uses, but not for transit-oriented development. The nature of mixed-use TOD is more complex, requiring analysis of modal split and trip internalization and externalization. The transportation profession lacks a widely accepted and relatively straightforward method, although the Institute of Transportation Engineers has published some guidelines and a limited mixed-use trip reduction method. Over time, with the compilation of empirical and demographic data on built TOD projects throughout the country, a systematic approach can be developed, disseminated, and eventually accepted.

Conduct cross-training for traffic and parking professionals. Engineers are often unfairly targeted as an obstacle to pedestrian and transit orientation because of their adherence to conventional design standards and lack of flexibility. This perception is changing as more engineers learn about and promote context-sensitive street design. Engineers and other planning professionals alike can benefit from interdisciplinary training in the fundamentals of architecture, urban design, traffic engineering, transit planning, economics, and subjects such as place making and livability.

Effective parking management for different TOD types. Probably the single biggest challenge is addressing parking issues both for land uses and for transit facilities. Because there is no one prototype that works for all types of TOD projects, planners and engineers need to understand fully the array of parking management tools and how to apply them effectively. The case studies in chapters 7 through 11 provide some perspective.

NOTES

1   Transportation Research Board. 2000. *Cost of Sprawl*. Washington, D.C.: Transportation Cooperative Research Program, Report 74.

2   Institute for Metropolitan Studies. 1994. Effects of Residential Density on Transit Usage and Residential Trip Generation. San Jose State University.

3   L. D. Frank and G. Pivo. 1994. Impacts of Mixed Use and Density on Utilization of Three Modes of Travel. *Transportation Research Record* 1466:44–52.

4   California recently passed legislation (SB 1636) that helps infill and transit-oriented development by relaxing Congestion Management Program level-of-service standards in "infill opportunity zones."

REFERENCES

Brown, Matthew and Cheryl Cort. 2001. Building Healthier Neighborhoods with Metrorail: Rethinking Parking Policies. A Chesapeake Bay Foundation Report. November 1.

Charles, John A. and Michael Barton. 2003. The Mythical World of Transit-Oriented Development: Light Rail and the Orenco Neighborhood in Hillsboro, Oregon. Cascade Policy Institute. April.

Dow, Alexis. 2001. Metro Transit-Oriented Development Program: Improving Accountability Through Enhanced Measures of Service Efforts and Accomplishments. Metro Office of the Auditor. March.

Holtzclaw, John, Robert Clear, Hank Dittmar, David Goldstein, and Peter Hass. 2000. Location Efficiency: Neighborhood and Socio-economic Characteristics Determine Auto Ownership and Use—Studies in Chicago, Los Angeles, and San Francisco. *Transportation Planning and Technology*. March 1.

Institute of Transportation Engineers. 1998. *Trip Generation Handbook*. Washington, D.C.: Institute of Transportation Engineers.

Lapham, Michael. 2001. Transit-Oriented Development: Trip Generation and Mode Split in the Portland Metropolitan Region. Portland State University. March.

Luscher, Daniel R. 1995. The Odds on TODs: Transit-Oriented Development as a Congestion Reduction Strategy in the San Francisco Bay Area. *Berkeley Planning Journal*. Volume 10.

Niles, John and Dick Nelson. 1999. Measuring the Success of Transit-Oriented Development. American Planning Association National Planning Conference. April 24.

Niles, John, Dick Nelson, and Aharon Hibshoosh. 2001. A New Planning Template for Transit-Oriented Development. Mineta Transportation Institute. September.

Parker, Terry, Mike McKeever, G.B. Arrington, and Janet Smith-Heimer. 2002. Statewide Transit-Oriented Development Study: Factors for Success in California. California Department of Transportation. September.

Thompson, Gregory L. 1998. TOD's Importance to Transit; Transit's Importance to TOD: Planning Scenarios for Sacramento. 98th Meeting of Transportation Research Board. January.

7.1
Aerial view of Rosslyn-Ballston
Corridor in Arlington County,
Virginia.
(Photo: www.globeXplorer.com)

THE ARLINGTON COUNTY CASE STUDY

Rosslyn-Ballston Corridor

Dennis Leach

This case study is about a transit-oriented redevelopment initiative undertaken over three decades in a low density commercial corridor in Arlington County, Virginia, just outside Washington, D.C. The government of Arlington County became an early proponent of transit-oriented development (TOD) as a strategy that could be used to retrofit the three-mile-long corridor—a commercial center that had never been incorporated as a city—in order to reverse significant declines in both population and commercial activity. Once consensus on the redevelopment plan was reached with all stakeholders, the county established and then refined a consistent and supportive policy framework over the next thirty years—creating stability and predictability that engendered trust in the county government among developers and the community. As a result there has been limited controversy over proposed projects and the corridor has remained a magnet for development, even during recessions and despite the fact that developers are required to pay for significant improvements to public infrastructure as a condition of site plan approval.

> The sheer amount of mixed-use development that has occurred is noteworthy, and the corridor has become as densely populated as many city centers in the United States. Between 1972 and the end of 2002 there has been a net increase of more than 11,000 housing units, 16 million square feet of office, 950,000 square feet of retail, 1,900 hotel rooms, and an 81 percent increase in the assessed value of land and improvements. Vacancy rates are generally lower than anywhere else in the region except in the District of Columbia, and rents are higher. Because this development has been channeled into an area with well-defined boundaries, surrounding low density single-family neighborhoods have been preserved. If all the development in the two-square-mile corridor area were constructed instead on vacant suburban land at standard densities, it would cover more than fourteen square miles.

> Most remarkable of all is the fact that all this development has generated only modest levels of additional traffic on local streets. Transit ridership in the corridor is higher than anywhere else in the region other than the District of Columbia, and most transit users get to stations on foot or by bus—there is little long-term commuter parking. There are some outstanding issues that need to be resolved in order to ensure the corridor's long-term success—including

affordability, aesthetics, the cohesiveness of the retail environment, and coordination of station area plans with countywide policies. But by most measures Arlington County's redevelopment initiative has surpassed the county's goals and expectations. The story of how the county succeeded in retrofitting its low density commercial corridor is instructive for other jurisdictions involved in planning for station area development.

Redevelopment Context

Arlington County's transit-oriented redevelopment initiative was undertaken with the intent of using the public investment in the Metrorail subway as a catalyst for the redevelopment of the county's low density commercial center. The corridor is centered around Wilson Boulevard, a four-lane arterial. It extends from Rosslyn in the east, a commercial center just across the Potomac from Georgetown and the District of Columbia, to Ballston, another commercial center to the west. In the 1960s, this corridor consisted of a mix of street-front retail, several major shopping centers, garden apartment complexes, and single-family homes. These buildings were mostly one- or two-story structures. Only Rosslyn had higher density commercial development.

> When redevelopment was initiated in the 1960s and '70s, both retail sales and population in the corridor had begun to decline due to the rapid suburbanization of surrounding region. Department stores, grocery stores, and other major retailers were leaving the corridor for the newly developing suburbs. Between 1972 and 1980, the Rosslyn-Ballston (R-B) Corridor lost more than eleven thousand residents, 36.4 percent of its population. The twenty-six-square-mile county lost about 21,500, or 12.4 percent, of its residents—a decline similar to that occurring across the country in inner-city areas.

> The county began discussing how transit and TOD could be used to revitalize the corridor as early as the mid-1960s, and a number of concepts were investigated in a series of white papers prepared for the board and the public. The "bull's-eye" concept proposed focusing the most intense development in the immediate station area, with building height and development density tapering down as it approached existing low density residential neighborhoods. It was also proposed that redevelopment should occur within a quarter-mile walking radius of stations, and include a mix of uses with a major residential component. These ideas are basic to our understanding of TOD today, but at the time they were brand-new and untested, as was the idea that public transit could be used as impetus for the redevelopment of a suburban area.

> Planning for a regional rail system had begun in 1960, and in 1966 the Washington Metropolitan Area Transit Agency (WMATA) was created to build and operate the ninety-seven-mile heavy-rail system. The first segment of the Red Line opened in the District of Columbia in 1976, the Blue Line opened from the District to Rosslyn in 1977, and the Orange Line from Rosslyn to Ballston opened in 1979, with an extension to Vienna in Fairfax County in 1986. Wilson Boulevard provided much of the right-of-way for the Orange Line.

Major Players

Five sets of actors have been involved in the planning and implementation of the redevelopment initiative: the Arlington County Board, the staff of several county departments, citizen commissions, other community representatives, and developers and business and property owners. Other stakeholders have been involved at different points, but only these five sets of actors have played an ongoing role in all the planning and project review and approval processes.

> The five members of the Arlington County Board, who are elected at-large, set policy and provide leadership on issues including development and capital investments. The board established the redevelopment framework, and longtime members have been able to provide institutional memory about early decisions, which has helped ensure policy consistency over time. By 2002, however, no board member had served prior to 1995. The county manager also has a major role in decisions about redevelopment and is responsible for all staff departments.

> The staff of the county's Community Planning, Housing and Development Department, the Economic Development Department, and the Department of Public Works advises the county manager and board and plays a major role in the redevelopment processes. The staff also provides technical and administrative support to board-appointed citizen commissions, and facilitates ongoing community involvement. Much of the early research regarding TOD was done by the staff.

> The citizen commissions review development and infrastructure projects, provide comment on new policy initiatives, and help forge community consensus on difficult issues. The Planning Commission and the Transportation Commission review most projects that go through the development process. The involvement of other civic interests has varied over time, though extensive community input has been solicited for most projects and public opinion has been weighted heavily by the county board.

> Developers have played a major role in pushing the development envelope in the corridor. There are two options available when developers propose projects. Proposals that are consistent with existing low density zoning regulations can be approved through an administrative process. But if developers want to negotiate for the higher densities that are permitted in the county's General Land Use Plan they can file for a site plan review and participate in a structured set of negotiations with the county board and staff, citizen commissions, and the community over the project's design and community benefits. As a result of these negotiations developers typically agree to pay for significant improvements to public infrastructure. The list of improvements that has been tied to approval of individual projects includes undergrounding utilities, redesign and signalization of intersections, and provision of sidewalks, crosswalks, street trees, street lighting, and other amenities. The county board reviews and approves all site plan submissions.

> The densities allowed in the General Land Use Plan are much higher than the densities permitted for by-right development in the zoning ordinance, creating a tremendous incentive for

developers to participate in the site review process, which takes three to six months and can result in a very detailed site plan requirements document.

Major Attributes

By the end of 2002, the Rosslyn-Ballston Corridor had attracted a significant amount of development. From 1972 to 2002, the amount of office space had increased from 4.9 million to 21.1 million square feet, the amount of retail and commercial space had increased from 2.5 million to 3.4 million square feet, the number of hotel rooms had increased from 1,300 to 3,200, and the number of residential units had increased from 13,400 to 24,400. And there was a tremendous amount of construction under way in 2003—more than 1.1 million square feet of commercial development, and 1,400 housing units.

> The intensity of development and mix of uses is quite varied by design. Following the station area bull's-eye concept, the highest intensity development is focused around the Metro stations, where there are a number of eighteen- to twenty-story residential buildings and ten- to twelve-story office buildings, with some developments achieving a floor area ratio (FAR) of 6.0. Floor area ratio is a measurement of the intensity of use of the land; a one-story building on a 10,000-square-foot site has an FAR of 1.0, whereas a four-story building on the same site would have an FAR of 4.0.

> Regulations require that development taper down as it moves away from the station. For example, there are 170- and 180-feet-tall residential buildings flanking the Virginia Square Station, while one block to the south the maximum building height is 110 feet. Continuing to the south, two- and three-story apartment buildings line Wilson Boulevard, and then two-story duplexes, and then two-story single-family houses. Residential neighborhoods with two- and three-story buildings comprise 30 to 40 percent of the corridor. Land-use and zoning regulations have preserved these neighborhoods, which were built from the 1920s to the 1950s.

> The mix of uses is specified in the General Land Use Plan. In the 1980s, when development was skewed toward office space, the county enacted special zoning districts that required developers to build residential space first before they could get the maximum allowable office density. These policies have paid off, resulting in a rich mix of uses in the corridor. Over the last twenty years the square footage of residential construction has roughly equaled the amount of office and retail construction, which is very atypical. Between 1972 and 2002, there was a 8.2 percent expansion of the housing supply, an unusually high rate for a mature community.

> Assuming that all vacant and underutilized parcels will eventually be redeveloped, the R-B Corridor is at 60 or 70 percent of build-out. A new land-use classification has been created to allow development up to 10.0 FAR for redevelopment projects in the Rosslyn Station area that provide major benefits to the community. With the development regulations in effect in 2003, an additional 25 million square feet of commercial and residential space could be accommodated in the corridor.

AFFORDABLE HOUSING

During the 1990s the county increased its focus on the preservation of existing affordable housing and the construction of new affordable housing, partnering with nonprofits, developers, and
property owners. Maintaining affordability has proven challenging given the rapid escalation of
property values for all types of residential housing throughout the Washington, D.C., region, and
in the corridor in particular. As of the first half of 2001 the vacancy rate for apartments in
Arlington County was 1.4 percent, the average rent for an apartment was $1,161, the average sale
price for a home was $268,800, and the supply of affordable units provided by the open market
had declined rapidly.

> The county encourages the preservation and development of what it calls "community
benefit units" or CBUs, apartments or houses owned by nonprofits or individuals and governed
by agreements with the county that guarantee their affordability for up to thirty years. By the end
of 2001, 7.9 percent of the 22,708 housing units in the corridor, or 1,783 units, were CBUs. The
fact that the county has channeled new development into the corridor has helped preserve existing affordable housing in the neighborhoods outside, and the fact that the county has encouraged residential development has increased the supply to match the demand—which also has
helped maintain affordability.

> The county has used the site plan review process to preserve affordability, requiring devel-
opers to either provide affordable units on-site or contribute to an affordable housing fund to pay
for construction of affordable units off-site in return for increases in density. The first such action
dates back to 1977, when Colonial Village, a large and historically significant garden apartment
complex, was designated a "Coordinated Development and Preservation District," allowing construction of higher density offices on a portion of the site in return for the preservation of 90 percent of the existing garden apartment units with some of these designated as affordable. The
issue of affordability was not revisited until 1990, when the county board tied approval of another redevelopment proposal to the replacement of a portion of its affordable units. That same year
the board created the "Special Affordable Housing Protection District," a designation requiring
one-for-one replacement of affordable units.

> In 2001, the county board adopted an expanded density bonus of up to 25 percent for the
development of affordable housing in market-rate projects. In addition to these initiatives, the
county has provided $1 to $2 million per year for the development and preservation of affordable
units in the county.

PUBLIC SUBSIDIES

Construction of the Metrorail extension through the R-B Corridor and ongoing capital maintenance and operation of the system have required major public subsidies from the federal, state,
and county governments. Arlington County issued more than $100 million in capital bonds to

support Metrorail construction, and funded the long-term financing of those bonds. In addition, the county benefited from more than $1 billion of the District of Columbia's Federal Highway Interstate Substitution funds—the largest such diversion of funding from highway to rail in the country—that were used to pay for the design and construction of much of the core Metrorail system, an investment that had regional benefit. The county also issues capital bonds to pay for its share of Metrorail construction and capital renewal funding to pay for improvements to tracks and stations. Ongoing operating expenses are funded on a pay-as-you-go basis out of the county's operating budget. The county also provides ongoing subsidies for WMATA's Metrobus and its own ARTS Bus system.

> WMATA has no tax-raising authority and relies on fares and on funding from the state and from local service jurisdictions such as Arlington. However, the Commonwealth of Virginia considers transit service mostly to be a responsibility of local government. As a result, operating support for transit is a major transportation line item in the county operating budget, which constrains spending on other transportation improvements, including streets. The county has shifted much of the burden of paying for these infrastructure improvements to developers through the site plan negotiation process, as discussed above. Because these improvements are negotiated on a project-by-project basis, however, areas that have not been redeveloped have not been improved, and the improvements often vary in their geometry and their treatment from project to project, leading to inconsistencies in the streetscape.

HISTORIC PRESERVATION

There was little interest in preserving the corridor's early- to mid-twentieth-century commercial buildings when the redevelopment framework was created. Perhaps this was because retail sales were declining, and there was an increasing perception that the corridor had become outmoded and needed to be redeveloped. Moreover, the basic agreement that was brokered between county government and the community was that the corridor would be redeveloped while the surrounding residential neighborhoods, which date back to the early twentieth century, would be preserved. These neighborhoods have been preserved and have benefited from significant reinvestment. There has also been a shift in ownership away from absentee landlords to owners who live in their homes. Early-twentieth-century commercial facades and buildings have been lost, however, including some art moderne and other period styles.

> The National Environmental Policy Act, passed by Congress in 1970, required environmental impact statements for the construction of Interstate 66 and Metrorail, both of which affected the Rosslyn-Ballston Corridor. The result was a protracted lawsuit filed by environmental and community groups against the Virginia Department of Transportation over its proposal to build an eight-lane freeway through residential neighborhoods in North Arlington. That lawsuit eventually resulted in a scaled-down design that also accommodated the construction of Metrorail.

The Interstate 66 proposal stirred up tremendous interest in historic preservation, and in 1976 the county board modified the zoning ordinance to address concerns about historic preservation. The county also created a Historic Landmark Review Board to direct and oversee the process of designating and monitoring local historic landmarks and districts. In 1978, the county designated the Colonial Village garden apartment complex as its first historic district.

> During the 1990s, both the county and the community became even more interested in encouraging architectural diversity in the corridor and in preserving the remaining early-twentieth-century structures and districts. The county board initiated a countywide architectural survey to identify historically and architecturally significant buildings. Numerous districts have been nominated for National Register landmark status.

Transportation

The wealth of transportation services in the R-B Corridor provides residents, workers, and visitors with an array of convenient options and incentives not to use their cars. This excellent service underpins the ongoing economic success and functionality of the corridor.

TRANSIT

Arlington's Metro stations are spaced as close together as stations in more highly urbanized areas like the District of Columbia. The five stations are two-thirds of a mile to seven-eighths of a mile apart, which means that every point along the corridor is within a ten- or fifteen-minute walk of a station. Metrorail service to destinations within the R-B Corridor is frequent: The four stations between Courthouse and Ballston are on the Orange Line—running from Vienna in Fairfax County through the District's core and on to New Carrolton, Maryland—which operates with five- to six-minute headways during peak periods of travel, and twelve-minute headways during off-peak. Rosslyn, at the eastern end of the corridor closest to the District of Columbia, is served by both the Blue and Orange lines, which converge before crossing the Potomac. The Blue Line provides service to points south and west, including the Pentagon, Pentagon City, Crystal City, National Airport, Alexandria, and Springfield. Because Rosslyn is served by two lines, it has two- to three-minute peak headways to and from the District, with six-minute headways off-peak.

> Metrorail stations are surrounded by pedestrian-friendly development. Some land was used for surface parking for commuters, but by 2002 the last two remaining lots had been redeveloped into residential and commercial uses, and there was no long-term surface public parking for commuters in the corridor. This does not appear to have had a negative effect on Metrorail ridership. Between 1990 and 2002, the average number of weekday passenger trips rose from 67,600 to more than 79,000 at the five corridor stations. A survey of Metrorail passengers showed that a majority walked to the station, while the next highest percentage traveled there by bus. Transit ridership was higher at R-B Corridor stations than many suburban stations; both

Rosslyn and Ballston were in the first quartile of Metrorail stations when they were ranked according to ridership.

> Both Rosslyn and Ballston are major bus transit hubs; twenty-three buses served the Rosslyn Transit Center between 7:00 and 8:00 A.M. in 2002, and twenty-seven buses served Ballston. The average number of weekday bus passengers at the Ballston station was 16,300 in 2000; there were 4,368 bus passengers at Rosslyn. More than 60 percent of the bus lines provided ten- to fifteen-minute headways in the morning and evening peak, with half-hour service at other times. A few lines provided thirty-minute peak-hour service and hourly off-peak service. All bus lines provided evening and weekend service. The Georgetown Metro Connection also provided service between Rosslyn and destinations in Georgetown, with ten-minute headways throughout the day. And because of its early success in attracting riders, Arlington County was planning further expansion of its local ART Bus service in the corridor and adjacent neighborhoods in 2002.

STREET AND HIGHWAY ACCESS

The corridor has excellent highway and arterial access. Four-lane Interstate 66 parallels the corridor, with exits at Ballston, Clarendon, and Rosslyn. During peak hours of travel Interstate 66 operates as a high-occupancy-vehicle facility, allowing only those vehicles with at least two occupants on eastbound lanes in the morning and on westbound lanes in the evening. In addition, highways parallel the corridor to the north and south, four boulevards serve the central part of the corridor, and a grid of local streets serves the corridor and adjacent neighborhoods. Despite efforts to minimize traffic in the corridor there is an increasing volume of regional traffic passing through Arlington. The benefit of this road network is that it permits numerous travel options and serves to disperse traffic trying to access destinations in the corridor. The major challenge, particularly on the east-west highways, is the increasing volume of regional traffic.

PEDESTRIAN AND BICYCLE ACCESS

Recognizing that the success of future development in the corridor is contingent upon minimizing the growth in vehicle traffic, the Arlington County Board, staff, and citizens have become increasingly interested in making the corridor more accessible and attractive to pedestrians and cyclists. The county has developed pedestrian and streetscape guidelines to guide the significant investments that are being made in landscaping, upgrading sidewalks, and undergrounding utilities around all projects approved through the site plan review process. The county has also funded a series of improvements to eliminate pedestrian hazards. More than half of the sidewalk network has been improved with wider sidewalks, curb ramps, pedestrian lighting, street trees, and other amenities, and by 2002 there were sidewalks on more than 90 percent of all streets. Areas that have not been redeveloped have not been improved, however, and present substandard conditions.

> The Rosslyn-Ballston Corridor is at the center of an extensive regional bike trail system that serves both commuters and recreational riders. The Custis Trail parallels the corridor to the north and connects to the forty-two-mile WO&D Trail, which extends west through Fairfax and Loudoun Counties. The eighteen-mile Mount Vernon Trail extends south from the Custis Trail at Rosslyn to Alexandria and Fort Belvoir. Easy connections can also be made across Key Bridge to trails in the District of Columbia and Montgomery County. These trails make it possible to safely and easily commute from numerous locations in the region. Whereas bridges often pose major barriers for pedestrians and bicyclists, all four bridges between Arlington and the District accommodate bicyclists and pedestrians. The county has focused on providing bike lanes throughout the corridor to connect to the trail system, and bike lanes have been approved to connect Rosslyn to Ballston and the corridor to residential neighborhoods as streets are resurfaced. Commercial and residential projects in the corridor are required to provide secure indoor bicycle parking as part of the site plan review process.

TRANSPORTATION DEMAND MANAGEMENT

Transportation demand management (TDM) is the establishment of measures to influence travel behavior so as to make more efficient use of the transportation system. Arlington County's TDM policy has focused principally on workplace commuter travel with the goal of reducing peak-hour single-occupancy vehicle trips. Transit users, employers, developers, building managers, residents, and county staff all work together to implement the program.

> The county first made implementation of a TDM program a condition for site plan approval for a proposed commercial project in the Courthouse Station area in 1989. In the same year, a collaboration between the county, the Northern Virginia Transportation Commission, and a business organization called the Ballston Partnership led to the opening of the Ballston Transit Store, which sells transit tokens and passes and provides schedules and information on ridesharing programs.

> Since then Arlington's approach to TDM has become more formalized and comprehensive. The county has instituted the Arlington Transportation Partners Program to provide employer transportation program assistance and to staff transit stores. The county also maintains a Web-based program, www.CommuterPage.com, to assist commuters. The county requires TDM plans for all major commercial and residential developments that go through the site plan review process. (See table 7.1.)

> Arlington County conducted a study of the effectiveness of its TDM and commuter services programs in 2000, surveying employers in the Rosslyn-Ballston and nearby Jefferson Davis corridors. There were 1,196 surveys collected from twenty-four employers, a number of which were not required to provide TDM. Employers offering no or low employee TDM incentives generated 2.17 vehicle trips per 1,000 square feet of gross floor area (GFA), while employers

LAND USE CATEGORY CODE

A General Land Use Plan (GLUP) consistent, no forecast traffic problem

B GLUP consistent, forecast traffic problem

C GLUP amendment requested, no forecast traffic problem

D GLUP amendment requested, forecast traffic problem

Footnotes

1 Less than 100,000 sq.ft. gross floor area

2 100,000–200,000 sq.ft. gross floor area

3 More than 200,000 sq.ft. gross floor area

TABLE 7.1—TRANSPORTATION DEMAND MANAGEMENT PROGRAM MATRIX

STRATEGIES	LAND USE CATEGORY			
	A	B	C	D
I RIDESHARING MARKETING				
a information dissemination				
· distribute/display brochures, posters	x	x	x	x
· conduct employee transportation surveys	x	x	x	x
b operate a vanpool program		x		x
c subsidize vanpool program				
· match state subsidy program		x		x
· double state subsidy program				x
· backup, reserve maintenance vehicle				x
d employee transportation coordinator				
· designate a part-time coordinator		2	x	x
· designate a full-time coordinator				x
· on-site ride matching				x
e contribute to a transit store or transportation management association				
· $5,000 per year	2	x		
· $10,000 per year			x	
· $15,000 per year				x
f locate/operate a transit store				
g emergency ride home (taxi, bus)		3	3	x
II PREFERENTIAL PARKING MANAGEMENT				
a unlimited reserved rideshare parking	x	x	x	x
b market rates for single occupant vehicles	x	x	x	x
c lease agreements reserved parking space		x	x	x
d deserved vanpool parking space	x	x	x	x
· one-half market rate	x		x	
· free, no cost	x		x	
e variable rate parking for carpools (2+ employees)				
· market rate	x			
· one-half market rate			x	x
· free, no cost				x
III TRANSIT PROGRAMS				
a contribute to operation of an employer shuttle bus				
· $5,000 per year	2	1	1	1
· $10,000 per year	3	2	2	2
· $15,000 per year		3	3	3
b operate an employer shuttle bus service				x
c fare media subsidy (Metrorail/bus, Commuter rail)				
· 25 - 50 percent		x		
· 50 - 75 percent			x	
· 75+ percent				x
IV ON-SITE CONSTRUCTION				
a bike lockers, racks	x	x	x	x
b shower facilities	x	x	x	x
c van accessible garage	x	x	x	x
d off-street delivery loading facility	x	x	x	x
e roadway improvements adjacent to site	x	x	x	x
V OFF-SITE CONSTRUCTION				
a pedestrian systems (SKYWALK)	x	x	x	x
b direct connections to Metro				
· existing knockout panels to stations	x	x	x	x
· new connections (elevator, escalator, tunnels)			x	x
c intersection improvements (i.e., turn lane)			x	x
d new facility construction				x
e new Metrorail Station				x
VI LEASE AGREEMENTS: PROGRESSIVE EMPLOYEE POLICIES				
a monitoring contribution				
· $1,000 / Year	2	1	1	1
· $5,000 / Year	3	2	2	2
· $10,000 / Year		3	3	3
b performance guarantees				x
c zoning compliance fines	x	x	x	x
d contingent phasing			x	x

offering incentives generated 1.97 vehicle trips per 1,000 square feet of GFA—a 10 percent reduction. While TDM is not the sole solution to the traffic problem, it does complement other county land- use and transportation policies.

> Table 7.1 is a matrix that defines standard county policy for TDM, outlining the strategies that are required. However, if there is clear and convincing evidence that these strategies are inappropriate, the developer may propose other ideas.

PARKING REGULATIONS

Arlington has been able to reduce the amount of parking required for development because most destinations are accessible by transit, walking, or biking and because the mix of uses allows people to run errands without having to drive. Arlington's parking standards are lower than standards for comparable development in nearby suburban jurisdictions. Most of the parking for high density uses is provided in below-grade parking structures, which minimizes the impact on the pedestrian environment.

> Table 7.2 describes the parking precedents for projects that go through the site plan review process, compared with requirements in neighboring Fairfax County.

TABLE 7.2—PARKING PRECEDENTS

LAND USE	ARLINGTON R-B CORRIDOR SITE PLAN & ZONING PRECEDENTS	FAIRFAX COUNTY, VA
Commercial Office–R-B Corridor	1 space/580 sq.ft. of gross floor area (GFA)	1 space/385 sq.ft. of GFA for projects over 125,000 sq.ft. 1 space/333 sq.ft. of GFA for projects between 50,000 sq.ft. and 125,000 sq.ft.
Commercial Office–Rosslyn	1 space/1,000 sq.ft. of GFA	*
Hotel–R-B Corridor	1 space/2 hotel rooms	1 space/hotel room plus additional spaces for other ancillary uses
Restaurants–within 1,000 feet of Metro	No requirement if there are less than 200 seats	*
Retail–within 1,000 feet of Metro	No parking required for the first 5,000 sq.ft. of GFA	*
Grocery Stores–within 1,000 feet of Metro	No parking required if this is not the primary site use and it is under 15,000 sq.ft. of GFA	*
Retail–beyond 1,000 feet of Metro	1 space/580 sq.ft. of GFA	1 space/200 sq.ft. of GFA on average
Multi-family apartments and condominium units	1.125 off-street spaces per dwelling unit for the first 200 DUs, 1 space for each unit over 200	1.6 off-street spaces per dwelling unit
Townhouses	2 spaces for each dwelling unit and 1/5 space per DU for visitors	2.3 spaces per dwelling unit
Single-family detached units	1 off-street space per dwelling unit	2 off-street spaces per dwelling unit

* Indicates no comparable zoning category for Metro accessible sites.

OTHER TRANSPORTATION ATTRIBUTES

The policies employed to concentrate development around stations and minimize automobile use have yielded results. A 2001 study of commuting behavior by WMATA provides some insights. Of those surveyed who work in Arlington, 41 percent use transit to get to their jobs, a percentage likely to be even higher in the Rosslyn-Ballston Corridor given the level of transit accessibility. This percentage was higher than any other jurisdiction in the region except the District of Columbia, which had a 62 percent transit share. When sorted by the location of residence, 36 percent of Arlington residents got to work using transit. The most comprehensive information about the commuting patterns of residents comes from the 2000 U.S. Census Journey-to-Work Survey, which showed that 47.2 percent of residents in the corridor used transit or modes of travel other than the automobile to get to work, and 2 percent worked at home.

> In 2000, a more limited study of trip generations was conducted at three large apartment buildings. The average number of auto trips into or out of the garage on weekday mornings during the peak hour was eighty-five, or one auto trip for every 5.9 units. In the evening peak, sixty-four trips were generated, or one trip for every 7.8 units. These generation rates are much lower than in more suburban locations.

> According to one major residential developer and property manager in the corridor, between 40 and 60 percent of the tenants of their buildings did not use their cars on a daily basis in 2002, preferring instead to walk or take transit. However, residents of these apartment complexes are fairly affluent and mobile and want access to a car for leisure activities. As a result, the market for high-rise residential units requires somewhat less parking than developments in other locations in Arlington, and significantly less parking than other locations in the region.

How the Job Got Done

Once consensus on the redevelopment plan was reached with all stakeholders, the county established and then refined a consistent and supportive policy framework for TOD over the next thirty years—creating a stability and predictability that engendered trust in the county government among developers and community members. As a result there has been little controversy over proposed projects and the corridor has remained a magnet for development.

METRORAIL ALIGNMENT DECISION

The Arlington County board and staff agreed early on that the Wilson Boulevard corridor, which runs through Arlington's commercial center, was the preferred route for Metrorail, that the alignment should be underground, and that stations should be closely spaced. This put Arlington County at odds with the regional transit agency, then called the National Capital Transit Agency (NCTA), which was in charge of planning the system. NCTA's preferred alignment followed the planned Interstate 66 corridor, north of Arlington's commercial core, which would have been at-grade in existing public right-of-way, and therefore cheaper. This alignment ran through low density residential neighborhoods that did not offer the same redevelopment potential as the Wilson Boulevard alignment. Arlington succeeded in getting its preferred alignment in 1968, shortly after WMATA was created to build and operate the system.

PLANNING PRINCIPLES

After several concepts for the redevelopment of Arlington's commercial corridor were identified in the 1960s, there was an extensive outreach effort conducted over several years in order to help all stakeholders in the community reach consensus around a broad set of assumptions and expectations that became the framework for policy. These planning principles have been maintained and respected for thirty years, even though there have been updates to station area sector plans and modest changes to the General Land Use Plan and zoning. The focus has been on refinement of the planning principles instead of wholesale change, with the intent of producing a more desirable built environment. For example, the board has adopted corridorwide streetscape standards and a Retail Action Plan, and has prioritized improving the pedestrian environment. The planning principles that guide redevelopment include the following:

- The Rosslyn-Ballston Corridor would have clearly defined boundaries.
- There would be a major increase in density, with virtually all nonresidential acreage around stations subject to redevelopment.
- Highest density uses would be concentrated within walking distance of Metro stations, with building heights and densities tapering down as development approached existing single-family residential neighborhoods.
- Mixed-use development would be required, coupled with design guidelines intended to create high-quality pedestrian environments, in order to produce an active, vibrant core area during the day and evening.
- Existing single-family neighborhoods and most apartment complexes would be preserved and improved.
- Commercial revitalization would come about through parcel redevelopment.
- Each station area would serve a unique function and have a well-defined identity: Rosslyn as a major business and employment center; Court House as a government center; Clarendon as an urban village; Virginia Square as the focus for cultural, recreational, and educational activities; and Ballston as a new downtown in central Arlington.
- Only minor adjustments would be made to the street system. Visual continuity would be achieved by instituting standard building setbacks, requiring ground floor retail and consistent signage, and by providing landscaped gateways at Rosslyn and Ballston.

7.2-A, B
Aerial perspective shows development in the Rosslyn-Ballston Corridor.
(Photo: Sky High Studios, Laurel, MD.)

7.3
The original "bull's-eye" development concept.
(Rendering: Albert Benedict / Center for Neighborhood Technology.)

Rosslyn Metro Station

Court House Metro Station

Clarendon Metro Station

Virginia Square Metro Sta.

Ballston Metro Station

0   0.5   1
miles

THE PLANNING PROCESS

Four levels of planning were undertaken in the corridor. First, a basic policy framework for redevelopment was established. Second, sector plans were created for station areas to provide guidance on land use, urban design, streetscape, public facilities, transportation, and other infrastructure. County staff led these planning efforts with substantial input from residents. Each station area sector plan was done separately and then adopted by the board. The first round of plans was completed by 1984 and sector plan addenda have been produced for several stations. A third level of planning has been focused on specific functional aspects of the corridor such as affordable housing, retail development, parking policy, pedestrian and bicycle access, and safety. An ongoing challenge is the coordination of station-focused sector plans with corridorwide planning initiatives.

> The fourth level of planning is the site plan review and approval process, where many of the site-specific decisions get made. The Planning Commission's Site Plan Review Subcommittee, which informs this process, includes staff from the county's planning, economic development and public works departments, representatives from other citizen commissions and civic associations, property owners, and other interested citizens. It has also been an ongoing challenge to coordinate these site-specific project reviews and approvals with the larger policy framework.

CONSISTENCY

Arlington County's redevelopment policies and process have been remarkably consistent and predictable over time, and developers, property owners, and the community generally know what to expect. As a result the redevelopment process has generated little controversy as compared to other jurisdictions in the region, and the focus of most project reviews is on project-specific planning and design issues. Most of the projects that are considered are approved in a reasonable amount of time. Developers have expressed some concern about the growing list of amenities they are required to pay for as a condition of site plan approval and that erodes the profitability of projects. The site plan review project pipeline remained full through the last recession, however, suggesting that development profit margins were still acceptable.

PUBLIC PARTICIPATION

The community had a major role in informing the original planning framework—more than sixty public meetings and workshops were held leading up to the adoption of the revised land-use plan and transportation policies. County staff took the time to educate citizens on how to be effective in the process and worked with residents to develop the planning principles. Board members and staff believed that this intensive public education and involvement was essential to the redevelopment initiative's success, in part because educated and involved citizens have provided invaluable feedback and there has been minimal conflict.

> In 2002, community members had several avenues for involvement. They could participate in updates to station area sector plans or in other corridorwide planning initiatives, or they could participate in the site plan review process if they lived in the community that would be affected by a project. Developers were strongly encouraged to consult with all civic and neighborhood associations during the site plan review process. Citizens could also attend planning commission and county board meetings and testify. Citizens continued to commit considerable time and energy to the redevelopment process.

Evaluation Factors and Results

By many measures, the redevelopment of the Rosslyn-Ballston Corridor has been highly successful. The county has achieved or surpassed most of the community objectives it set out to accomplish. Some measures of success are described below.

MARKET DEMAND

The corridor in 2002 was truly mixed-use with 21.1 million square feet of office space, 3,200 hotel rooms, 3.4 million square feet of retail and, most remarkably, 24,400 housing units. Housing was the strongest market sector in the corridor, with apartment rents commanding a premium over apartments located outside the corridor. In 2002, there were more than 1,400 housing units under construction in the corridor, with several thousand additional units in the development pipeline. Homes were often sold within thirty days for more than the asking price. In 2002, the residential population density of the R-B Corridor put it in the top five most densely populated downtowns in the United States, with more than 17,250 persons per square mile, according to the 2000 Census.

> The office market in the R-B Corridor historically has had very low vacancy rates, similar to those in downtown Washington, D.C. Before the 2001–2002 recession, the rate was 5 percent. Even with the economic downturn and the residual affects of the 9/11 terrorist attack—which affected Arlington directly because of the bombing of the Pentagon and the subsequent shutdown of National Airport and several major arterials—the vacancy rate in June 2002 was less than 10 percent, half the rate at suburban office centers such as Tysons Corner and Reston in outlying Virginia. Office rents in the corridor also commanded a premium over offices elsewhere in Northern Virginia.

> The retail sector has lagged behind other development sectors. Despite the more than 3 million square feet of retail space and low vacancy rates there is no cohesive shopping environment. Supermarkets, however, have done very well. In the 1980s the corridor had only one aging market, but in 2002 there were four full-service markets, so that no destination was more than a ten-minute walk away, which has made shopping very convenient for residents. Restaurants have also done well, there are more than one hundred in the corridor.

FINANCIAL RETURN

The redevelopment initiative has had a very positive effect on property values and tax revenue. Arlington County conducts a countywide reappraisal at the beginning of each year to assess the value of land and improvements. In 2002, the assessed value of the corridor was $8.88 billion—$2.18 billion for land and $6.7 billion for improvements. This represents an 81 percent increase in value over 1992. The average annual change in valuation was 6.1 percent, well above the inflation rate. In 2002, of the total projected real estate tax levy of $277 million in the county, $90.9 million, or 32.8 percent, came from the Rosslyn-Ballston Corridor. The corridor also produces hotel taxes, meal taxes, and business and household personal property taxes (taxes on personal property such as cars, not real estate). In FY02, Arlington County had one of the lowest real estate tax rates in Northern Virginia, $1.023 per $100 of assessed value. Only Fairfax City's rate was lower, $0.98 per $100 of assessed value. The Fairfax County rate was $1.23 and Alexandria was $1.11 per $100. Most rates went down by two cents in FY03 due to rising real estate assessments.

> Redevelopment has also increased transit ridership, which has generated increased revenues for WMATA. The average weekday ridership at the five Metrorail stations was more than 79,000 in 2002.

> According to developers and real estate attorneys who have worked here in the Rosslyn-Ballston Corridor, it remains attractive for development because of its central location, excellent transportation access, good government services, and predictable development review and approval process. The fact that vacancy rates for all types of development (office, retail, apartments) tend to be lower in the corridor than in the surrounding area, even during recessions, also contributes to its attractiveness.

7.4
Clarendon Market Common features pedestrian-oriented retail on the ground floor and residential development on the upper stories.
(Photo: Dennis Leach.)

7.5
Clarendon Market Common also includes townhomes.
(Photo: Dennis Leach.)

7.6
The Courthouse Station has also become a key node for development. Until recently, pedestrian and bicycle amenities were not a priority in the corridor.
(Photo: Dennis Leach.)

FUNCTIONALITY OF THE TRANSPORTATION SYSTEM AND LAND-USE PATTERNS
A tremendous amount of development has been absorbed over the last twenty years with only modest increases in traffic. On some local streets and arterials the volume of traffic has remained relatively flat, and there is limited congestion. Car ownership is similar to rates in nearby Alexandria and lower than everywhere else in the region except the District of Columbia.

Outstanding Issues

There are outstanding issues, many of which have been discussed above, that need to be addressed if the corridor is to remain attractive and economically successful over the long term: perhaps the greatest shortcoming of the redevelopment initiative is that it has failed to ensure that the built environment is cohesive and of consistently high quality. When, as a part of this study, sixteen members of the community—representing all the major stakeholder groups— were asked their opinion about the redevelopment effort, the corridor received high marks for its residential neighborhoods, transit access, range of services offered, and impact on regional transportation and air quality. The corridor received less favorable responses when stakeholders were asked about the attractiveness and cohesiveness of the new development, the success of efforts to preserve and integrate historic buildings into new development, and the quality of the pedestrian environment. Affordability is another major concern. Success has its downside. Corridor redevelopment has driven up land prices to the point that the free market no longer provides inexpensive housing or low cost locations for business start-ups.

Lessons Learned

Rail investment can be used as a catalyst for redevelopment. The investment in fixed rail was not viewed as just another transportation alternative in Arlington County. The Arlington County Board and stakeholders were very clear that the investment was going to be used to reshape and redevelop Arlington's commercial center and the county's economic base, and it has. Once a low density commercial corridor, Arlington is now one of the most densely populated commercial centers in the United States, and the redevelopment initiative has had a very positive effect on property values and tax revenues.

A predictable development and review process is important for both developers and the community. Arlington County created clear boundaries and a consistent planning and policy framework for the Rosslyn-Ballston Corridor, which has assured stability and predictability over time. This has engendered trust, minimized controversy and risk, and made the corridor a magnet for further development.

A rich mix of uses promotes a balanced use of the transportation system. Arlington's policy framework has focused on promoting mixed-use development around stations and has encouraged residential development in particular. This emphasis was challenged in the 1980s when commercial office was more marketable than other uses. But instead of changing the General Land Use Plan, the county created additional incentives to further encourage residential development in conjunction with commercial projects. The result is that over the last twenty years the county has matched commercial construction (of office and retail) on a roughly one-for-one basis with residential—for every square foot of commercial space built there is one square foot of residential space. This is atypical. This rich mix of uses has promoted a balanced use of the transportation system so that not everyone is arriving and leaving from the same place at the same time by the same mode—a situation that occurs daily at the suburban station in Vienna in Fairfax County, where most transit riders use Metro during the morning peak period to head to work in the R-B Corridor and Washington, D.C.

Continued public involvement is critical. A broad public education and involvement program was central to getting the original planning and policy framework approved for the Rosslyn-Ballston Corridor. The framework represented a major departure from Arlington's traditional low density development pattern and it was important that all stakeholders reached consensus on the planning principles before proceeding. Continued community involvement has been essential— through sector plan updates and the site plan review process—in order to keep the community on board and providing valuable feedback.

7.7

Bus service is a key ingredient in the success of Arlington County's TOD strategy, as it connects residential neighborhoods to the rail system.

(Photo: Dennis Leach.)

Density supports transit use. Focusing density and mixed-use development around transit stations as part of a regional network has yielded substantial transportation benefits by providing choices for residents and workers so that they do not need to use private vehicles for all trips. This development pattern produces fewer vehicle trips than lower density single-use suburban developments. Transit ridership in the R-B Corridor is very high. Despite the amount of development that has occurred, there have been only modest increases in traffic.

Design is important; so are pedestrians. Good urban design and an attractive and functional pedestrian environment are necessary to creating a coherent urban environment, especially when station area redevelopment involves a diverse set of interests and occurs over a long period of time. The redevelopment initiative has fallen short by this measure.

Historic preservation maintains community character. Preserving and integrating historic buildings and places into station area plans is essential to maintaining community character or creating an identity. This was not a focus of the planning and policy framework for the core commercial area in Arlington, and the community lost some of its most significant early-twentieth-century commercial structures before it became a priority.

Economic diversity is important. Successful station area development and redevelopment can drive up land values and may ultimately limit the economic diversity of households and businesses. Proactive policies are required to protect affordable housing and affordable business locations.

REFERENCES

Acurio, Gabriela (Assistant County Manager). 2002. Interview by the author, January 28.

Arlington County. 2002. Inter-Departmental Memorandum. April 29.

Arlington County. 2001. Proposed Outcome Measures for Affordable Housing Goals. August 22.

Arlington County Department of Community Planning, Housing and Development. 2002. Arlington County Major Statistics, 2000–2025. March.

Arlington County Board. 1996. C-O Rosslyn Zoning And Land Use Changes. May 11.

Arlington County Department of Community Planning, Housing and Development Planning Division. 2001. Draft: R-B Corridor Streetscape. May 8.

Arlington County Department of Community Planning, Housing and Development Comprehensive Planning Section. 1995. Development Capacity in the Metro Corridors. Planning Information Report 32, September.

Arlington County Department of Environmental Affairs Planning Division. 1976. Goals and Objectives; Planning Process. March.

Arlington County Department of Environmental Affairs Planning Division. 1974. Rosslyn- Ballston Corridor Commercial Study, June.

Arlington County Department of Community Planning, Housing and Development. 2002. Planning Information Report 52. March. At www.co.arlington.va.us/cphd/planning/development_highlights01/Dev2001.htm.

Arlington County Department of Community Planning, Housing and Development. 2002. Round 6.3 Cooperative Forecasts of Households, Population and Employment. 2002. Planning Information Report 53. May. At www.co.arlington.va.us/cphd/planning/publications/pir53/pir53.htm.

Arlington County Department of Public Works. 2002. Transportation Demand Management Policy Statement.

Arlington County Department of Public Works Planning Division. 1999. Arlington County Pedestrian Initiative. At www.co.arlington.va.us/dpw/planning/ped/ped.htm.

Arlington County Department of Public Works Planning Division. 2000. Review of the Street Element of the Arlington County Comprehensive Plan. February.

Arlington County Department of Transportation. 1977. Secretary's Decision on Interstate Highway 66, Fairfax and Arlington Counties. January 5.

Arlington County Transit Program, Department of Public Works. 2002. Transit Program Slide Presentation. January 22.

Arlington Department of Economic Development in cooperation with the Arlington Bus Tour Committee. 2001. Real Estate Showcase 2001. March 30.

Baker, Gail (Citizen Activist; AC Historical Affairs & Landmark Review Board, 1985–1994). 2002. Interviewed by the author, February 13.

Berghoefer, Fred. 1975. Report of the Rosslyn-Ballston Corridor Committee. June.

Brosnan, Robert (AC CPHD Department Head; AC CPHD staff, 1978–present). 2002. Interviewed by the author, January 23.

Bozman, Ellen (Arlington County Board, 1974–1997; Arlington County Planning Commission, 1971–1974). 2002. Interviewed by the author, January 23.

Chesapeake Bay Foundation Report. 2001. Building Healthier Neighborhoods with Metrorail: Rethinking Parking Policies. November 1.

Cho, David. 2002. Homeowners Feel Tax pain in N.Va., Empty Offices, Housing Shortage Drive Shift. *Washington Post* March 10, page C1.

Cohn, D'Vera. 2002. Happy to Pound the Pavement. *Washington Post* July 7, page C01.

Cushman & Wakefield, Inc. 2002. Northern Virginia, Office Market—Second Quarter 2002. At www.cushmanwakefield.com.

Department of Real Estate Assessments. 1992. 1992 Metro Station Area Taxable Property Assessment. March 11.

Department of Real Estate Assessments. 2002. 2002 Metro Station Area Taxable Property Assessment. March.

Eisenburg, Al (Arlington County Board, 1986–1999; Chair, Arlington County Affordable Housing Task Force—1999). Interviewed by the author, January 2.

Fisette, Jay (Arlington County Board, 1998–present). Interviewed by the author, January 30.

Freshley, Katherine (Citizen Activist—Ballston Civic Association, 1973–present). 2002. Interviewed by the author, February 15.

Freshley, Katherine T., and Don Alexander Hawkins. N.d. Ballston: A Community Plan. The Ballston-Page Civic Association, The Arlington Committee on Optimum Growth, and the Urban Design Studio of Catholic University.

Hamre, Jim (AC DPW Transit Program Coordinator). Interviewed by the author, February 1.

Hulme, Henry (AC Department of Public Works Director, 1977–1989; AC DPW staff, 1954–1989). 2002. Interviewed by the author, February 13.

Huslin, Anita. Study Forecasts Huge Loss of Land by 2030. *Washington Post* May 1, page B01.

Jacobson, Jason (Vice President, Development; Charles E. Smith Realty Companies). 2002. Interviewed by the author, February 13.

Jenkins, Chris L. Urban Villages Sprout Near Metro Stations. *Washington Post* July 7, page C01.

Johnson, Carrie (AC Planning Commission, 1986–present). Interviewed by the author, January 23.

Kellogg, Mark (AC DPW Planning Section Chief; DPW staff, 1977–present). 2002. Interviewed by the author, January 23.

Leventhal, Michael (AC CPHD, Historic Preservation Program Coordinator). 2002. Interviewed by the author, February 14.

Lynford, Lloyd. 2002. Pre-Release Analysis of Second-Quarter 2002 Reis Findings in the Office Sector. At www.reis.com.

Northern Virginia Transportation Commission. 1966. Potential Rail Transit Corridors In Northern Virginia. April 4.

Parker, Tom (AC Economic Development Division Chief, 1981–1995; AC Planning, 1965–1981). Interviewed by the author, January 29.

Partners for Livable Places. 1989. The Rosslyn-Ballston Corridor, Threshold of Opportunity: Mid-Course Review. May.

Rhodes, Wayne (AC Economic Development Department Head; AC Economic Development staff, 1971–present). Interviewed by the author, January 23.

Tang, Tzung-Wen (Amy) and Mark Kellogg. 2000. Travel Demand Management: Experience in Arlington, VA. May.

Terpak, Nan (Legal Counsel, Walsh, Colucci, Stackhouse, Emrich & Lubeley; Arlington Zoning & Land Use Law, 1985–present). Interviewed by the author, January 23.

The Brookings Institution Center on Urban and Metropolitan Policy and the Fannie Mae Foundation. 1998. A Rise In Downtown Living. November.

Washington Metropolitan Transit Authority. 2002. Capsule History of WMATA. January.
At www.wmata.com.

Zimmerman, Christopher. 2002. The neo-traditional response (New Urbanism/Old Urbanism). Excerpt from Urban Village Talk. October.

———. (Arlington County Board 1996–present, Current Chair).

8.1
Aerial view of Mockingbird
Station and surrounding
single-family neighborhoods.
(Photo: www.globeXplorer.com)

THE DALLAS CASE STUDY

Mockingbird Station and Addison Circle

Gloria Ohland

The Dallas–Fort Worth metroplex—sprawling, polynuclear, crisscrossed and encircled by belt-ways, expressways, turnpikes, and tollways—has at the turn of the century embarked on an improbable experiment: It is seeking to reinvent itself around rail- and transit-oriented develop-ment (TOD). Judging from the "facts on the ground," as one developer calls the region's sever-al examples of TOD, it's an experiment that shows incredible promise. The importance of this experiment in the suburbs of the Sunbelt cannot be overstated as low density cities worldwide struggle to establish more sustainable transportation systems and land-use patterns.

> One caveat: The experiment is in the early stages. Dallas Area Rapid Transit (DART) had in place only twenty miles of light-rail in 2002, and the system had been operating only since 1996, with an additional twenty-four miles opening to the suburbs by 2003 and other corridors in the planning stages. But in part because the starter lines served a transit-dependent population on the city's south end and employment centers to the north, ridership was well above the projec-tions, and DART, once a four-letter word among residents, had become so popular that 77 percent of voters passed a bond proposal in 2000 to dramatically accelerate the expansion of light-rail. DART had become the transit industry's "golden-haired agency," and it was considered a model for other cities struggling to establish transit systems.

> Trained as an urban planner, DART executive director Roger Snoble understood the transportation/land use connection. At DART he did market research and analysis to identify development opportunities at each station, information that was published—along with aerial maps, demographics, land-use distribution, and other information about each station area—in substantive brochures for developers. DART designated a staff person to act as liaison to devel-opers who shared the agency's vision of high density, mixed-use, transit-oriented development, and who could make available to them the agency's engineering and real estate expertise.

> Economic development was within the scope of the agency's mission, and by 2001 DART boasted that more than $1 billion in new development was either built or under construction near stations. The agency advertised this success often and early, beginning with a 1999 study by the

University of North Texas (UNT) that showed property valuations within a quarter mile of DART stations were 25 percent higher than a control group of properties. The study found that land values around DART stations when considered alone (not including rents or occupancy rates) were double that in non-DART rail neighborhoods.

> A follow-up study in January of 2003 showed that the value of office properties near DART stations increased 53 percent more than comparable properties not served by rail between 1997 and 2001, and that the value of residential properties increased 39 percent more than a group of control properties. "Dallas-area business leaders, planners and elected officials are committed to public transportation, both for mobility and developmental goals," wrote study authors Bernard Weinstein and Terry Clower of UNT's Center for Economic Development and Research. "Host communities view the existing and soon-to-open DART rail stations as tremendous assets and ... non-DART cities want to be an integral part of the region's public transit future."

> Some would say DART's success included a hefty dose of Texas braggadocio. Putting it in perspective, one bus line down Wilshire Boulevard in Los Angeles, where Snoble went to head the Metropolitan Transportation Authority after leaving DART in 2001, carried more riders than the entire light-rail system in Dallas. And it could be argued that much of the $1 billion in investment occurred in transit-adjacent downtown neighborhoods because investments were flowing into downtowns all over the United States—not because of the proximity of rail in Dallas—and because the opening of rail service coincided with an economic upturn that caused the real estate market to boom all over the city in the late 1990s.

> Regardless, even communities that had fought to keep DART out when the rail line was planned in the early '90s were clamoring for stations by 2003, and more than a dozen fast-growing suburbs as well as the City of Forth Worth were eagerly positioning themselves as rail-ready and marshalling local support for TOD. They mounted ambitious transit-oriented development visioning and planning and design exercises around proposed rail lines and stations, sent their elected officials on tours of successful TOD in other cities, and hired the Urban Land Institute and architects Peter Calthorpe, Andres Duany, and other New Urbanist gurus to show them how TOD could be implemented in their cities.

The Suburbs Rush to Embrace TOD

Thirty of DART's thirty-four stations are located within the City of Dallas. But despite the fact that the city was a leader in 1987 in helping to develop Dallas's very first New Urbanist development—a walkable, pedestrian-friendly, mixed-use downtown neighborhood served by a trolley and called State/Thomas—the city did not promote TOD around its stations through either special planning or zoning, and at the writing of this case study in 2002 no one was assigned to work on TOD projects. Rather, the success of TOD in Dallas seemed to have been

entirely driven by the market—though facilitated by a developer-friendly transit agency—and implemented by the city's savvy developers.

> The suburbs, however, seemed poised to do whatever was required to encourage TOD even if it meant making significant public investments in streets, landscaping, and other infrastructure. "The suburbs are leading the way because they are highly competitive," said Marcos Fernandez, traffic engineer and DART liaison for the Dallas suburb of Plano. Added Dallas developer Art Lomenick, who had worked on State/Thomas and was in 2002 managing director for Trammell Crow, the nation's largest commercial developer, "The suburbs are anxious to get transit and TOD because the cost of sprawl has put their tax bases at risk. Addison, Plano, Farmers Branch, Richardson, Irving—they all see transit-oriented development as a big economic engine that can help pull their tax bases back into balance."

> The prairie town of Plano had invested $800,000 in public improvements around the already completed first phase of a 3.6-acre transit village, with the second phase under construction, almost a year before the rail station was due to open in 2003. In an indication of the way the market was moving, some of the businesses that signed leases in the first development canceled when they realized rail service was still a year away. Like nearby Richardson, Plano had studied and planned for transit-oriented development around its three station sites over several years, but Richardson had encountered more opposition to the idea of building multifamily housing, especially at the densities proposed.

> In Richardson, however, Hunt Petroleum was at work developing the 500-acre Galatyn Urban Center mixed-use development around the city's two stations, and a hotel and performing arts center had already been built in a 2-acre public plaza at the center. These two fast-growing commuter towns are located in Dallas's Telecom Corridor, surrounded by gigantic corporate campuses for telecommunications and other companies—including Perot Systems, Nortel

Networks, Ericcson, Frito-Lay, and JC Penney. These corporations provided tens of thousands of jobs and a mighty tax base, but employees were driving long distances for food and housing and to run errands—generating continual traffic problems.

> It had been a bruising blow to civic pride when Boeing announced in 2001 that it was choosing to locate its corporate headquarters in Chicago, not Dallas, because Chicago had a lively downtown and a sophisticated urban culture—the implication being that Dallas had neither. But, in fact, living in the middle of a prairie and surrounded by fast-food restaurants, strip malls, garden apartments, and not much else was not especially appealing to the younger generation of hotshot telecom workers. Many had moved to Dallas from more urban environments, and their 24/7 work styles were much more suited to the way of life offered by transit-oriented development, which provided for the commingling of life and work without driving.

> Fernandez said most of the renters in Phase 1 of Plano's transit village were not native Texans, and indeed the attractive red brick mixed-use project with 450 units was more ambitiously urban than any other development in ultra-low-density Plano—the two phases together would double the size of downtown. The Plano transit village was being built by Dallas developer Robert Shaw, who was working with an architectural and planning firm named RTKL Associates. Shaw had headed up the team—including RTKL and developer Art Lomenick—that was responsible for the State/Thomas New Urbanist experiment in downtown Dallas in 1987, and which had then gone on to build the first four phases of the impressive 80-acre TOD project called Addison Circle in the Dallas suburb of Addison. Shaw, then CEO of a real estate investment trust (REIT) called Columbus Realty Trust—Lomenick was development director—had merged his company with Post Properties in 1999, and then left Post to form his own development company, Amicus Partners.

> Shaw said he believed the interest in TOD in Dallas had been enhanced by the fact that the city was home to more than its share of national developers and aided by the fact that development in Dallas is "development by right," meaning that if a project meets code it can be built— the developer does not need to go through separate entitlement and approval processes. "You have to understand that developers don't mind guidelines or restrictions," Shaw said. "But they need predictability—they need to know that if they do 'x' they will get 'y'—and the approval process is not predictable."

> He said that he also believed that the presence of rail in Dallas had definitely been the incentive that made cities begin to think and plan for more sustainable development, and that rail had made the market interested in providing financing. "Transit is definitely the hook that created the opportunity for interest in this kind of development, and it is the reason these projects will be successful in the long term," Shaw said. "Transit is an essential part of telling the story of these developments. And it's been my experience that if you can tell a good story, and if you can get control of the land, you can always attract capital. That is, as long as you're not stuck with unrealistic rents or infrastructure costs."

Addison Circle and Mockingbird Station

Of the $1 billion in transit-adjacent and transit-oriented projects built in Dallas since the opening of the rail line, two stood out in 2002 because they are ambitious, well designed, and because they function so successfully as mixed-use environments: they are Shaw's Addison Circle, now one of Post Properties's flagship properties, located in a northern suburb of Dallas, and Dallas developer Ken Hughes's Mockingbird Station, located about four miles north of downtown Dallas. Both projects were designed by RTKL and each has won a dozen design awards.

> Both projects are especially interesting because they work as auto-oriented *and* transit-oriented environments. Mockingbird Station is immediately adjacent to the light-rail line with service every ten to twenty minutes, and Addison Circle is a short walk from a bus transfer center that is slated to become a rail station in 2010 or 2012. Both projects provide parking at ratios typical of suburban developments, but the parking is mostly underground at Mockingbird and incorporated into the interiors of buildings at Addison Circle. Cars do not threaten the pedestrian orientation of either development.

> There are two other similarities: both Shaw and Hughes are charismatic and visionary developers. And both projects were built in affluent neighborhoods. Mockingbird is adjacent to Dallas's old and wealthy Park Cities neighborhoods and Southern Methodist University. Addison Circle is in Addison, the largest center of business and retail activity in the Dallas area.

> Aside from these similarities, the two projects could not be more different. Whereas Mockingbird was an entirely private venture completed with no public subsidy, Addison Circle was a public-private partnership from start to finish and was built "by the book" and with a significant public infrastructure investment: there were visioning exercises, a master plan, economic impact studies, development of a new zoning code, and standards to guide everything from building design, scale, and setbacks to building materials and exterior finishes. Whereas Mockingbird, at 10 acres, is relatively small and oriented toward retail and entertainment, Addison Circle covers 80 acres and consists mostly of residential development, with office and neighborhood-serving retail. Finally, while Mockingbird is an adaptive reuse project, Addison Circle is a greenfield development.

MOCKINGBIRD STATION: *THE* PLACE TO BE SEEN

Mockingbird Station is a $105 million "urban village" consisting of 211 loft-style apartments, 150,000 square feet of office space, an eight-screen independent film theater, and 183,000 square feet of retail, a half-dozen restaurants, a bank, and a dry cleaner. There is a full-service grocery store and ninety other shops within a five-minute walk. There are 1,440 parking spaces, nearly all of which are located underground.

> It did not take long for Mockingbird Station to establish itself as *the* place to see and be seen in 2001, because the urban village was smart and slick and unlike any other destination in Dallas. "With the opening of Mockingbird Station the city's urbanity quotient shot up dramatically," enthused *Dallas Morning News* architecture critic David Dillon. Mockingbird developer Ken Hughes had begun his career as a commercial leasing agent, an experience that made him adept at creating the right chemistry of uses—an eight-screen independent film theater, Virgin Megastore, the state's first Urban Outfitters, a Gap, Starbucks, other youth-oriented retail, and popular local restaurants. "Cocked a little to the left—a sanitized version of hip," is how he described it, and the development brought in the students from nearby Southern Methodist University (SMU) as well as the older, more sophisticated residents of the nearby Park Cities.

> RTKL had transformed the trapezoidal site and its motley collection of existing buildings into a complex, citified, and intriguing environment that made the visitor want to explore and that was full of the kind of "messy vitality" architect Robert Venturi advocated. The impressive visual centerpiece was a renovated brick warehouse circa the 1940s that supported an additional five floors of lofts, "which seemed to explode from the top of the masonry warehouse in a panoply of shiny galvanized metal and glass," wrote Willis Winters in *Texas Architect*. "The sleek upper floors are uniformly set back from the brick parapet, giving the building the look of a massive ocean liner, including a pool on the stern deck... the penthouse floor consisting of two-story mezzanine units sporting dramatic views toward downtown and the SMU campus." The lofts began at $1,500 per month, with the penthouses renting for $5,000. That was about 30 percent over market rate in 2001, leading some to joke that Mockingbird Station was injecting a healthy dose of per-capita income into DART's ridership profiles.

8.3
Mockingbird Station is wedged on a 700-foot-wide strip of land between the rail line and Central Expressway.
(Photo: Dallas Area Rapid Transit)

> In retrospect, Mockingbird Station seemed like the obvious choice for exactly this kind of development, but Hughes had difficulty convincing partners and investors—he went through several—and the project metamorphosed repeatedly. Hindsight also makes clear the rightness of the decision to recycle the brick warehouse and an ugly '70s glass office building attached to a parking structure, which forced design decisions that led to a rich and varied environment and views in which "the vertical continually contends with the horizontal," wrote Winters. But integrating the existing structures with the new buildings and making them suitable for the proposed uses required a lot of "careful plastic surgery," in the words of Mockingbird architect Randy Shortridge.

> Only the Angelika Film Center and a wedge-shaped restaurant pavilion, located on a plaza above a modest version of the Spanish Steps and a cascading fountain, are new structures. Immediately beyond is a pedestrian bridge over the rail station, which is located below grade in order to accommodate the train's immediate descent into a three-mile-long tunnel to downtown. Exiting the train and ascending the escalator or elevator to the Angelika affords dramatic views of the project—the pavilion, film center, and lofts looming overhead. Hughes studied architecture in college and was keenly aware of the importance of the "arrival sequence" for those entering the project either by car or from the light-rail station, as well as both the emotional and psychological impact of the orientation and design of the buildings.

> Hughes advocates the use of computer graphics so that at the end of every day the developer and architect can "walk through" the project. He was also sensitive to details like the development's kinetic quality, which contributed to his decision to locate two double bays of surface parking accommodating about 150 cars in the center of the project. Hughes said he was inspired by his experience of Avenida Presidente Masaryk in Mexico City, one of the world's great streets, where people throng sidewalk cafes and shops despite parked cars and bumper-to-bumper traffic. Hughes believes that it is important to provide for movement so that people can enter and move through a space. "All that activity breeds a sense of excitement and of security," he said, "and everybody likes convenience."

> Although this decision can be challenged, it does highlight one of the project's most striking qualities—it's equally convenient for those arriving by car or by public transit. The siting could not have been more fortuitous: wedged on a 700-foot-wide strip of land between the rail line and the Central Expressway and bordered on one side by Mockingbird Lane, a major east-west thoroughfare, Hughes was able to sell the development as freeway-adjacent to financial partners who had little appreciation for the value of its proximity to transit. Hughes said he had to "shroud the transit connection in secrecy." "I talked about the project's accessibility to the Central Expressway and to Mockingbird Lane, and then at the end I'd say, 'Oh, by the way, there's also a rail station.'"

> Hughes did not solicit any public involvement. And he raised the bar for other Dallas developers because he did not ask for public assistance, even though the Angelika theater could

Top to bottom, left to right

8.4
With the opening of Mockingbird Station, one architecture critic said, "Dallas's urbanity quotient shot up dramatically."
(Photo: Tim Street-Porter.)

8.5
Ascending the escalator from the below-grade station area to the film theater.
(Photo: Dallas Area Rapid Transit.)

8.6
Mockingbird's visual centerpiece, a 1940s brick warehouse supporting ground floor retail and five additional floors of lofts.
(Photo: RTKL Associates, Inc.)

draw 1,200 patrons on a weekend night, which justified significant street improvements, and even though the town of Addison was at the same time poised to provide developer Robert Shaw with $9 million in public infrastructure improvements.

> Hughes said he simply did not want to go to the trouble of getting the city involved, and it is true that without the complexities caused by a public-private partnership, Mockingbird was a fairly straightforward project. But it is unlikely Hughes would make that choice again, given the amount of public subsidy provided for transportation improvements at other TOD projects around Dallas and elsewhere in the country. At the time this case study was written, Hughes had helped the City of Dallas secure federal transportation funding and was working with RTKL landscape architect Paul Shaw, brother of Addison Circle developer Robert Shaw, to turn Mockingbird Lane into a boulevard with raised medians, wide sidewalks, landscaping, and traffic calming— thereby connecting the project with the wealthy communities and 9,500 university students on the other side of the Central Expressway.

> These transportation improvements would address one of Mockingbird's most severe short-comings: Mockingbird's pedestrian connections to its surroundings were tenuous at best. Construction of the project's proposed third phase, an L-shaped eighteen-story hotel with ground floor retail on the northwestern side of the site, would address another shortcoming: the project is surrounded by noisy, hostile automobile infrastructure—the freeway, the heavily trafficked arterial, and a DART surface parking lot for 700 cars. Phase 3 would enclose the site and insulate it from traffic noise. The proposed extension of a hike-and-bike trail along the rail line from White Rock Lake to the north would also enhance the project's connectivity to its surroundings.

ADDISON CIRCLE: A SUBURB GETS A CENTER

Addison Circle is a European-style town center built around a linear park lined with shops and cafes in the northern Dallas community of Addison. The project's first phase included 460 apartments in three buildings, 25,000 square feet of retail space, the park, street improvements, and a huge public sculpture in the middle of the traffic circle that is Addison Circle. The second phase included another 607 residential units, including luxury units, a live-work loft building, six for-sale townhouses, an additional 90,000 square feet of retail, 42,000 square foot of office space, a self-storage building, an esplanade, and sidewalks. This phase also included a ten-story, 300,000-square-foot office building and adjacent six-level parking garage with 1,400 spaces. Phase 3 included another 250 residential units in three buildings. Since then, 86 condominiums and 18 townhomes have been constructed; at full build-out there will be 4,000 residential units.

> Both Mockingbird Station and Addison Circle have a direct lineage to the work done by Robert Shaw and his team on the State/Thomas district. State/Thomas proved that investments in the urban core pay off and that there is a market for something other than garden-style apartments in Dallas.

> A historic African-American neighborhood, State/Thomas had been leveled in the late 1970s and early '80s by developers hoping to capitalize on the downtown market for office space. Then the savings and loan debacle caused the bottom to fall out of the real estate market, and the office market moved to the suburbs in the north. Suddenly this land became affordable, and in an attempt to recoup from the failed redevelopment attempt, the City of Dallas worked with Shaw and RTKL planner John Gosling to create a special urban neighborhood that permitted mid to high density housing in four- to eight-story buildings and a reduction in the size and scale of residential streets.

> This was before New Urbanism and before the term transit-oriented development was in common usage, but there was already disenchantment with garden apartments, and State/Thomas was to offer a new kind of in-town living with a careful mix of residential and commercial uses, including street-level retail, cafes and offices, and landscaping standards that were much higher than usual for Dallas or any other city. To raise funding for public improvements, the City of Dallas created the city's first tax increment financing district. Shaw had to go all the way to Japan to find financing for his first residential projects, but by 1991 State/Thomas had become Dallas's most popular in-town residential neighborhood, with 1,100 market-rate apartments and townhomes and several thousand square feet of new commercial space.

> By 2002, development had spilled outside of the State/Thomas district and the neighborhood had become known as "Uptown," a name Shaw coined, and had attracted $1 billion in investment, boosting downtown's population by 5,000 residents. A historic trolley that had carried mostly tourists and conventioneers was being taken over and improved by DART. As the density and activity in downtown and Uptown increased, an expanded trolley system seemed the right mode of transportation to complement light-rail and make these neighborhoods truly transit and pedestrian oriented.

8.7
Aerial view of Addison Circle—
a new town center for a
"boomburb."
(Photo: www.globeXplorer.com)
8.8
Addison Circle is a public-
private partnership, with
substantial dedicated
public space.
(Rendering: RTKL Associates, Inc.)

Building Second Floor Plan

Scale

Retail/ Restaurant
Residential
Office
Open space
Parking
Storage
Future Bldg.
Existing Bldg.
Townhouse

> It was the work of Shaw and his team on State/Thomas that inspired Addison officials to contact Shaw in 1991. Addison had prospered during the '70s and '80s because it was located at the terminus of the Dallas North Tollway and because it was one of the few suburbs permitting the sale of liquor by the drink. At the epicenter of Dallas's northward growth corridor, it had become Dallas's largest center of retail activity, boasting 4,000 hotel rooms and 130 restaurants. But there was definitely no "there" there in Addison, and the city had little appeal or identity. And while the daytime population was 100,000, the nighttime population fell to just 5,000. As the extension of the tollway to the north made cheap undeveloped greenfields accessible, the town of Addison saw its popularity and tax revenues drop.

> The then-mayor of Addison was a well-traveled airline pilot who had visited walkable, densely populated, mixed-use neighborhoods in cities around the world, and she and other city officials really liked State/Thomas. They wanted to increase their residential population and create a sense of place in Addison, and they did not want garden apartments. They came up with the idea of creating a special urban district in their 1991 Comprehensive Plan, and asked Shaw if he could do it. The site was Addison's last large parcel of undeveloped land, next to the town's tiny historic main street and a new conference center and theater, on what used to be a sharecropper's cotton and sorghum fields. Gaylord Properties of Oklahoma City, Oklahoma, owned the entire 120 acres.

A Small Piece of Land Yields Big Tax Revenues

When Addison officials approached Shaw in 1991 he put together a planning team, working with consultants and town staff over an eight-month period, surveying potential demand for a high density mixed-use New Urbanist development. It was the public funding for pedestrian-friendly streets and landscaping that helped define and make State/Thomas attractive to developers, but officials in Addison wanted to make sure a similar investment on their part was a sound business decision. The survey indicated a high demand, so the team set up a consensus-building planning process, educating elected officials and staff and the public about the benefits of high density, walkable communities.

> Design and development standards were encoded into a new zoning ordinance by the city. The economic benefits of the development plan and phasing strategy were analyzed and a cost/benefit analysis was prepared to compare the effect of various development options on the municipal budget. The developer identified potential financing gaps and worked with the town to reach agreement on a public improvement funding strategy to seed the initial development. The City of Addison agreed to pay for high-quality public infrastructure—parks, a districtwide pedestrian-friendly street grid, wide sidewalks, paved crosswalks, shade trees, benches, signage, outdoor lighting—linking improvements to developer performance. It took two years to reach a developer's agreement.

> The key planning imperative was to avoid the isolated, self-contained development pattern of the typical North Dallas garden apartment complex. The development framework

8.9

Addison Circle is a town center built around a linear park lined with shops and cafes.
(Photo: © 2000–2002 Steve Hinds, Inc., all rights reserved.)

8.10

Housing at Addison Circle is architecturally distinct, with details far beyond those of the typical "garden" apartment.
(Photo: RTKL Associates, Inc.)

was based on a traffic impact analysis and composed of public infrastructure costing three times the normal streetscape allocation. Over the first two phases of the project Addison invested $9 million out of the city's general fund in a high-quality, districtwide, pedestrian-friendly street grid. In return, Shaw promised architecturally distinct housing that would be built to last, employing high-quality building materials and finishes with life cycles beyond the typical garden apartment.

> "Addison Circle will age, and it will transition, but it will not become obsolete and worn out. It will stand the test of time and ultimately it will pay off," Shaw said. "These are not garden apartments. These are permanent structures. Yes, the infrastructure cost was significant but it was doable because the amount of land involved was small—and it will provide the city with a good return on its investment. As in Uptown, it's the infrastructure that gives the development a good bone structure. And because it has good bones not every building will have to be great in order for the development to succeed as a whole."

> Construction began in 1996. The project consists of fifteen buildings ranging from four stories up to ten stories near the tollway, and it is organized around open spaces—an esplanade, roundabout, park, and interior courtyards—and a hierarchy of gridded streets and pedestrian corridors: the "ceremonial street" or esplanade, a four-lane, tree-shaded boulevard with a wide median; two-lane residential streets with parallel parking on each side, wide sidewalks, and trees; very narrow streets called "mews" without curbs and gutters; motor courts with rear entrances; and carriageways and open corridors cooled by ceiling fans leading through the buildings and connecting all parts of the project.

Proving the Market

Extraordinary attention to detail is evident throughout Addison Circle. Shaw's brother Paul, a landscape architect, designed the outdoor spaces. Each courtyard has a pool, fountain, fireplace, trees and vines, and some gathering place—a billiard room or indoor/outdoor living room—and each courtyard is different. Some are paved with wood-mold bricks, their edges softened and already covered with moss; some are paved with stained, scored, and sealed concrete; and some are stone. Some of the swimming pools are Caribbean blue; others have a pebble-tech finish. Some have mosaics; some have fog-emitters. Fountains create white noise. Streetlights suspended from cables create an overhead plane and dramatic lighting; courtyards have gas lamps. Numerous entrances to each building ensure privacy.

> If fault can be found with Addison Circle it might be that it is too perfect; nervous about the quality of the product, the city required facades to be 90 percent brick, giving it the uniform look of a college campus. Otherwise, the development is nothing short of enchanting, the courtyards and motor courts drenching each building with light and providing visual access into the interiors. Addison offers every type of real estate product and they are not segregated by price: a luxury townhome is next to a 600-square-foot apartment that is next to flex space for home or office. Ground floor flex space offers the additional benefit of providing for more residential space in the early project phases but can be turned into retail space in the latter phases when the project can support more retail. The efficiencies and smaller one-bedrooms were renting for about 80 percent of county median income in 2003. The first phase of the project was fully leased in a record six months when it opened.

> "Everybody says, 'We want an Addison Circle in our city—what does it take?'" said Paul Shaw. "And I say, 'Are you willing to spend a dozen extra million dollars and a few extra years of your life? Most developers—if they took as many meetings as we did—would think there was something really wrong with the project. But that's how long it takes. Detail matters. Collaboration matters. Fortunately, we had enlightened clients: a property owner with a long-term vision and a city that could write the checks because it had an incredible tax base."

> Robert Shaw's Columbus Realty Trust had succeeded in creating a very high quality and high profile product that was also profitable because the city had funded the public infrastructure of streets, parks, and plazas that contributed to its success and the design and planning process that minimized the risk. The payback for the city was that it had succeeded in reinventing itself by creating an appealing city center that proved attractive to new residents. Addison Circle put this formerly anonymous suburb on the map as a desirable place to live, sparking the interest of every other suburb in the Dallas–Fort Worth metroplex as well as suburbs across the United States.

> When Columbus Realty Trust and Post Properties merged midway through the huge second phase of the project, there were "a few bumps in the road," said Addison Development Director Carmen Moran. She added that Post wanted to build garden apartments for Phase 5, and that it was likely that the city would choose other developers for the project's remaining six phases, which include a nineteen-acre outdoor performance space and park and a mixed-use corridor in between the first four phases and the bus transfer center. "We remain confident that we will get the kind of development we want," Moran said. "Because even

8.11
Addison Circle gave this formerly undistinguished suburb a new identity.
(Photo: RTKL Associates, Inc.)

if the new developers don't get it, we have all of the guidelines in place to protect everybody's investment."

> Developer Art Lomenick had left Post shortly after Shaw to promote mixed-use and transit-oriented development nationally for Trammell Crow. "Real estate development is like an oil tanker that takes twelve miles to change course. The industry is hard-wired to deliver certain kinds of product," Lomenick said. "But in the last ten years there's definitely been a guerilla movement among developers, and we've been part of it. The lesson of State/Thomas and Addison Circle and Mockingbird Station and Plano is that there is market demand for the lifestyle offered by TOD. Baby boomers, Generation Xers, and Millennials don't want garden apartments. It's lonely and boring. They want to live somewhere more engaging and interactive. In America that's the first step—proving there's demand. Now the industry has to figure out how to go about providing for it."

Lessons Learned

Unless the TOD site is promising real estate, like Mockingbird Station, the public sector has to share the cost of building TOD by investing in infrastructure and other public improvements. TOD's complex design and higher densities—and the sometimes time-consuming process and collaborations required to coordinate it—make it more expensive to build than garden-style apartments and strip malls. In addition, the return will be lower and slower, and the risk will be higher. For these reasons and because TOD achieves many public objectives and can increase tax revenues, public funding for infrastructure and other improvements is justified and necessary in order to level the playing field for TOD and make these projects attractive to developers. Mockingbird Station was a rare site, situated as close by a freeway and major arterial as it was to a rail station, and immediately adjacent to some of Dallas's wealthiest neighborhoods as well as 9,500 university students. Developer Ken Hughes was able to raise the money to complete the project without public investment. Shaw said TOD requires a new covenant between cities and developers: Cities must agree to provide incentives, create a pedestrian-friendly environment that supports neighborhood services, and provide zoning flexibility to encourage mixed uses and higher densities. Density is important because it is how both parties will fund their obligations. In return, Shaw said, developers should invest more money in exteriors and build for long-term ownership, build structured parking that's hidden from the main street, privatize very little space, and "take a big tent approach to consensus building."

If cities want to develop sustainable communities, they must play a proactive part in the development process. Visioning and master-planning exercises, and the development of special codes and design guidelines, help create certainty for both public and private partners. Addison Development Director Carmen Moran said the planning, zoning, and design guidelines that were hammered out before construction began ensure that the city's investment will be protected, despite the fact that new developers will come in with new ideas for subsequent phases. Robert Shaw said that the development of special codes and guidelines in the State/Thomas district was critical for the same reasons. The close working relationships that develop during these collaborations permit the exchange of technical and political advice, and assure agreement and understanding on the form and substance of the planning concepts, traffic issues, and development standards. Ken Hughes, who paid RTKL to create a master plan for Mockingbird Station, said his job would have been much easier had the city completed a station area plan. Most important, he said, it would have served to put all city departments on notice about the city's goals for the site, it would have helped to coordinate their disparate objectives, it would have helped ensure political support, and it would have made clear the necessity of transportation improvements, some of which were paid for by Hughes.

Having "facts on the ground" is important, as is telling stories about other successful TOD projects. In Dallas, the success of State/Thomas was key to proving that there was demand for other than garden-style apartments and that investment in the urban core could provide a good return. Dallas developers credit State/Thomas for seeding both Addison Circle and Mockingbird Station, and said Addison Circle seeded Plano's TOD, which will seed TOD in Richardson, which will seed projects in all the other suburbs. Developer Robert Shaw said that telling stories that create a sense of success about these projects is especially important until there is enough critical mass to create real success. Developer Ken Hughes, who visited TOD projects all over the world before building Mockingbird Station, recommended sending city officials on similar tours because "everybody makes decisions in the end that are based on their personal experience." Hughes also said that it is critical that transit agencies and other TOD advocates spend more time educating the financial community about the benefits and the successes of the development that is occurring around transit, because investors often put up the most resistance.

TOD projects can be both auto-friendly and pedestrian-friendly. Seeing is believing. Mockingbird Station works, despite the fact that there is ample parking, and Addison Circle functions well as a pedestrian-friendly environment even though it is unlikely that many, if any, residents use transit. Whether these are destinations that will promote transit use is less certain, though a parking study completed shortly after Mockingbird Station opened suggested that about 10 percent of patrons were arriving by transit.

Cities that are against multifamily housing can be persuaded if it is sold as TOD. RTKL's Paul Shaw said the construction of too many shoddy garden apartment complexes has prejudiced cities against multifamily housing. But he said that when multifamily housing is presented as part of an urban center that is transit-adjacent and that has mixed-use development, cities become much more interested. This works especially well when the time is taken to market the urban center concept, with slides and videos from successful developments in other cities, and with information about proposed quality standards, tenant profiles, and various design features. He said it is critical to use the term "urban housing" instead of "apartments."

Retail is the most difficult part. RTKL architect Randy Shortridge, who designed Mockingbird Station, compared designing retail space to designing one home for twenty different families, each with their own ideas about what works. He said that a lot of thought should be given to which shops will go where, their relationship to other shops, to the street, to the street corner, and to the rail station, and who will be walking past the shop at what hour of the day or night. Major credit tenants will also exercise demands about what other kinds of shops can be located within the development and where. These constraints make it difficult to create a successful mix of uses. In Addison Circle it also proved difficult to make retail work because the city and developers had to zone for retail that would not compete with the surrounding business community, and that would not bring too much traffic into the development. That left neighborhood-serving retail like dry cleaners, personal services like nail and hair salons, a copy center, sandwich shops, and a few restaurants. Shaw said that in small-scale projects, and in early phases of larger projects, the residential has to subsidize the retail. At Addison Circle, ground floor "flex space" was built to accommodate live-work arrangements in the early phases and retail if and when there is demand for it.

Transit agencies need to site stations carefully if they want to encourage TOD. Ken Hughes said transit agencies need to be very careful about siting stations, noting that if the station at Mockingbird had been built even 50 feet closer to the Central Expressway, there would not have been enough site to build on. As of the writing of this chapter, he had begun working with the City of Fort Worth and its transit agency on siting that city's proposed rail line, because the city wanted to maximize the opportunities for development. "Few transit agencies realize the extent to which they need to ally themselves with developers so they can take development issues into consideration before stations are built," Hughes said. "Stations shouldn't be built by Joe Transportation Engineer without input from people who may have other points of view, because then the ship is out of the harbor—stations are too expensive and inflexible to change."

TOD projects take time. Collaboration is important. Detail is important. For this reason, small developers are best suited for TOD. Robert Shaw said that the fact that TOD projects take so much time is the reason that very large developers like Post Properties or Federal Realty Trust, both of which entered the TOD market in the late '90s but then abandoned it, have little advantage over smaller developers. TOD requires expertise, skill, and relationships more than it requires a huge capital outlay, he said. "TOD projects require the developer to be very entrepreneurial," he said. "The developer must be able to respond to local circumstances, and to be involved day to day, even hour to hour." The amount of internal review this necessitates at a large company, where the development project would be handled by junior staff, makes the projects unwieldy and expensive. In fact, there's a dis-economy of scale, he said, because TOD is so site-specific that TOD can't be institutionalized or made formulaic in the same way that shopping centers or strip malls or garden apartments can. Art Lomenick added that large national developers with strong local branches that have the autonomy to function like smaller developers are also well suited to do TOD. The point, he said, is that the developer must have relationships in place in order to put together the public-private partnerships and agreements that TOD requires and to negotiate the consensus-building process. But he said that while large developers don't want to build TOD, they definitely want to own it. "Wall Street capital, the public capital market—including real estate investment trusts—want mixed-use and infill projects and are willing to pay for it—that kind of development is on the top of their list," he said. "They are willing to partner with smaller developers and be their capital source."

REFERENCES

Brink, Tom (Vice President, RTKL, Dallas). 2002. Interviewed by the author, March.

City of Addison. City of Addison Economic Development Online Business Network. At www.addisontexas.com.

City of Plano. 1999. Downtown Plano: A Vision and Strategy for Creating a Transit Village. Adopted May 10.

———. 1998. Downtown Plano Light Rail Stop, Development Vision and Objectives. April.

Dallas Area Rapid Transit. N.d. Homepage. At www.dart.ort.

Dillon, David. 2001. This Year's AIA Award Winners Share a Decidedly Fresh Approach to Design. *Dallas Morning News* October 20.

———. 2001. An Urban Space That Sings. Mockingbird Station Creates Harmony from Old and New, Odds and Ends. *Dallas Morning News* July 1.

———. 2001. Shock of the New. The Downtown Housing Boom Has Forged Winners and Losers. *Dallas Morning News* January 14.

Dunklin, Reese. 2001. Tour Offers a Taste of Things to Come: Carrollton Officials Studying How DART Has Sparked Development. *Dallas Morning News* September 28.

Fernandez, Marcos (Traffic engineer, City of Plano). 2002. Interviewed by the author, March.

Frisco, John (Associate, RTKL, Dallas). 2002. Interviewed by the author, March.

Gosling, John (Vice President, RTKL, Washington, D.C.). Interviewed by the author, March.

Griffin, Laura. 2001. A Change of Heart about DART Rail. Some Neighborhoods That Once Were Opposed Now Beg for Stations. *Dallas Morning News* October 20.

Hall, Cheryl. 2001. Back on Track. Ken Hughes Aims to Re-Energize Dallas with His Vision of Eclectic Urban Living. *Dallas Morning News* March 11.

Hughes, Ken (Developer and President of UC Urban). 2002. Interviewed by the author, January.

Lomenick, Art (Developer, Trammell Crow). 2002. Interviewed by the author, January.

Melton, Annie (Transportation advocate, Trans Texas Alliance). 2002. Interviewed by the author, April.

Mid America Regional Council. Addison Circle Case Study. At www.qualityplaces.marc.org.

Moran, Carmen (Economic Development Director, City of Addison). 2002. Interviewed by the author, February.

Morris, Mike (Director of Transportation, North Central Texas Council of Governments). 2002. Interviewed by the author, June.

Post, Sarah. 2001. Mixed Uses on Their Minds, DART Offers a Chance to Get on Board. New Approach to Development Mixes Old, New Ideas. *Dallas Morning News* December 6.

———. 2001. Developments Are on Track. Residential and Commercial Merge along DART Route. *Dallas Morning News* June 3.

Ronan, Courtney. 2002. Addison: The Town within the City. *Realty Times* March 27.

Rutherford, Paris (Vice President, RTKL, Dallas). 2002. Interviewed by the author, March.

Shaw, Paul (Landscape architect, RTKL Associates, Dallas). 2002. Interviewed by the author, January.

Shaw, Robert (Developer and President of Amicus Development). 2002. Interviwed by the author, January.

Shortridge, Randy (Architect, RTKL Associates, Los Angeles). 2002. Interviewed by the author, February.

Urban Land Institute. 2000. Richardson, Texas: A Plan for Transit-Oriented Development. June.

Walmsley, Ann. Plano Goes Urban, *D Magazine* March.

Weinstein, Bernard (Director, University of North Texas Center for Economic Development and Research). 2002. Interviewed by the author, February .

Weinstein, Bernard and Terry Clower. 2003. DART Light Rail's Effect on Taxable Property Valuations and Transit-oriented Development." Prepared for DART. January.

Weinstein, Bernard and Terry Clower. 1999. The Initial Economic Impacts of the DART LRT System. Prepared for DART. July.

Weirzinski, Jack (Assistant Vice President of Planning and Economic Development, DART). 2002. Interviewed by the author, January.

Winters, Willis. 2001. Urban Living at Its Most Vibrant. *Texas Architect* November–December.

9.1
From the air, Lindbergh Station is ringed with freeways and big arterials and hemmed in by low density development.
(Photo: www.globeXplorer.com)

THE ATLANTA CASE STUDY

Lindbergh City Center

Sharon Feigon and David Hoyt
with Gloria Ohland

The building boom that had caused the Atlanta metropolitan region to sprawl over twenty-two counties seemed unstoppable in the late 1990s, when it took an unusual twist. BellSouth, a regional telecommunications company and Atlanta's second-largest employer, announced it would consolidate its many suburban offices into six towers built on three sites, all within Atlanta proper, and as near Atlanta's rail stations as possible. Lindbergh City Center, a joint development effort of BellSouth and the Metropolitan Atlanta Rapid Transit Authority (MARTA), would house 1 million square feet of offices right on top of the Lindbergh Metro station, making it Atlanta's most recent and, at forty-seven acres, most ambitious transit-oriented development project. Furthermore, it was a conspicuous sign that development was moving back into the center city, which hadn't been the focus of the market in thirty years. Even farther south, the site of a defunct downtown steel mill was being cleared to make way for Jim Jacoby's mixed-use Atlantic Station, which would be the biggest development in Atlanta in fifty years.

>   Viewed charitably, these events suggested that the forces driving sprawl were no longer operating unchecked, and that considerations of business efficiency, residential quality of life, and regional air quality were now being factored into development decisions. Most Atlanta residents were becoming aware of the downsides that had accompanied their city's entry into the ranks of great American boomtowns. Throughout the '90s Atlanta had achieved a number of dubious distinctions. Residents of Atlanta were now driving more than residents of any other U.S. metropolitan area, including Los Angeles—thirty-five miles per day per capita—and Atlanta had some of the worst air quality in the nation. Experts conjectured that Atlanta had undergone the greatest geographical expansion of any urban area in history. And Atlanta ranked second only to hollowed-out Detroit in the volume of office space that existed outside the city.

>   In 1998, there were high expectations for the Lindbergh Station project all around, in no small measure as a hopeful response to the region's aggravated transportation crisis. No longer the sole concern of traffic engineers and Department of Transportation bureaucrats, by the late '90s Atlanta's growth-related transportation problems had visibly encroached on general issues of public health, corporate livelihood, and municipal fiscal solvency. Atlanta's newfound notoriety garnered it the kind of negative publicity in the national media that business leaders dread:

a lead article in the Wall *Street Journal*, "Is Traffic-Clogged Atlanta the New Los Angeles?" on June 18, 1998, and "Sprawling, Sprawling..." in *Newsweek* on July 19, 1999. Not long after the *Newsweek* essay, the Centers for Disease Control, to which Atlanta plays host, announced to the world that Atlanta was the third most dangerous metropolitan area for walking in the United States, behind Fort Lauderdale and Miami, Florida. The report advised Atlanta to protect its pedestrians by carrying out "engineering interventions... to separate pedestrians from traffic"—in other words, by building the sidewalks so many neighborhoods lacked.

> But not only was the auto-dominated environment of Atlanta a mortal threat to its pedestrians, it was a growing disincentive to the corporate expansion that had fueled Atlanta's real estate boom in the '90s. BellSouth's much-heralded 1998 decision to locate at the Lindbergh MARTA station took on even more significance by contrast with Hewlett-Packard's choice, that same year, to cancel expansion plans in the Atlanta suburbs, explicitly on account of the area's traffic congestion and long commutes. It was becoming apparent that Atlanta's gridlock directly affected not only the lives of its residents, but also the future of its economy.

Atlanta's Crisis Year

All of this was only a prelude, however, to one of the greatest civic crises to affect the city since the Civil Rights movement. In 1996, the U.S. Environmental Protection Agency (EPA), as executor of the Clean Air Act (CAA) amendments of 1990, declared the Atlanta metropolitan region to have entered a "conformity lapse," which meant that planners at the Atlanta Regional Commission (ARC) had until mid-1998, when the plan then in effect expired, to come up with a long-term transportation plan to bring Atlanta into conformity with CAA standards. Under the CAA, federal funds could be spent only on road projects that were part of a regional plan that could be shown to stay within limits on vehicle emissions. Until Atlanta came up with a plan, it would receive no transportation funding from the federal government for new road capacity.

> At the root of Atlanta's multiple problems were at least two decades of unplanned growth and road building. While endless gridlock was certainly an inconvenience for commuters, it became clear that there were graver consequences. Commentators despaired of Atlanta's dozens of Balkanized municipalities ever being able to come together to work out a passable transportation improvement plan under the guidance of the beleaguered ARC. In the absence of this kind of cooperation, and despite the 1998 deadline, Atlanta continued to build. Suburban Atlanta municipalities and the Georgia Department of Transportation pushed forward dozens of transportation projects, claiming that a Clean Air Act loophole allowed for the grandfathering of projects that had been initiated, or only approved, prior to the conformity lapse.

> In 1999, two lawsuits filed by environmental groups against the U.S. Department of Transportation, the Georgia Department of Transportation, and the Atlanta Regional Commission—charging these agencies had abused the EPA's grandfathering provision—resulted in the

blocking of forty-four of these projects, worth more than $700 million. Three months earlier a decision in a related suit brought by the Environmental Defense Fund had declared the grandfathering process illegal. These decisions made it clear that the Atlanta region simply could not do what it had done for decades: build its way out of its congestion problems. In order to receive the federal funding on which the region depended for as much as 80 percent of the cost of road projects, plans for emission-reducing transportation alternatives had to be given serious consideration.

MARTA: A Solution to Traffic

Most of the reforms then under discussion had to do with creating a state agency that would have broad powers over regional transportation and land-use planning. The ARC had ultimately been subject to the whims of the local politicians who made up the board and had not been able to direct growth in a comprehensive and sustainable fashion. In the absence of an effective regional planning body, MARTA, Atlanta's twenty-three-year-old cash-strapped transit agency, had emerged as a key player in the campaign to do something about the city's traffic congestion. Making transit more attractive to Atlanta residents was key to improving both congestion and air quality, and MARTA's assets—a forty-eight mile rail system, thirty-eight stations and adjacent property—could be exploited for regional benefit.

> More than most transit agencies, MARTA operated under severe financial constraints—it is the only large metropolitan transit system in the country that receives no money from state government. The agency was dependent for funding on a one-cent sales tax in the two counties—Fulton and DeKalb—where most of its operations were located, but MARTA also served commuters from many of the surrounding counties (especially Gwinnet, Cobb, and Clayton) that did not have similarly dedicated sales taxes. Any increase in ridership meant an increase in ever-scarce operating revenue. As young professionals began returning to the city core to live in the '90s, MARTA recognized that there was a market for transit-oriented development at its rail stations. The agency established a director of what it called "transit-related" development and received a grant from the Federal Transit Administration's (FTA) Livable Communities Initiative to study how to develop the Lindbergh site.

> For as long as MARTA existed, it had planned for transit-oriented development, convinced that developing station properties was in the agency's own financial best interest. A decade earlier MARTA had completed several joint development projects, leasing the air-rights over several stations, and interfacing several more stations with adjoining retail stores and office buildings. This activity had ended in the late '80s with the downturn in the real estate market as growth moved out of the city. But with the return of bullish markets in Atlanta proper in the '90s, MARTA's various parking lots and unused parcels became tremendously valuable. Hemmed in financially, the transit agency began to push the legal envelope in terms of what a transit agency could do with land it had acquired for right-of-way and other operational needs, aggressively leas-

9.2

The master plan for Lindbergh was ambitious, dense, and mixed use—although the uses were separated on the site.

(Rendering: Cooper Carry Architects.)

ing and even selling land for development. This activity, however, ran afoul of an FTA mandate that transit agencies should sell excess land that had been purchased for right-of-way but which was not being used for transportation purposes and reimburse the federal government for its share of the purchase price. In 1994, MARTA was audited and instructed to divest itself of excess property.

> Existing FTA rules permitted transit agencies to develop land as long as the projects were "physically or functionally related to transit," which had been narrowly interpreted to mean that land had to be developed for a purpose explicitly related to transportation, such as a transit station or station parking lot. But MARTA as well as other transportation agencies began lobbying the FTA for a broader interpretation that would allow agencies to develop the land for mixed use or sell it and keep revenues for operations and capital improvements. In 1997, the FTA agreed, and issued a statement clarifying its policy, a change that sent transit agencies scurrying to get into the real estate business. MARTA immediately put out a request for proposals to develop the forty-seven acres at Lindbergh station.

> The rationale for choosing Lindbergh was clear. The station, the second busiest in the system, was situated at the junction of two MARTA lines, and it was located immediately adjacent to the wealthy Buckhead neighborhoods seven miles north of downtown Atlanta. "I told everybody that we should go with our best property first," recalled Paul Vespermann, the director of transit-related development. "If anything was going to generate interest, it had to be our best piece of property." What shape the Lindbergh TOD would take was less certain. Larry Frank, then on the faculty of Georgia Tech's City Planning Program, authored a 1999 study of the Lindbergh

site that incorporated the most current thinking on land use and its relationship to transportation. Frank's recommendations for Lindbergh conformed in many ways to the TOD ideal: a high density mixed-use development integrating transit with the commercial and residential life of surrounding neighborhoods using a grid plan of highly interconnected surface streets to enhance the pedestrian environment and create a sense of place. Traffic calming would be employed to slow busy traffic on the area's congested Piedmont Road. Lindbergh's housing would be designed for people with a mixed range of incomes.

> The plan that MARTA's developer, Carter and Associates, first took to community groups in the mostly affluent neighborhoods surrounding Lindbergh in 1998 did not look much different from what Frank described in his study. Some residents were apprehensive about the potential for aggravated traffic congestion around the site, and the lack of improvements for pedestrians along Piedmont Road, which served as the main entrance to the project and separated Lindbergh from the moderate- to low-income neighborhood to the east, where many residents were transit-dependent. But most of the groups were charmed by the pleasant watercolor renderings of the transit village Carter then intended to build. The overall response to Lindbergh was generally positive. "Initially, we thought the Lindbergh project was fantastic," said architect Peggy Whitaker, a resident of Peachtree Heights East, one of the neighborhoods adjacent to the project. "But then MARTA and Carter added, under their breath, 'There are going to be some offices.'"

BellSouth: Building Great Places to Work

Neither MARTA nor neighborhood groups could have anticipated that the Lindbergh site would attract Atlanta's second largest employer as a tenant. BellSouth made local history when it announced that, contrary to the investment trends of the previous three decades, it was going to make a major investment on property within the I-285 perimeter that encircled the city of Atlanta. "The plan was such a departure from the norm," *Atlanta Journal-Constitution* reporter David Goldberg wrote in a case study of the project, "and so important a symbol of positive change, that it was front-page news for several days in the local papers." The decision was interpreted by many as an indication that the economics of sprawl no longer made sense, even in the corporate boardroom. Running a technology firm with 20,000 employees scattered across seventy-five suburban locations, argued BellSouth's strategists, incurred costs and inefficiencies that could be avoided by centralizing operations. And, in an industry that had evolved from a basic service provider to a technological hothouse over the course of the Internet boom, there was a sellers' market for skilled talent. The workers BellSouth needed to attract in order to remain competitive most likely would not want to settle down to a life of suburban commuting.

> About a third of the leases on BellSouth's regional offices were set to expire between 2001 and 2003, and BellSouth had outgrown what space it had. While putting together a strategic plan for corporate real estate, BellSouth had considered moving into a one-hundred-story office tower

9.3
Lindbergh Station under construction in spring 2003.
(Photo: Aerial Innovations of Georgia, Inc.)

9.4
The scale of Lindbergh Station is in marked contrast to the surrounding low density development.
(Photo: Aerial Innovations of Georgia, Inc.)

9.5
The project incorporates more than ten thousand parking spaces in four massive garages.
(Photo: Aerial Innovations of Georgia, Inc.)

in downtown Atlanta, or into a classic suburban corporate campus. Both ideas were rejected in favor of consolidating offices somewhere in between the Midtown, Lindbergh, and Lenox MARTA stations. Though not the only factor considered, proximity to transit weighed heavily in the final decision of where to locate all three "business centers." "We wanted people to have choices about how to get to work," said Richard Gilbert, coordinator of BellSouth's Metro Plan. "We took all the employees in Atlanta . . . took all their home locations, and determined the geographic center of our employee base, which was just about at Lindbergh, which also is in the middle of the three business centers we are building." Locating at the MARTA stops would make it cheaper, easier, and more productive for BellSouth employees to move between offices during the day.

>   Both MARTA and BellSouth were clients of Carter and Associates, and when Carter helped bring the two parties together, the deal was closed quickly. Market forces had brought the part-ners together without any particular effort on the part of ARC or any other state or local officials. Plans were drawn up for two office towers totaling 1 million square feet, with an option to build another 1.2 million square feet during a second phase of development, 330,000 square feet of retail along the center's "main street," 259 condominiums, and 566 apartments. While the inte-riors of BellSouth's towers were promoted as avant-garde workspaces, the arrangement of retail, commerce, and offices along a villagelike "main street" was organized in accordance with the principles of the New Urbanism. "The mall will be an incredibly alluring place to be," insisted MARTA's Vespermann.

>   When MARTA and Carter came back to the neighborhood groups with this significantly expanded development plan, the neighbors were alarmed. "Things were progressing fairly well," recollected Carter's Chuck Konas, "until BellSouth announced that there was actually going to be some density at this station." The project was too big and had too many parking spaces, protest-ed residents, and there were not enough pedestrian improvements or green spaces. All of these became points of contention between MARTA and the neighborhoods as they entered first into negotiations, and then into court. "It was a done deal," reflected Libba Grace, a resident of Garden Hills, the Buckhead neighborhood that eventually brought suit against MARTA. "They didn't want public participation. . . . It was all over and done, no questions asked."

The Politics of Parking

What had stunned neighborhood groups about the expanded project was the plan to build more than 13,000 parking spaces. The conflict that ensued turned on what effect those parking spaces would have on traffic congestion and quality of life in the neighborhoods abutting Lindbergh. Everyone agreed on one thing: the present situation along the main access to Lindbergh, Piedmont Road, was intolerable, and getting worse. An estimated 42,000 vehicles passed through the intersection of Piedmont Road and Lindbergh Drive each day in 1999, and planners estimated that the new development would draw an additional 33,000 daily trips. In the summer of 1999, in an effort to stave off a lawsuit, MARTA and the developer entered into conflict nego-tiation with five groups representing the adjoining neighborhoods—Garden Hills, Peachtree Heights East, Peachtree Park, Peachtree Hills, and a tenants association from Lindbergh Gardens, a large apartment complex in the neighborhood to the east—over the issue of parking as well as the need for more pedestrian and traffic improvements.

>   The groups took a range of positions. Some worried about the effect of the project on their property values, and wanted to preserve the quiet, residential character of their streets, which were likely to become commuter shortcuts. Others wanted to ensure there would be pedestrian access from lower-income neighborhoods to the east. Many were disturbed by what they felt had been the unilateral nature of the Lindbergh planning effort—that MARTA and Carter had pre-sented the project design as a fait accompli. Others supported the idea of TOD at Lindbergh, and argued that the long-term benefits of building a high density project so near transit were worth the short-term adjustments that would be required as the region became more transit-oriented. But even they felt that MARTA and the City of Atlanta had settled for something that fell too far short of the ideal. It was as if, complained Peachtree Heights representative Peggy Whitaker, "They went out and hired a consultant—because they didn't know anything about what they were doing—and put together something they called TOD when it's just a BellSouth office park with a transit station stuck onto it."

>   As a result of six months of mediation, Carter agreed to reduce the parking at Lindbergh from 13,000 spaces to 10,461. But the company ultimately preserved the total number of parking spaces it wanted by relocating the disputed 3,000 to what it called "interceptor parking decks" at MARTA stations farther out—Doraville, North Springs, College Park, and Indian Creek. BellSouth argued that in order for its Metro Plan to work, the company needed to assure employ-ees they would have parking at outlying stations in lots that frequently filled up by 8:30 A.M. MARTA's Paul Vespermann said it would have been impossible to secure financing for the project unless lenders were guaranteed that commuters could find ample parking. "Lenders don't trust the mode split that we believe transit will enjoy," said Vespermann. "Once we can prove that, and we are confident that can be proven . . . they will see the empty parking, and when Phase 2 arrives, less parking will be built." BellSouth estimated only 30 percent of the employees working at Lindbergh would use transit—a number no higher than the average transit use at the other BellSouth offices located near transit stops. Vespermann estimated ridership would be as high as 40 to 50 percent.

>   Leon Eplan, Atlanta's former planning director, said he believed the plan could have worked with as few as 5,000 to 6,000 spaces, and he questioned how 10,000 more cars would negotiate the interchange of heavily trafficked Piedmont and I-85 and then traverse another half mile to Lindbergh's parking decks without creating gridlock. Moreover, Lindbergh Plaza Mall, built in 1958 and located across the street from Lindbergh Center, was being redeveloped as a gigantic

shopping mall with big box stores and other national retailers. "I live just south of Lindbergh," Eplan said during an interview in 2001, "and it's already jammed up. And here we're going to add another 10,000 parking spots. And there's a new mall coming in." Ed Ellis, vice president of the firm responsible for traffic engineering at Lindbergh, summed up the dilemma: "This is the right project, in the right place, at the right time. But, yes, it has the potential to increase congestion in the immediate area."

> Aside from convincing Carter and BellSouth to reduce the parking from 2.75 spaces per 1,000 square feet of space—the same ratio applied at the suburban-style Lenox shopping mall one stop to the north—to 2.24 spaces, the neighborhood groups extracted several other concessions during negotiations. Carter and Associates agreed to a range of improvements for pedestrians and bicyclists in the surrounding neighborhoods, including wider sidewalks along Piedmont, traffic calming, medians, textured crosswalks, and bike lanes in the residential neighborhoods, which would be funded through impact fees paid by the developer and money set aside in the Regional Transportation Improvement Plan. Though the developer had wanted to widen Piedmont from six lanes to nine lanes, neighborhood opposition resulted in a compromise—the addition of two turn lanes at the intersection of Lindbergh and Piedmont.

Providing Affordable Housing

Homeowners in affluent neighborhoods were not the only ones worried about the impact of the project, however. Affordable housing advocates worried that so much development would gentrify less-affluent neighborhoods to the east and south, which provided a variety of housing types for people with a wide range of incomes—including some older apartment complexes that accepted Section 8 vouchers (housing assistance in the form of direct payments to private landlords, which low-income people can get from a local housing authority and use in the private market)—all within walking distance of Lindbergh. There was no affordable housing planned at Lindbergh. This greatly concerned the Atlanta Neighborhood Development Partnership (ANDP) and other advocates who argued that affordable housing was an important component of any TOD. The ANDP had a very different take on the reason it was necessary to build four interceptor parking decks: "What they built instead of affordable housing was satellite parking decks outside the central city, so that those who can't afford to live at Lindbergh can live somewhere cheaper and ride MARTA to work," said ANDP's Hattie Dorsey. "My question has always been, 'Can your secretary afford to live there?' Or 'Can she live somewhere nearby and walk across the street to work?'"

> Working with the city, these neighborhood groups succeeded in obtaining a Special Public Interest (SPI) zoning designation for the residential area immediately to the east of Lindbergh, which offered a density bonus to developers if they built new affordable housing as a part of their projects; the housing would have to remain affordable for twenty years. The SPI provided no

guarantee, however, that new development would include affordable housing, or that existing affordable housing would not be torn down. And shoppers and tenants at the Lindbergh Plaza Mall, which was slated for redevelopment, were worried that they, too, would be priced out.

> Many of the new immigrant and low-income residents who lived in this neighborhood walked to the old shopping center from nearby apartments, and they worried whether the new shops would carry the goods and services they needed. Taking a bus to a supermarket farther away was not really an option, Karime Benitez told the *Atlanta Journal Constitution* in 2001: "Sometimes you don't have money for a bus. You have just enough money for the groceries," she said. Lino Dominguez, publisher of the Spanish-language weekly *Mundo Hispánico*, told the *Atlanta Journal Constitution* that he believed the development of both Lindbergh Center and the redevelopment of Lindbergh Plaza meant that people would be displaced. "It's not just the displacement of immigrants, but the displacement of poorer residents," he said. "Also, small businesses that cater to these residents will lose their clientele and have to move or close their doors."

MARTA's Role: Leadership or Self-Interest?

Late in 1999, three of the five neighborhood groups involved in mediation declared themselves satisfied with the reduced parking ratio and other changes agreed to by MARTA and Carter, and signed off on the plans for Lindbergh. The two remaining groups, Garden Hills and Peachtree Heights East, felt that the parking ratio was still too high and they were angered by what they felt had been MARTA's heavy-handed dealings with the community. When the Atlanta City Council voted in favor of granting Carter a development permit for the first phase of the Lindbergh project, the Garden Hills Civic Association decided to take both MARTA and the city to court and in December of 1999 filed suit. The group also sought a restraining order to block demolition of several buildings on Piedmont Road, charging that the city had not followed proper procedure when changing zoning in the area several months before. This request was denied by a Fulton County judge.

> There were no illusions about what was at the center of this dispute: 10,461 parking spaces. Once the city had approved the number of parking spaces, however, and the court upheld the city's zoning procedure, the legal ground on which to contest the parking ratio diminished considerably. With this more measured avenue closed to them, Garden Hills decided to enter into a full frontal engagement with MARTA, challenging that MARTA's 1965 state charter did not authorize the agency to lease its property for a commercial development at Lindbergh or any other site. The plaintiffs sought, in effect, to reinstate the limitations on development that MARTA and other transit agencies had convinced the FTA to drop two years earlier. The attorney for Garden Hills argued that while MARTA had condemned the land in order to build a transportation system, it was spending public funds on parking decks and other infrastructure that would benefit the developer. "What they are doing is converting public property into private use," argued Garden Hills attorney Richard Hubert.

> The lawsuit touched on what all of the neighborhood groups felt to be the central injustice of the Lindbergh project: it was designed by a public agency and built on public land, and site improvements were funded with $81 million from MARTA, and yet the plan was formulated and approved through a process that was very difficult for the public to influence. BellSouth was also getting $14.5 million in tax breaks. Hubert argued that if there were not so much public funding, the project would have to be downscaled to a degree that was more palatable to the surrounding neighborhoods.

> MARTA countered Hubert's charge that public money was being used for private profit, arguing that all the revenue generated by the leases and the increased ridership at Lindbergh would be used to fund transit operations and improvements. The Fulton County Superior Court agreed, and rejected Garden Hills's request for an injunction against construction at the Lindbergh site. In November of 2000, Garden Hills appealed to the Georgia Supreme Court, which also ruled in MARTA's favor. The outcome of the lawsuit clearly had implications for future development. MARTA wanted to build TODs at two dozen stations, and smaller projects were already under way at the Medical Center station, and at Sandy Springs and North Springs at the end of the North Line. MARTA's court victory, however, did not discourage opposition to Sandy Springs and North Springs, where neighbors worried—just as they did at Lindbergh—about traffic congestion, property values, and preserving the single-family character of their neighborhoods.

> The *Atlanta Business Chronicle* chastised Sandy Springs in a July 2001 editorial entitled "Don't Let Not-In-My-Backyard Mentality Stop Smart Growth In Atlanta": "Metro Atlanta taxpayers have made a $1 billion investment in MARTA's north rail line," wrote Steven French, a Georgia Tech professor in city planning who had been working with the developer to create a project the community would accept. "There is no better way to maximize the public's return on that investment than by moving people and jobs within easy reach of the train stations. . . . In the Perimeter Center area alone there are some 70,000 jobs but very little housing. By providing housing closer to jobs, and locating both closer to transit, we shorten or eliminate car trips."

Winning Hearts and Minds for TOD

The fiscal exigencies that motivated MARTA to pursue TOD worsened in the latter half of 2001 when the economic downturn led to a reduction in the sales tax revenues on which the agency depended. The agency found itself $12 million short of its annual $300 million budget, and was forced to hike fares, cut back on service, and encourage staff to take early retirement. The $9.5 million the agency would bring in annually from leases and increased ridership at Lindbergh and three new TODs on the North Line would go a long way toward making up the budget shortfall. But the office market had crumbled and BellSouth had cut its workforce, raising another concern—was it wise to have designed such a large project for one particular corporate tenant? What if BellSouth went out of business? BellSouth's offices had been designed so they could be sublet to other tenants, but the project would not have been skewed so heavily toward office uses had it not been for BellSouth. As the Internet boom turned bust, Garden Hills began pressuring MARTA to reconsider building a second phase.

> Atlanta's conformity lapse lasted only two years, from 1998 into early 2001, at which time ARC, together with the Georgia Regional Transportation Authority (GRTA)—the state agency created by Governor Roy Barnes and the General Assembly in 1999 in response to the Clean Air Act crisis—produced a twenty-year transportation plan that met CAA standards. This new plan was a dramatic departure from previous plans, dedicating 40 percent of funding to transit and 10 percent to bicycle and pedestrian projects, and only 26 percent to roads. But it was just a long-range plan, and the document approved by GRTA in 2001 that actually authorized expenditures for projects—the 2003–2005 Transportation Improvement Program—made no allocations for either capital or operating expenses at MARTA.

> GRTA had been given broad powers over regional transportation and land-use planning, including authority to issue bonds to finance mass transit and veto power over regionally significant transportation and real estate projects. But the agency was proving a disappointment to those who had expected leadership, and an $8.5 billion bond proposal put together by the governor in 2001 was weighted heavily toward road building, including improvements to rural highways, an HOV network on urban highways, and what critics called a "massive sprawlway" in the wealthy, white, northern suburbs. There was no money for pedestrian improvements or streetscape projects. Metro Atlanta, still in dire need of reducing traffic and air pollution, was not making much progress. "What's wrong with this picture?" business reporter Maria Saporta asked rhetorically in the *Atlanta Journal-Constitution* in December of 2001. "The flaw is simple. MARTA's base of funding is inadequate, and the Atlanta community needs to do something dramatic to fix it, once and for all."

> As population and investment continued to move back into the City of Atlanta proper, MARTA boasted that investments in new construction and renovation around its stations totaled $885 million in 2000, with another $102 million in proposed development—up from $537.5 million in 1996. The city had amended its zoning ordinance in 1982 to create "public interest" overlay districts around stations, which permitted very high densities and reduced parking requirements. The result, almost two decades later, was extensive transit-adjacent development with high densities and some mixed uses, especially in midtown Atlanta. But there were almost no pedestrian or streetscape improvements to link up Atlanta's destinations and transit stations in a dense, interesting, and walkable urban fabric, and the increasing number of high density projects were not integrated into the surrounding communities—dooming the city to continued auto dependence and congestion.

> The unwillingness of communities to link up with transit and TOD was due to predictable concerns about density and traffic, but also belied deeper divisions having to do with class and

race. Atlanta contined to be a deeply segregated place that was "sorted by income and race and separated by vast stretches of highway, and increasingly, locked behind guarded gates," *Atlanta Journal-Constitution* reporter David Goldberg wrote in a briefing paper for the Atlanta Metropolitan Regional Forum in 1997. "Suburban sprawl has left behind the lower-income residents who can't afford large lots, new homes and late-model cars that are the passports to life on the suburban frontier. To preserve exclusivity, mass transit doesn't go there. Meanwhile, jobs go wanting in the suburbs." Lindbergh would at least address one of these concerns, bringing good jobs within reach of low-income workers—BellSouth had an aggressive training program and employee retention policy, and was advertising jobs on MARTA's trains and buses.

> One other legacy of the 1999 crisis was the ARC's exemplary if small Livable Centers Initiative, which awards $1 million annually for community land use and transportation planning efforts. By 2002 the seed funding had resulted in a network of two dozen communities that were implementing plans with a transit-oriented focus.

> "The potential to make Atlanta truly transit-oriented is incredible," said Larry Frank of Georgia Tech. "But there are major problems. Foremost among them is an alarming and woeful lack of connectivity between new development and the stations, and between the stations and the communities that surround them. It's like trying to cook soup when you've left the plastic wrappers on all the ingredients—there ends up being no chemistry between them." Frank pointed to the unfortunate juxtapositions of gated communities of single-family homes next to high density residential or office projects next to large commercial developments with vast parking lots, divided by wide arterials filled with fast-moving traffic. "It's really a worst-case scenario," he added. "There's lots of density and destinations that are close together but there's no safe way to walk. The result is that people drive to where they could throw a football."

Outcomes

Lindbergh was the very illustration of this "woeful lack of connectivity": situated at the junction of two MARTA lines, Lindbergh occupies an otherwise marginal space, separated in all directions from surrounding residential neighborhoods by transportation infrastructure. The property is shaped roughly like the quadrant of a circle, its arc formed by the Southern Railroad Corridor. Lindbergh Drive runs east and west; Piedmont Road runs north and south. There are no sidewalks bridging the railroad, which acts as a very effective barrier between Lindbergh and the affluent neighborhoods to the north and west of the tracks. Farther east, running parallel to Piedmont Road, is state highway Georgia 400, which intersects with Interstate 85 south of Lindbergh. These two freeways act as further infrastructure barriers closing Lindbergh off from easy communication with areas farther east and south.

> Lindbergh does not present an inviting facade to the pedestrian or bicyclist, who can access the site only by traversing heavily trafficked Piedmont Road, which is six lanes wide, or Lindbergh,

which is eight lanes wide. Lindbergh is designed for those who get there by car, or who are shuttling through on MARTA, but definitely not for those who might wander in from a surrounding neighborhood. Internally focused and modular, Lindbergh's centerpiece is the shop-lined "main street" that runs perpendicular to the sunken MARTA tracks. At one end stand BellSouth's twin fourteen-story office towers, across the street from ground floor retail with lofts above. This building will become an office tower in a later phase. At the other end of the main street will be the two planned condominium towers. MARTA's headquarters, and the station, are also located on the site, and smaller retail and residential buildings will eventually line the street.

> Critics point out that the project's relative isolation from surrounding neighborhoods, its massive parking structures and high density single-use buildings make it seem more suburban than urban—"suburban development plopped on top of a rail station," in the words of one critic. While it combines retail, residential, and office space, Lindbergh was not intended to be a 24-hour center. With the majority of the project's square footage occupied by one corporate tenant, the pedestrian life of the station will conform to the traffic cycles of the business day. It does not have either the mix of uses or the integration into surrounding neighborhoods that would serve to modulate surges in rush-hour traffic. Moreover, while the final design kept some of the elements of the original "urban village" concept, it is hard for the visitor not to feel intimidated and closed in by towering buildings and parking decks, heavily trafficked arterials, and the railroad trench.

> Given the project's shortcomings, it is not hard to understand the objections of the surrounding neighborhoods, who saw Lindbergh as exacerbating the problem—traffic congestion—instead of offering a solution. Perhaps it is remarkable that a project with Lindbergh's high densities got built at all in a metro area with some of the lowest density in the United States, and a city that had not—to quote Denise Starling of the Buckhead Transportation Management Association—"developed a transit mentality yet." Perhaps it was the wrong project. Or the wrong tenant. But MARTA's continued financial insecurity would motivate the agency to build more of the same: projects with very high densities and a mix of uses designed to maximize revenues, as opposed to projects that would meet community-driven objectives. Nor will affordable housing be a likely component. And given its budget shortfalls, MARTA is unlikely to prioritize TOD projects in the low-income ethnic communities that might, unlike wealthier neighborhoods, welcome the investment.

> "There's so much resistance to TOD from so many communities that I say let's just go for the low-hanging fruit and build projects in communities that want them," said M. Von Nkosi of the Atlanta Neighborhood Development Partnership. "Why bother trying to convince communities that freak out at densities above ten dwelling units an acre? They'll figure it out soon enough when they find they can't get to any other place in the city without a grueling commute. Because no matter how many highways the governor builds he isn't going to get rid of traffic." In the meantime, while no one seemed willing to condemn Lindbergh entirely, neither were TOD advo-

9.6

BellSouth headquarters: Lindbergh Center concentrates this major employer's workforce along transit.
(Photo: M. von Nkosi, NCARB, AIA/ Atlanta Neighborhood Development Partnership.)

9.7

Main Street has ground floor retail with loft/office space above.
(Photo: M. von Nkosi, NCARB, AIA/ Atlanta Neighborhood Development Partnership.)

cates eager to claim it as a model. Big, bold, and important—and a much-needed initiative to solve Atlanta's notorious problems—Lindbergh was born of the best intentions. It is hoped that, over time, it may evolve into a better project.

Lessons Learned

Community involvement is essential to creating good projects. The entry of BellSouth as a partner in the Lindbergh project effectively shifted the balance of power into BellSouth's court, and the very magnitude of the corporation's physical presence guaranteed the site would end up conforming to BellSouth's needs. It was as if MARTA was so eager to win and to accommodate this large corporate tenant that the opinion of the neighborhoods no longer mattered. MARTA didn't involve them in what turned out to be the most critical decision of all—whether BellSouth was the right tenant. The resulting furor has put community groups on guard around other MARTA stations and has given pause to developers and lenders. Time is money when financing is on the line, and the delays created by lawsuits are a developer's worst nightmare. One of the unintended consequences of Atlanta's 1982 rezoning of transit station areas to permit Manhattan-scale densities and reduced parking requirements was that it left communities and the city with little leverage when negotiating with developers over proposed projects. Because of the high densities permitted, the Lindbergh station area actually had to be down-zoned. The Arlington County case study illustrates how a comprehensive planning process and continued structured community involvement in a transit-oriented development initiative can create the stable and predictable environment that both developers and residents long for—despite the fact that the result was very high density development in an otherwise suburban environment.

Research shows that too much parking has a deleterious effect on transit ridership, aggravates traffic congestion, and drives up the cost of projects. Too much density is just as bad. Constructing parking at Lindbergh cost about $10,000 per space, driving up project costs. One of the results is that Lindbergh's apartments and condos will be priced above what many Atlanta residents can afford. As long as parking is convenient, and taking transit and walking around Atlanta is not, Lindbergh residents with the means to choose are not likely to choose transit. Too much density exacerbates the problem, because density combined with the transit access and increased mobility causes the value of the property to inflate, which creates pressure to create monocultures of offices or retail. At $40 a square foot, for example, space may be too expensive for any use other than high-end offices or a concentration of commercial activity that needs to draw patrons from a vast market area that is not serviceable by transit.

TOD projects should be integrated into their surroundings. Investment in pedestrian infrastructure and streetscape improvements is key. If a TOD project is not integrated into its surrounding neighborhoods by means of an interesting and walkable environment and pedestrian and bicycle connections to the world outside, it then becomes an island, and its relevance and importance to the rest of the city and the rest of the transit system is diminished. This hurts ridership and makes the project less attractive to tenants, shoppers, and other visitors. Any project with as much parking as Lindbergh is of necessity separated from its surroundings by parking structures and traffic: "The parking ratios are an index of Lindbergh's relative isolation from its surroundings," in the words of one observer. In order to extend the reach of the existing transit system and improve its usefulness to residents—every transit rider is a pedestrian—Atlanta has to get serious about investing in pedestrian infrastructure. Atlanta is becoming more dense but not more walkable, a situation that will result in even more unbearable congestion.

Affordable housing needs to be a component of TOD. TOD planning should include measures to preserve existing affordable housing and incentives to build new affordable housing, because significant new investment in neighborhoods will drive up property values and price low-income tenants out. BellSouth will bring thousands of jobs back into the city from the suburbs, but where will lower-income BellSouth employees live? If there were measures in place to guard against gentrification of the low- to moderate-income neighborhoods to the east and south, BellSouth could help preserve the socioeconomic diversity of those neighborhoods. One irony of Lindbergh is that it will surround the MARTA station with so much development and traffic that it will make it even more difficult for low-income residents living to the east and south to get to the transit on which they depend. Crossing the six lanes of Piedmont and the eight lanes of Lindbergh will be hazardous. The people who already use transit—and those who walk because taking transit is too expensive—are the ones who will lose the most.

TOD cannot solve congestion and emissions problems without supportive policies and investments at the regional and state level. One TOD does not a livable community make. MARTA needs the help of state, regional, and local transportation officials, who should maximize funding for transit and nonmotorized transportation projects and minimize funding for sprawl-inducing road improvements. Lindbergh looks best when viewed from a regional perspective: BellSouth is the civic-minded corporation willing to move jobs back into Atlanta proper and to encourage the use of transit to help address the region's problems with traffic and sprawl, and MARTA is an entrepreneurial transit agency interested in more than simply keeping the trains running on time. But the story of Lindbergh illustrates that solutions to regional problems have to provide local benefits as well.

REFERENCES

Brookings Institution. 2000. Moving Beyond Sprawl: The Challenge for Metropolitan Atlanta.

Brookings Institution, Center on Urban & Metropolitan Policy. 2000. Office Sprawl: The Evolving Geography of Business. October.

CDC. 1999. Pedestrian Fatalities—Cobb, DeKalb, Fulton, and Gwinnett Counties, Georgia, 1994–1998, Morbidity and Mortality Weekly Report (July 23) 48,28:601–605. At http://www.cdc.gov/epo/mmwr/preview/mmwrhtml/mm4828a1.htm.

Dobbins, Michael (Commissioner, Atlanta Department of Planning). 2002. Interviewed by the authors.

Dorsey, Hattie (President-CEO, Atlanta Neighborhood Development Partnership). 2002–2003. Interviewed by the authors.

Durrent, Jim (Executive Director of Atlanta Area Council, Urban Lands Institute). 2002. Interviewed by the authors.

Ellis, Ed (Vice President, URS Corp, Atlanta). 2002. Interviewed by the authors.

Eplan, Leon (Former Atlanta Commissioner of Planning and Development). 2001–2002. Interviewed by the authors.

Federal Register. 1997. Policy on Transit Joint Development. Volume 62, Number 50. pp. 12266–12269. March 14.

Frank, Larry (Associate Professor, Georgia Institute of Technology). 2002. Interviewed by the authors.

———. 1999a. Assessing Transit Station Area Redevelopment: A Case Study of the Lindbergh Station in Atlanta. *Journal of Public Transportation* 2,3:48.

———. 1999b. Land Use Impacts on Household Travel Choice and Vehicle Emissions in the Atlanta Region. Georgia Institute of Technology.

Gilbert, Richard (BellSouth Metro Plan Coordinator, Atlanta). 2002. Interviewed by the authors.

———. 2002. Case Study: BellSouth's Atlanta Metro Plan. A Case Study in Employer-Driven Smart Growth. February 1. At http://www.sprawlwatch.org.

———. 1999. Rethinking the American Dream. Environmental Journalism Center.

———. 1999. Ruling may halt metro roads. *Atlanta Journal-Constitution.* March 4.

———. 1999. 17 of 61 road projects OK'd. Truce with environmentalists?. *Atlanta Journal-Constitution.* June 22.

———. 1997. Briefing Paper. prepared for the Atlanta Metropolitan Regional Forum, July 28.

Grace, Libba (Representative, Garden Hills Neighborhood Group, Atlanta). 2002. Interviewed by the authors.

Konas, Chuck (Vice President, Carter & Associates, Atlanta). 2002–2003. Interviewed by the authors.

Local Government Commission. 1999. Livable Places Update. July. At http://www.lgc.org/freepub/PDF/Land_Use/lpu/lpu_9907.pdf.

McCosh, John. 2001. MARTA Development Poised to Pay Off Transit-Based Projects Seen as Revenue Boost. *Atlanta Journal-Constitution* June 4.

———. 2000a. Battle Goes to Supreme Court MARTA Fight: Neighbors Take Firm Stand against Commercial Project at Lindbergh Station. *Atlanta Journal-Constitution* November 15.

———. 2000b. BellSouth Insists MARTA Deal Stands. *Atlanta Journal-Constitution* April 21.

———. 1999a. Neighbors Split after Mediation on Lindbergh. Carter Development Plan Divides Groups Worried about Traffic near MARTA Station. *Atlanta Journal-Constitution* December 13.

———. 1999b. Judge OKs Site Clearing at Lindbergh. *Atlanta Journal-Constitution* December 11.

Moriarty, Kathleen (Representative, Peachtree Hills Neighborhood Group, Atlanta). 2002. Interviewed by the authors.

Nkosi, Von (Director Mixed Income Communities Initiative, Atlanta Neighborhood Development Partnership). 2002–2003. Interviewed by the authors.

Orenstein, Suzanne (Environmental Mediator, Prides Crossing, Massachusetts). 2002. Interviewed by the authors.

Pruitt, Kathey. 1999. Smog Plan Nibbles at Lifestyles—Bites Later. *Atlanta Journal-Constitution* October 17.

Racicot, Caleb (Tunnell-Spangler-Walsh and Associates). 2001. Interviewed by the authors.

Rader, Jeff (Vice President, Greater Atlanta Homebuilders Association). 2001–2003. Interviewed by the authors.

Saporta, Maria. 2001. Regional Funding, Not Cuts, the Answer for MARTA. *Atlanta Journal-Constitution* December 17.

Sibley, John (President, Georgia Conservancy, Atlanta). 2002. Interviewed by the authors.

Starling, Denise (Executive Director, Buckhead Area Transportation Management Association, Atlanta). 2002. Interviewed by the authors.

Stokes, Tom (President, EpiCity Real Estate Services, Atlanta). 2003. Interviewed by the authors.

Turner, Melissa. 2001. An ultra-modern future Atlanta, depicted by tabletop toys. *Atlanta Journal-Constitution.* September 24.

Vesperman, Paul (Former Director of MARTA Transit Related Development, Atlanta). 2001–2002. Interviewed by the authors.

Weyandt, Tom (Director of Comprehensive Planning, Atlanta Regional Commission). 2001–2002. Interviewed by the authors.

Whittaker, Peggy (Representative, Peachtree Heights Neighborhood Association, Atlanta). 2002. Interviewed by the authors.

Wilbert, Tony. 2001. BellSouth's MARTA Adventure: Consolidation near Transit Sites Still on Track Despite Derailed Economy. *Atlanta Journal-Constitution* November 19.

10.1
The City of San Jose targeted undeveloped land parcels along the light-rail line for higher density housing in 1991.
(Photo: www.globeXplorer.com)

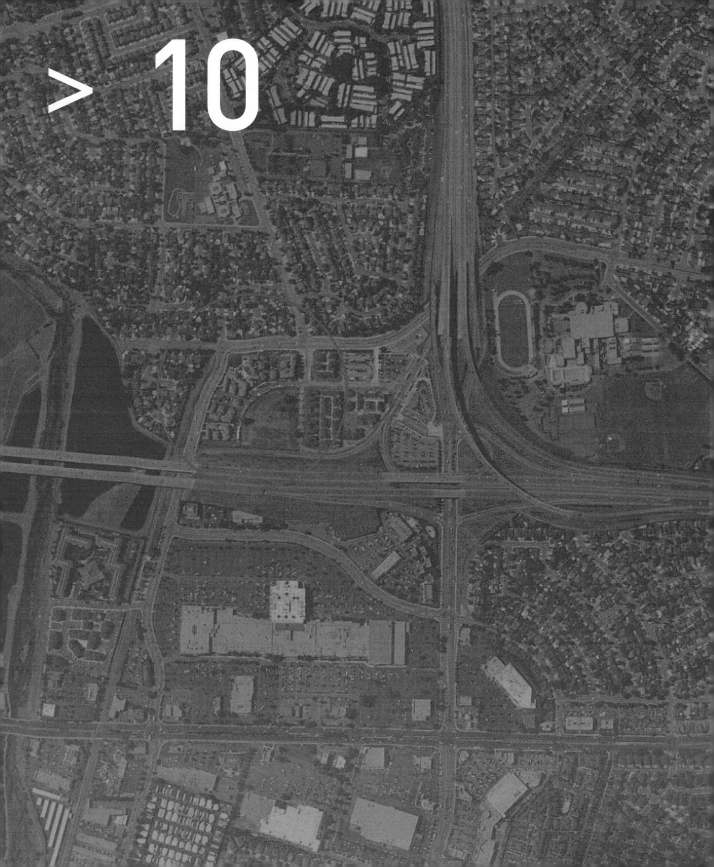

THE SAN JOSE CASE STUDY

Ohlone-Chynoweth Station

Shanti Breznau

San Jose, California, lies at the center of what was once a great agricultural valley, large swaths of which remained in agricultural production well into the second half of the twentieth century. San Jose, however, grew to become California's third most populous city, and as a result many of its neighborhoods and much of the housing stock date from the 1950s on. Even in the 1990s, small pockets of what was once farmland could still be found lying fallow in the midst of suburban development. One of the very last remnants of San Jose's agricultural past, a twenty-acre plot of land next to the Ohlone-Chynoweth light-rail station, became the site of three transit-oriented housing projects in the late 1990s, serving to pioneer both multifamily and affordable housing in what had been a suburban single-family neighborhood.

> The twenty-acre plot was a difficult development site due to the fact that it was squeezed in between the juncture of two freeways, the rail station, and a station parking lot. But the site proved a godsend for two intrepid nonprofit affordable housing developers searching for developable land in an increasingly tight housing market. Despite the economic slowdown that hit Silicon Valley in 2000, the median price for a single-family home in Santa Clara County in 2002 was still above $500,000. The fact that market-rate housing could command such high prices put affordable housing developers at a distinct disadvantage at the same time that it made the construction of new affordable housing even more critical. As a result, sites were often secured either through the intervention of a public entity or because the parcel in question had so many problems that for-profit developers were not interested.

While the freeways and rail station posed design problems for development, they also provide excellent transit and transportation access. The station is on the Guadalupe Corridor light-rail line, part of an integrated rail and bus system in the South Bay—the southern portion of San Francisco Bay that is the heart of Silicon Valley and which underwent tremendous development during the 1990s. Operated by the Santa Clara Valley Transportation Authority (VTA), the transit system links San Jose, Santa Clara, Sunnyvale, Milpitas, and Mountain View, and connects the residential areas of southern San Jose to the large Silicon Valley job centers in northern San Jose and surrounding cities. It also connects with Caltrain, a heavy-rail commuter train that runs north up the Peninsula to San Francisco and south to Gilroy.

> The two affordable housing projects that were built—Ohlone Court and Ohlone-Chynoweth

Commons—encountered many of the same challenges described in other chapters in this book. These included neighborhood opposition and problems involving the tension between the site's role as a node in a regional transit system and as a place in its own right. But due to the City of San Jose's innovative land-use policies and supportive city council, as well as the cooperation of all of the actors in the development process—the city, the transit agency, the private landowner, and the nonprofit developers—opposition was overcome and the projects were built. While neither is perfect—the second project is the more problematic in part because it is the more ambitious and complex of the two—both have won design awards and were accepted by the community. This success helped the private owner of part of the station area site begin construction of a market-rate apartment complex on his property in 2002.

Site History

While the VTA owned half of the Ohlone-Chynoweth development site, the other half was owned by Cilker Orchards, a family-owned-and-operated company headed by Bill Cilker, Sr., who had begun acquiring and operating orchards in Santa Clara Valley in 1946. Cilker had owned all the land, including the site of the light-rail station and freeway interchange, which had been part of a one-hundred-acre plum orchard. It was the last of his properties to be developed, the rest having been condemned for public uses such as the freeways and light-rail line, donated or sold for the construction of a hospital and housing, or developed as offices and a shopping center. In 2002, Bill Cilker was eighty-three years old and still heading the company, and a well-known philanthropist whose stature in the community was such that he was described as "straddling the Valley of Heart's Delight [as the valley was known because of its agricultural bounty] and Silicon Valley."

> Most of this orchard had been condemned by the California Department of Transportation in the 1950s for the construction of Highways 85 and 87. Another twenty-six acres was taken in the 1980s in order to expand the freeway interchange and construct the light-rail corridor as well as a fire station. Caltrans, as the state transportation agency is known, shared some of this land with the VTA, leaving the Cilkers approximately 10.5 acres. The Cilkers protested, unsuccessfully, that the portion taken was in excess of what was needed. In spite of this disagreement, Cilker Orchards later collaborated with the VTA on a development framework for the property.

> With completion of the light-rail corridor in 1991, the City of San Jose and the VTA began implementing new policies that made higher density transit-oriented development around the Ohlone-Chynoweth station possible. The City of San Jose had launched a housing initiative in 1989 that targeted underdeveloped parcels along the Guadalupe Corridor for higher density infill development. At about the same time, the VTA began looking for joint development opportunities.

> In 1990, the VTA ranked all the station area properties under agency control according to their suitability for higher density housing. Most of the 11.6 acres the VTA owned to the west of

the Ohlone-Chynoweth station was a significantly underutilized park-and-ride lot with 1,166 spaces, only 25 percent of which were used regularly. The VTA ranked Ohlone-Chynoweth as second most suitable after Almaden Station, which was immediately developed as market-rate housing. In 1995, in cooperation with the city, the VTA began working with the Cilkers and prospective developers on a joint development framework for Ohlone-Chynoweth. The plan called for the construction of a medium to higher density residential neighborhood that would enhance the station by linking it with the existing community and improving transit ridership.

> The framework designated 7.3 acres for housing and a small amount of retail, and the remaining 4.3 acres were to be used for 200 parking spaces for transit, bus bays, circulation, and access to the Cilker property. The Cilkers agreed that their 10.6-acre portion would also be designated for medium to higher density housing development. The Cilkers leased six acres to the Bridge Housing Corporation, a nonprofit affordable housing developer, for fifty-five years. Bill Cilker had been friends with Bridge's founder, Don Terner, a legendary figure in the state's affordable housing arena, who died in a plane crash in 1996, and the two had talked about developing some portion of the property for affordable housing. When the city rezoned the property for higher densities, Bridge quickly assembled financing and built the Ohlone Court Apartments, 135 very-low-income units, in 1997.

> In 2001, the VTA leased its 7.3-acre joint development site to Eden Housing, another nonprofit affordable housing developer, for seventy-five years at market rates. Eden developed Ohlone-Chynoweth Commons, 194 low- and very-low-income residential units, with partially submerged parking, as well as 4,400 square feet of retail and a 4,000-square-foot community building for residents.

San Jose's Housing Initiative

During the past thirty years and even today, as commuter rail systems have been extended out from urban job centers into suburban residential areas in the western United States, few suburbs have acted on the special development potential inherent in transit-adjacent sites. Because suburban stations are typically located in or near existing neighborhoods of single-family homes, and because land prices are cheaper than in urban areas, these sites are rarely zoned or developed to take advantage of the presence of transit. When the City of San Jose launched its Housing Initiative Program in 1989, it was a pioneering effort to accommodate growth, minimize traffic, and improve the jobs/housing balance by building higher density housing along transit corridors. No other city in the Bay Area had attempted this approach, and it was not until 2000 that the regional Association of Bay Area Governments did a growth modeling study that proposed a similar model of higher density transit-oriented development.

> The housing initiative was begun with a Housing Opportunity Study that analyzed the feasibility of accommodating growth along transit corridors. In Phase 1 of the study the city

10.2

Affordable housing and transit
are a good match: even owning
one less car per household can
generate significant savings.
(Photo: McLarand Vasquez Emsiek &
Partners, Inc.)

assessed the amount of land that was available along its transit corridors and calculated how much housing the land could support over and above the number of units provided for by existing land-use designations in the General Plan. In Phase 2 the city examined the housing market in San Jose and estimated current and future demand for higher density housing, then conceived as twelve to forty or more dwelling units per acre (dua). In Phase 3, development prototypes and cash-flow models were used to assess the financial feasibility of different types of housing.

> The city concluded that an additional 5,300 to 9,900 housing units could be built over the yield from existing General Plan designations. Based on these findings the City of San Jose Planning Department created a new General Plan designation called "transit corridor residential," which was applied along the Guadalupe Corridor line in the mid-1990s. Both urban and suburban versions of this designation exist. The urban version, which was put into effect in the core area of downtown or for sites within 2,000 feet of stations in other intensely developed areas, mandated a minimum of forty-five dua. The suburban version, also in effect within 2,000 feet of stations, mandated a minimum of twenty dua, and allowed commercial uses at the street level of residential projects, or neighborhood-serving commercial uses in freestanding buildings. The height limit for either designation was ninety feet for residential developments.

> According to San Jose's assistant planning director, Laurel Prevetti, the city learned early on that it is important to be specific about the desired densities in the General Plan and zoning code. She said that before the city had developed the transit corridor residential designation, there was

a property along the Capitol Corridor rail line that had been zoned for twelve to twenty-five dua. When a major single-family development was proposed at twelve dua, the city could not demand higher density. Because of this experience the city began redesignating property along the line as transit corridor residential so as to ensure a minimum density of twenty or more units per acre.

> As the result of the housing initiative, thirteen sites were rezoned for higher densities with the potential of adding 2,200 new units to the city's housing stock. The Ohlone-Chynoweth station was one of these sites and was redesignated as suburban transit corridor residential in the General Plan and rezoned as a planned unit development (PUD)—a zoning designation usually applied to large sites that would not be optimally developed under normal zoning and which provides for more flexibility in terms of what can be built. Although the site was located in an unincorporated part of Santa Clara County, it was already under the planning jurisdiction of the City of San Jose and it was subsequently annexed.

> In addition to creating the new General Plan designations, amendments and rezonings, the Housing Initiative Program also created specific plans for several transit-rich neighborhoods. Prevetti said that specific plans work well in neighborhoods that lack cohesion and are characterized by scattered vacant properties. A specific plan can be used to state upfront the city's policy objectives for the land and to establish criteria that can be used when negotiating with developers—criteria that aids developers because it provides them with certainty. Specific plans are not needed in more established neighborhoods and transit corridors, she said, because these already have an established structure and identity and General Plan amendments can be used to complement existing development.

> The planning department also staged several working sessions with the city council to ensure that the policies that came out of the housing initiative were fully understood and supported. This effort proved invaluable: not only did the council enact the policies but it has also supported proposed projects that take advantage of the density minimums and height increases. The housing initiative was intended to be an ongoing initiative, and a second Housing Opportunity Study was underway in 2002 and had resulted in General Plan amendments to fourteen more sites and the identification of an additional eleven sites that could be rezoned. These General Plan amendments had the potential of adding as many as 12,100 new units to the housing stock.

VTA's Joint Development Efforts

Shortly after the City of San Jose launched its Housing Initiative Program, the VTA completed its twenty-one-mile light-rail system and thirty stations, and began looking for joint development partners. The agency had separated from the county in 1995 and merged with the local congestion management agency, thereby taking on responsibility for minimizing traffic and analyzing the impact of local land-use decisions on the regional transportation system. The VTA's expanded mission dovetailed with the city's objectives in the housing initiative and the coordinated efforts of both city and transit agency were key to stimulating investment around several stations. The VTA owned large parking lots next to many of its stations, and the agency prepared station area plans that provided market data and prototype designs for development.

> The VTA's joint development framework plan for Ohlone-Chynoweth was intended to guide development of both the VTA and Cilker parcels by providing important site information while also allowing for developer initiative in the design of the projects. The framework explored a number of land-use and circulation alternatives for the whole site, and suggested building setbacks and streetscape and pedestrian improvements for the VTA property. At the city's urging, the framework also laid out special transit-oriented design principles for the VTA property, which the city intended to use as a model for other projects. The alternative development scenarios proposed in the framework plan were reviewed by the Cilkers, a group of developers, and transit agency staff, and each was evaluated with respect to the residual land value it created.

> The framework area is bounded to the north by Chynoweth Avenue, a four-lane road. On the other side of Chynoweth is a residential community of single-family homes built in the late 1960s. About eight blocks farther north is a community retail center anchored by an Albertson's supermarket. To the south is Highway 85, built on a twenty-foot-high earthen berm, beyond which lies a regional shopping mall. To the east is the light-rail station and tracks; farther east is Highway 87 and, slightly southeast, the interchange with Highway 85. To the west is a small pocket of single-family homes and then the Guadalupe River. The VTA's property is located on the eastern half of the site, immediately adjacent to the station; the Cilkers' property is to the west.

> The joint development framework assumed heightened importance because of the complexities caused by the fact that there were two landowners, three different development projects, a rail station, and a parking lot. Moreover, there was a need to integrate the new development into the adjacent single-family neighborhood. The circulation plan that was proposed connected the projects with the station and with Chynoweth Avenue via roads, pedestrian paths, and specially designated bus routes. The design principles specified the following guidelines for the relationship of the VTA site to the community and to the station:

- The project should be designed as part of the larger urban fabric, not as a self-contained enclave.
- The project should be designed in a scale and style compatible with the surrounding community.
- The project should include community services, to the extent that demand exists.
- The project should encourage transit use by residents of both the site itself and the surrounding community.
- The project should enhance the transit experience.
- The project should accommodate transit parking and bus transfers with no significant diminution of service.

> The development program for the VTA's property specified residential densities of twenty-five to forty dua, higher than the twenty dua minimum mandated by the suburban transit corridor residential General Plan designation. The development program encouraged but did not require the provision of community services, especially retail and child care. Because real estate market analysis had indicated that a strictly market-rate project would not be economically feasible, the program called for a substantial number of affordable units, which would be subsidized with government funding and money raised from the private sector through the issuance of low-income housing tax credits. These tax credits are sold to investors who use them to reduce their tax liability, thus generating equity.

> The framework plan was recognized by the Local Government Commission's Center for Livable Communities and awarded a 1995 Ahwahnee Community Design Award of Merit. Unfortunately, the planning process did not involve the community or solicit any community input, a decision that would be regretted. The framework plan had stated that "While intensive, multifamily development can be incompatible with adjacent single-family areas, in this case the interface is not as sensitive, because the existing homes turn their backs to Chynoweth and the joint development site. Still, the project should be scaled and designed to create a graceful transition to the existing community." These were not the only issues that came to concern residents, however. They were worried about the impact of traffic and the potential for parking problems, and they were especially concerned about the impact of so many new families and children on the nearby elementary school—concerns that flared up during meetings with the nonprofit developers.

> According to deputy planning director Laurel Prevetti, retrofitting the suburbs so that they can accommodate growth and higher densities and become more transit-oriented is a huge challenge, and locating and rezoning sites for higher density development is only a small part of the solution. The harder part, she said, is figuring out how to provide and fund additional services for new residents: "We also have to think about how to provide parks and other neighborhood services, because neighborhoods won't accept new housing unless they are assured that there will be adequate services."

Ohlone Court Apartments

Ohlone Court Apartments, Bridge Housing's project, moved forward first. Originally, 6.8 acres of the Cilker property had been designated "medium-high-density" residential, which called for eight to sixteen dua, and the remaining 3.8 acres was zoned high-density residential, which allowed twelve to twenty-five dua. The housing initiative had recommended the 6.8 acres be up-zoned to high density and the 3.8 acres be up-zoned to very high density, which allowed twenty-five to forty dua. The up-zoning increased Bridge's interest and assured the Cilkers that they could make sufficient revenue off the market-rate project they intended to build on their portion of the site. This prompted the Cilkers to donate half the land value for Bridge's affordable housing project, enabling them to lease the property to Bridge at half the market value for fifty-five years. According to their arrangement, if the project made any money—which was unlikely—25 percent would go to the Cilkers. Bridge also handled the entitlements on the Cilkers' project for a consulting fee.

> Ohlone Court was designed by Ernesto M. Vasquez of McLarand, Vasquez, and Partners, and consists of 135 very-low-income units, including 46 one-bedrooms, 48 two-bedrooms, 36 three-bedrooms and 4 four-bedrooms. The buildings are two to three stories tall and are arranged along a curvilinear street that traverses the site and also serves as a pedestrian promenade, and there is a pool, playgrounds, and several basketball courts.

> The residential density, including roads, is twenty-three units per gross acre. The framework plan had specified that a pedestrian path was to extend from the intersection of Winfield Avenue and Chynoweth Avenue at the northwest corner of the site through all three projects to the station, located in the northeastern corner. But the single-family neighborhood to the north—which was already separated from Chynoweth Avenue by a solid six-foot-high sound wall—did not want to encourage the residents of Ohlone Court to walk through their neighborhood, and as a result of their opposition the connecting path was struck from the plan.

> Had the neighborhood been included in the VTA's initial framework planning process—which had instead involved only the agency, the Cilkers, and developers—it may have been possible to work out a compromise and find an acceptable way to connect the project with the neighborhood. There was no neighborhood involvement, however, until Bridge Housing proposed the Ohlone Court project and arranged for meetings. Fortunately for Bridge Housing, Bill Cilker was an active participant and strongly advocated for the project, assuring neighbors that he would personally guarantee that there would be no negative impacts. This fact, as well as the Cilker family's willingness to be flexible, allowed Bridge and its architect to come up with a site plan that was eventually deemed acceptable to the neighborhood. The lack of pedestrian connections and interaction with the neighborhood across the street was unfortunate, however.

> The parking ratio for the project is about 2.05 spaces per unit, with all parking located at surface, either in garages or in spaces adjacent to the building. The city had not yet created its transit-oriented parking discount, which reduced the required ratio to 1.7 spaces per residential unit for residential developments that projected significant levels of transit ridership. But Brad Weblin, project manager for Ohlone Court, said that it was unlikely Bridge Housing would have wanted the parking reduction, given the developer's experience with other multifamily projects that included larger apartments. He said there had been problems at the multifamily project Bridge built at the Almaden Lake station, not because the project had not provided enough parking, but because residents who lived in the single-family neighborhood across the street did not use their garages, parking on the street instead, and they didn't like it when residents of the TOD or their guests used

street parking. However, because of the proximity of transit the Ohlone Court project was allowed a 10 percent reduction in the number of car trips projected to result from the project, which allowed Bridge to avoid building a right-hand turn signal that would have cost $50,000.

> There have been no surveys of residents to determine their travel behavior, but Weblin observed in 2002 that by and large adult residents drove cars while teenagers took the train. It may be that the very-low-income residents who live in Ohlone Court do not work in downtown San Jose or the Silicon Valley business centers that are served by the light-rail line. The potential for this kind of a mismatch between the transit system and the residents of transit-oriented affordable housing projects was not something that was ever considered during the planning process. Not that the teenage ridership is insignificant. After-school activities and socializing can generate a significant number of car trips, and given the number of family units in Ohlone Court the proximity of transit could be resulting in a significant decrease in auto trips as well as in the number of cars owned by families who live there. A family who owns even one less car can save significantly on transportation costs, a savings that would be particularly significant for very-low-income families. Proximity to transit also provides teenagers with increased mobility and independence, and liberates parents from the need to chauffeur their children around.

Ohlone-Chynoweth Commons

While neighbors had objected to the idea of being connected with Ohlone Court via the pedestrian path, they accepted the project once it was built and soon came to consider it a successful addition to the neighborhood. They liked that the project was well maintained and that managers were responsive to any issues that arose. Nonetheless, they were alarmed to discover that another multifamily affordable housing project was being planned for the VTA property immediately adjacent to the station. Some felt that it was unfair to ask them to accept a second affordable multifamily project into what had been a single-family neighborhood. Once the Cilkers finished the multifamily project they proposed to build on their property to the south, the number of multifamily units on the station area site would total 511, with a combined density of thirty dua— a significant number of units for a single-family neighborhood.

> Dave Fadness, a spokesman for the VEP Community Association, which represented the nearby neighborhoods of Vistapark, Encore, and Parkview, said that residents were concerned about the overall density of the three projects, the amount of traffic that would be generated, the potential for parking problems, and the impact on local schools. The VEP argued against giving the project a transit-oriented parking discount, arguing that the 20 to 30 percent ridership rate that was being projected for project residents was unrealistic. But the neighbors' biggest concern was about the impact that so many new families and children would have on the local elementary school. Despite the fact that the developer, Eden Housing, would be assessed a $250,000 impact fee that would go to the local school district, there was no

Clockwise from top left to right

10.3
Ohlone Court has 135 very-low-income units, a pool, playgrounds, and several basketball courts.
(Photo: McLarand Vasquez Emsiek & Partners, Inc.)

10.4
Ohlone-Chynoweth Commons contains 194 units, at a density of 25 units per residential acre.
(Photo: Jay Graham Photography, San Francisco.)

10.5
Bridge Housing's Ohlone Court pioneered both affordable and multifamily housing in a suburban single-family neighborhood.
(Photo: McLarand Vasquez Emsiek & Partners, Inc.)

10.6
The retail portion of the Commons has been problematic, as it is only visible from the track side, and not from adjacent streets.
(Photo: Jay Graham Photography, San Francisco.)

mechanism to ensure that the money would be spent on the school in the area where the project was built.

> The VEP lobbied against the project, and there were two years of public meetings between the developer and the community in an attempt to resolve the issues they raised. Although other community groups were more accepting, Eden Housing was never able to secure the VEP's support and community members, including students from the elementary school, spoke out against the project at the city council meeting where it was reviewed. In spite of this opposition, and in spite of the fact that the city council member representing the area voted against the project, as did the council member from an adjacent district, the San Jose City Council approved it, and ground was broken in early 2000.

> Five units had been cut from the plan in an attempt to appease the neighborhood, but the General Plan designation and the zoning were already in place, and the project was consistent with both. Moreover, the fact that the planning department staff and its team of consultants had engaged and educated the city council about the Housing Initiative Program and the need for locating high density housing near transit enabled council members to summon support for the project despite the opposition of the community and two council members. "It was extremely unusual for a project to be approved over the objections of the council member representing the district," said Linda Mandolini, the executive director of Eden Housing. "Having a city council that had political will and courage was key to the success of the project."

> One obstacle overcome, Eden Housing found another in its path. The developer had a hard time obtaining financing because it could not use the land—which was owned by the VTA and bought with federal funding—as security for the loan, since this would have required that the VTA subordinate its interest in the property. Eventually the problem was resolved by the lender's purchase of a first-right option to buy the land from the VTA for a set price should the project fail and the lender need to foreclose. Unfortunately, these complications caused the lender to charge a higher than usual interest rate, which had a negative effect on the project financing.

> Ohlone-Chynoweth Commons was finished in May of 2001, and contains 194 units affordable to households at 50 to 60 percent of area median income, with a density of almost twenty-seven dua. There are 20 one-bedroom units, 63 two-bedrooms, 77 three-bedrooms, and 4 four-bedroom townhouses interspersed with terraces and interior open spaces. There's a small community center with on-site staff offices, a computer center, and an affordable daycare program serving both residents and the neighborhood. Through a clever but expensive design conceit, the buildings are cantilevered out over the edge of a partially submerged parking garage, hiding it from view. The parking ratio at the Commons, because of the transit-oriented reduction, is 1.7 spaces per dwelling unit. The parking is structured and halfway submerged under the building and the upper floor of the parking lot is open to the outside, letting air and light in. There are three storefronts, a total of 4,400 square feet of retail space, built near the station.

> While aesthetics were important, the main reason that Eden built structured parking was that the project needed to reach a density of twenty-five dua, which had been specified by the VTA's joint development framework and in the request for proposals for the project. If the project had included 150 units instead of 194, all the parking could have been located at surface; Ohlone Court's surface parking was not obtrusive. Even if the project had 168 units—creating a density similar to Ohlone Court's and requiring only a little submerged parking—there still would have been a significant cost savings and the money could have been used to build much nicer housing units. Of course there would not have been as many units, and the project would not have reached the desired density.

> The irony, however, was that while the extra money was spent on structured parking, Ohlone-Chynoweth Commons looked out over the VTA station's parking lot. According to Mandolini, the trade-off—more units, more density, and hidden parking—wasn't really worth the expense. "The cost of building the structured parking combined with the cost of the cantilevered space that hangs out over it was very high," she said. "The improvements that could have been made to the units with all that money would have been extensive."

> But there were other, more significant problems, mostly having to do with the failure to resolve the tension between the site's function as a node in a regional transportation system and its role as a place in its own right: Ohlone-Chynoweth Commons was located immediately adjacent to the transit station and needed to accommodate intermittent crowds of transit riders in an open and welcoming space at the same time that it provided privacy and security for residents. This tension was exacerbated by the fact that the station was used by many high school students who took the train to Gunderson High School across Highway 87 to the east. The station had become a popular place to congregate after school, and in November 2000, just before the project opened, a student was fatally stabbed at the station. This tragic incident raised concerns not only about the safety of students but also about the safety of residents.

> A security guard was hired to patrol the site, with the cost shared by both Ohlone-Chynoweth Commons and Ohlone Court, and concerns about safety eventually abated. And as was the case with Ohlone Court, once Ohlone-Chynoweth Commons was built, the community developed a more welcoming attitude, especially when it became clear that the impact on the schools, especially the elementary school, would not be as significant as had been feared. "We are very pleased with the project overall," Mandolini said in a 2002 interview. "The one concern we do have is the project's openness to transit users who are not residents and who walk through the project or wait there in order to transfer from the train to the bus or vice versa. The station is a major switching center and, especially in the afternoon when school lets out, things can get a little crazy. The VTA wanted a very open, pedestrian-friendly design that wouldn't separate housing from the transit, and while that's desirable, it also raises security concerns."

One Pearl Place

In 2002, the Cilkers began to build One Pearl Place, a luxury apartment complex project located adjacent to and immediately south of Ohlone Court and designed by the same architect. At forty-one units per gross acre, including roads, the project will include 182 predominantly one-bedroom and two-bedroom apartments, with a parking ratio of 1.7 spaces per unit. The Cilkers decided to move forward with their project, and to develop it themselves, despite the fact that the VTA's 1995 market research had concluded a market-rate project would not succeed. It took them some time to complete the predevelopment work because of their inexperience, and that inexperience together with the negative market study made it difficult to secure financing. In the end, the Cilkers decided to finance the project themselves. It is to be completed by the end of 2003.

Node versus Place

The Ohlone-Chynoweth Station site was becoming increasingly complex, with three separate projects totaling more than 500 units, and involving two different property owners (the Cilkers and the VTA) and three different developers (Bridge, Eden, and the Cilkers). Pearl Avenue cut the site roughly in half, with the Cilkers' parcel to the west and the VTA's to the east. Ohlone Court formed an "L" shape, wrapping around the western and northern sides of the Cilkers' parcel. One Pearl Place was in the southeastern corner of that parcel, facing Pearl Avenue and flanked to the south by Highway 85. Ohlone-Chynoweth Commons fronted the length of Pearl Avenue on the other side and took up the entire VTA site, except for the northeastern corner of the property, which was the VTA's 200-space station parking lot. The station was located just below the parking lot, and the three storefronts were located across from the station and at the back of the Commons.

>   The layout had looked good on paper when the joint development framework had been promulgated: "The two projects [the Cilkers' and the VTA's] should create an inviting gateway to the station area and a visual terminus for Pearl Avenue," stated that document. "Major streets within the project should have a public character, with sidewalks, formal landscaping and residence entrances facing the street." But this layout should have been thought through more carefully. The VTA had required that its 200-space station parking lot be located immediately adjacent to and visible from Chynoweth Avenue, and that it not be obscured from view by the retail space. But because the retail is not easily accessible or visible, except from the station, the space has been hard to lease.

>   Moreover, in addition to the parking lot to the west of the station, there is another 350-space lot to the east, in between the station and the junction of Highways 85 and 87. While the presence of the residents of the Commons certainly helps guard against undesirable activity in the imme-

diate vicinity of their residential units, residents can hardly patrol this huge uncontrolled expanse of blacktop, which acts as a draw for teenagers who take the train to and from school. Had the two sides of the Commons that faced the parking lot faced another multifamily unit, a single-family neighborhood, or the station, it is unlikely there would have been so many safety problems. Integrating park-and-ride lots into TOD projects is an especially important design issue in suburban locations where the lots tend to be large. If not treated carefully, these large lots can blight a new project.

> These concerns aside, the VTA and the City of San Jose are happy with the degree of openness achieved at the Commons, which provides the opportunity for connections between the station and the community as well as among the various projects and uses on the site. "Part of the success of Ohlone-Chynoweth Commons is its outward feeling and orientation," said Prevetti. "We have to build interconnected neighborhoods, not just developments that sit next to each other. We have to ensure that new projects fit together and into existing development." Ohlone Court, in contrast, is more internally oriented, with courtyards that set the units back from the curvilinear street. What is most unfortunate, however, is that the openness of the Commons serves mostly to connect it to the VTA's large parking lot, which makes it vulnerable to undesirable activity and makes it feel unsafe.

> The framework plan had encouraged the incorporation of retail if there was sufficient demand, and suggested retail could be converted to housing if it did not succeed. The request for proposals, however, required the inclusion of retail near the station and specified that it be located away from the street. According to Eden Housing's Laura Mandolini, the fact that the storefronts were in the interior of the project made it difficult to lease the space. "We knew from the beginning it wouldn't be easy to find tenants, so it wasn't a surprise when high-profile tenants like Starbucks weren't interested. Everyone wants mixed use, but it's still quite hard to make it work." The conversion of this space to housing also proved difficult. Housing requires a different configuration of space. Moreover, there are subsidies available to convert space to affordable housing, but not for such a few units. However, over time, as more multifamily projects are built and more people use light-rail at the station, the retail space may become more successful.

> Both Ohlone Court and Ohlone-Chynoweth Commons succeed on many counts and introduced affordable multifamily rental housing into an established single-family neighborhood where most people owned their own homes, a significant accomplishment in the suburbs. Furthermore, the fact that Bridge and Eden were able to build high-quality affordable housing anywhere in the Silicon Valley was a considerable achievement given the inflated land values. When combined with One Pearl Place the site will be a mixed-income development, which could provide for supportive social networks among people of different means. Additionally, the Commons managed to satisfy the design requirements that had been set out in the VTA's joint

development framework plan, and was able to surmount the financing challenge caused by VTA's refusal to subordinate its interest in the property. But had the Commons been designed for a better balance between its role as a node and a place it might have been a more comfortable place in which to live.

Lessons Learned

Affordable multifamily housing can help to pioneer market-rate multifamily housing in suburban single-family neighborhoods. The public subsidies that were used to build Ohlone Court and Ohlone-Chynoweth Commons paved the way for the market-rate One Pearl Place, thereby serving to leverage private investment. It is not likely the Cilkers would have been willing to invest so much of their capital in a market-rate multifamily project in the midst of a single-family neighborhood unless the other two projects had been built first. This indicates that well-designed and well-maintained affordable housing may be used to stimulate market interest, and that the public subsidy invested in affordable housing projects can help leverage private investment in market-rate projects.

Include the community from the get-go. The success of all three projects was undermined by the lack of community participation in the initial joint development planning process. Because the neighborhood did not understand what the VTA intended to build on the site, they were blindsided when the second project was proposed, which made them angry and served to delay the second project by two years. Had the community been included from the beginning, their concerns and insights could have been dealt with early on, and perhaps solutions could have been found and incorporated into the projects' designs. Had the neighbors been involved and felt that their concerns were being addressed, they might not have been so opposed to the proposed pedestrian connections between the site and their neighborhood.

Balance the needs of all users. Because the VTA had the upper hand as landowner of the Commons site, the needs of transit users and the function of station and transit system ended up being privileged at the expense of project residents, retail tenants, and the surrounding community. Suburban TOD does not have the benefit of the high levels of pedestrian traffic that urban TOD does—where the continual presence of people creates a space that is self-policed. In suburban environments the flow of foot traffic into the station is sporadic, and the rest of the time there may be no one in the public spaces around the station. This leaves the areas around the station and in front of residents' units vulnerable to undesirable activity. The creation of "defensible space" has been the subject of architectural study for many years now, and one of the fundamental conclusions is that large, unprogrammed, unused areas, such as the park-and-ride lot, are vulnerable. An area that large cannot be made safe solely by the watchful eyes of residents. Park-and-ride-lots need to be broken up by development or active uses that claim the space.

Implement a comprehensive parking strategy. The residential units at the Commons had to bear the construction cost of the structured parking, resulting in a decrease in unit amenities—yet the complex looked out on the VTA's surface lot. Had there been a comprehensive parking strategy developed for all three projects and the station, this incongruity may have been avoided. The lower density of the Commons allowed for less-expensive at-grade parking, and more money was available to spend on building materials, unit details, and landscaping.

Locate retail to succeed. Isolating small increments of retail away from street traffic is not likely to work in a suburban area with little demand for retail. The amount of subsidy necessary for such unmarketable space makes its value questionable. Retail may not have been appropriate for this site, given the proximity of a shopping center just a few blocks away. TOD does not have to include retail to be successful, especially if there is existing retail nearby.

Innovative public-private for-profit and nonprofit partnerships are beneficial in the TOD arena. All three projects are the result of innovative partnerships between the public and private, for-profit and nonprofit sectors, showing how these partnerships bring together diverse visions, talents, and resources to produce innovation in the built environment. None of the projects would have been possible without the City of San Jose's housing initiative, the VTA's joint development strategy, the Cilkers' long-term vision, initiative, and investment in the community, or each non-profit housing developers' expertise and willingness to work together despite difficulties.

TOD projects like these have regional implications. As TOD projects significantly ahead of the curve in Bay Area development practice, both Ohlone Court and Ohlone-Chynoweth Commons serve as prototypes for transit-oriented infill multifamily development at the lower density edges of rapidly growing cities. Further study of these projects, especially of the travel behavior of residents, could lead to more accurate transportation demand modeling for transit-oriented growth scenarios as well as a deeper understanding of the difference between urban and sub-urban TOD. As was suggested in the Bay Area Association of Government's study of several regional growth scenarios in 2000—ranging from a status quo growth model to one that chan-neled all development into transit-oriented development—a significant number of projects like these could shift new growth away from far-flung single-family greenfield developments with poor access to jobs and toward revitalized and transit-supported neighborhoods in what had been auto-oriented suburbs.

REFERENCES

Cervero, Robert. 2000. Transport and Land Use: Key Issues in Metropolitan Planning and Smart Growth. University of California Transportation Center Research Paper.

City of San Jose Department of Planning, Building and Code Enforcement. 1994. Focus on the Future San Jose: 2020 General Plan.

City of San Jose Unified School District Communications and Accountability Office. 2001. School Accountability Report Card, 2000–2001, Erikson Elementary School. School Wise Press: San Francisco.

City of Seattle Station Area Planning Program. 1998. Building a Community Vision: Transit-Oriented Development Case Studies.

Cook, Mary Ann. 1997. Abundant Harvest: Leadership Forum honors orchardist, philanthropist and developer Bill Cilker. *Los Gatos Weekly-Times* March 26.

Fadness, Dave (Vistapark, Encore and Parkview Community Association). 2002. Interviewed by the author.

Federal Transit Agency. 1998. Innovative Financing Techniques for America's Transit Systems.

Mandolini, Linda (Executive Director of Eden Housing, Inc.). 2002. Interviewed by the author.

Pang, Ron (Joint Development Division, Santa Clara Valley Transportation Agency). 2002. Interviewed by the author.

Prevetti, Laurel (Deputy Director of Planning, City of San Jose). 2002. Interviewed by the author.

Render, Julie (Transit-Oriented Development Manager, Santa Clara Valley Transportation Agency). 2002. Interviewed by the author.

Valley Transportation Authority. 1995. Ohlone-Chynoweth: Design Framework for Joint Development. Final Report. March.

11.1
From the air, it is clear that Barrio Logan is squeezed between the waterfront industrial complex, the I-5 Freeway, and the Coronado Bridge.
(Photo: www.globeXplorer.com)

THE SAN DIEGO CASE STUDY
Barrio Logan's Mercado Project
Gloria Ohland

As the new millennium dawned in San Diego, planners were proposing two ambitious strategic plans—one for land use, one for transit—that sought to ease sprawl and traffic by accommodating growth in walkable, mixed-use village centers served by bus and trolley. Sunny San Diego had grown twice as fast as the rest of the United States during the late 1990s and was no longer viewed as an irrelevant cul-de-sac at the far end of the nation, known mostly as a retirement community for golf-club–wielding military officers. The city had become more diverse, less Republican, and was booming. Named the No. 1 "Best Place in America for Business and Careers" by *Forbes* in 2002, the magazine cited San Diego's diversified high-tech economy, educated workforce, gateway for international trade, "unrivaled high quality of life," and quantity of open space.

> But on its way to becoming the nation's sixth largest city San Diego had been rapidly developing what remained of its open space. The high cost of housing was forcing people to commute to homes as far away as neighboring Riverside County and across the border into Tijuana, which now boasted a population of 1 million. Traffic and subdivisions were threatening the pine- and oak-covered valleys and canyons of San Diego's environmentally stunning "backcountry," not to mention hundreds of endangered habitats and species—and San Diego County had more of them than any other U.S. county. As the city's planning department prepared for an impending update of the city's general plan, just 10 percent of land within city boundaries remained undeveloped. The question increasingly on everyone's mind was where could San Diego put the million more residents and 500,000 new jobs that were projected by 2030?

> Fortunately, residents of the San Diego region, as elsewhere in the nation, were increasingly prioritizing "quality of life"—they wanted more sense of community, less time in traffic, more housing options, and to ensure the preservation of open space. Because of harrowing commutes and changing demographics—more empty nesters, nontraditional households with fewer children, and new immigrants—suburban living was losing its appeal. Regional growth modeling scenarios by the San Diego Association of Governments (SANDAG) showed that only a modest increase in densities—from the existing regional average of 3.7 units per acre to 4.3—would reduce land consumption by 400,000 acres and reduce vehicle miles traveled by 22 percent.

>	There was increasing awareness in the city and in the region that in order for San Diego to maintain its competitive edge it would have to maintain high quality of life. If housing was too expensive in the city but suburban housing was no longer as viable for the reasons listed above, then new housing products were needed that made in-town living appealing, including live-work spaces, townhouses, lofts, and other choices in higher density residential buildings around public transit. Mixed use could provide for jobs, shops, services, and restaurants within easy walking distance. The city came up with the name "City of Villages" for this growth strategy, which would be used to guide its general plan update, and it proposed increasing densities as well as funding for parks, schools, transit, and other community improvements.

>	San Diego's transportation planning agency, the Metropolitan Transit Development Board (MTDB), supported the approach outlined in the City of Villages plan, and had adopted its own strategic plan to accommodate travel, called "Transit First." This plan proposed investments that would dramatically increase the relevance of transit: it promised waits of no longer than ten minutes at bus and trolley stops, increased the percentage of residents living within a quarter mile of transit from 3 percent to 17 percent in twenty years, and increased the percentage of jobs located within a quarter mile of transit from 15 to 43 percent. The plans were intrinsically linked: the City of Villages was predicated on adequate transit. Transit First was predicated on adequate density. If funded, they would chart a very different course for growth.

>	These new plans would reinforce planning efforts of the previous two decades. San Diego was the first U.S. city to build a light-rail system in 20 years when it opened the Blue Line south to Tijuana in 1981, and then the Orange Line east to El Cajon. In 1992, it became the first U.S. city to adopt transit-oriented development design guidelines, developed by renowned New Urbanist Peter Calthorpe. The working relationship between the city and MTDB, which built the forty-seven-mile trolley system, served as a model of how land use and transportation could be voluntarily linked. MTDB paid for two full-time city staff to serve as planning and engineering liaisons between the city and transit agency. The city adopted TOD guidelines and supportive zoning, forwarded relevant site plans to MTDB for review, and directed staff to regard transit as an integral component of all major planning initiatives and to seek right-of-way dedications where needed through the development permitting process.

>	But there was not really enough of a rail system to influence decisions about where to locate jobs or housing, and both trolley lines were built along freight corridors that were not attractive to developers. Then the recession of the early '90s slowed all growth. As a result, in the two decades following the trolley's debut, stations attracted only a modicum of development while most growth continued outward. The city's TOD-friendly zoning and guidelines had not yet been implemented in most community plans, and, being optional, they were in limited use—mostly in redevelopment project areas and for master-planned developments, where city planners were allowed more influence.

> The market was still "hard-wired" to finance suburban greenfield development instead of more complicated infill; it had not been retooled to support changing demographics and preferences. As a result, the public investment in the light-rail system had not succeeded in leveraging much investment in transit-oriented development. "We don't have any real TOD," opined one MTDB staff member attending a national TOD convention in 2002. "The codes are there if developers want to use them. But they don't."

Natural-Born Transit Village

There were notable successes, however, especially where the city and the San Diego Redevelopment Agency were able to take a more proactive role, employing strategies that made TOD more convenient or affordable for developers and minimized risk. The ninety-three-acre Rio Vista West project on the Mission Valley rail line—its site plan designed by Peter Calthorpe and its mixed-use phase nearing completion in 2002—was being heralded as one of this country's best suburban TODs, with a mixed-use core, 1,800 high density apartments and condos, a public commons and transit plaza, and walkable streets, abundant trees and landscaping, small offices, and even a Kmart. San Diego's Uptown District and City Heights urban village were probably this country's best proof that you could build TOD around bus transit. And downtown San Diego had so much transit and so many new developments—the number of residential units was doubling from 11,000 to 21,000 in ten years—that it was described as "one big TOD."

> Downtown boasted two joint development office towers incorporating trolley stations—the Mills Building, which housed the MTDB's headquarters, and America Plaza. The developer of America Plaza paid for most of that station, which was built in the grand European style and surrounded by retail and an art museum. Located immediately adjacent to the historic Mission-style Santa Fe Station, which was served by Amtrak and commuter rail, America Plaza was a particularly impressive gateway into the city via rail. A downtown ballpark under construction to the east in 2003 stimulated lots of interest in mixed-use TOD around its trolley station. And there were several other large projects—some more, some less, transit-oriented—along the Mission Valley segment of the Blue Line, which, unlike the first segment, had been sited specifically to encourage TOD.

> Planners were particularly excited about the fifty-three-acre transit village slated to be built for students and faculty at the San Diego State University Station, one of four new stations along a six-mile Mission Valley line extension to be completed in 2004. The extension will connect the Blue and Orange lines in one large loop north of downtown and is expected to boost trolley ridership significantly. And there were other projects built in outlying cities along the trolley lines—a transit village in a redevelopment project area in La Mesa, an adult education center built by the Redevelopment Agency in National City, and a huge master-planned community called Otay Ranch in Chula Vista that had reserved rights-of-way for transit, though funding had not been secured to pay for it.

> In addition, the City of Villages plan targeted many older, urban-core neighborhoods adjacent to the trolley and bus in San Diego for transit-oriented infill development. One such "village" was Barrio Logan, the historic heart of San Diego's Latino community, located just one stop south of the new downtown ballpark and hard up against the Port of San Diego. Barrio Logan was tiny and it was poor, but it was a natural-born transit village, and a place with a definite "sense of place." Both transit-dependent and well-served by transit—with a trolley stop and two major bus lines that took riders literally anywhere in the city—Barrio Logan was already mixed-use and live-work. There were jobs, schools, healthcare and social services, churches, houses, mom-and-pop grocery stores, and even a bank, all within walking distance.

> And Barrio Logan already had a TOD project just a block from the trolley—an award-winning New Urbanist–style affordable apartment complex and a soon-to-be-built retail center across the street. The ten-acre nonprofit Mercado Apartments and for-profit retail center were conceived in 1989, more than a decade before the City of Villages plan, and two years before the TOD guidelines were adopted. "Barrio Logan is testament to how much sense transit-oriented development makes in urban communities," said city planner Nancy Bragado. "People who knew the community recognized—before the TOD ordinance and without agency influence—that mixed-use, pedestrian-oriented New Urbanist development is just good common sense."

> Tell that to the bank. Barrio Logan, like many of the older communities slated to become transit villages, had been neglected both by the city and by investors. The neighborhood needed basic public infrastructure like parks and recreational facilities, street improvements, more quality affordable housing, and home-ownership opportunities. Aside from the Mercado Apartments, which were constructed in 1993, there had not been any major investments or construction in Barrio Logan in fifty years. It had been a long and difficult struggle to line up a major credit tenant to anchor the Mercado del Barrio retail center, and an even longer search to secure financing. But in 2003, after more than a decade of trying and failing, the developers succeeded in obtaining a funding commitment. The Mercado del Barrio project was a hopeful sign that not only was the market beginning to respond to changing preferences by investing in transit-oriented development in the city, it was also willing to build TOD in low-income ethnic communities.

Building "More Than Housing" in the Barrio

Until the early 1960s Barrio Logan was part of the vibrant community of Logan Heights, home to many Mexican immigrants and their families. But disinvestment began in the late '50s following the decision to construct the Interstate 5 freeway through the community, severing Barrio Logan from Logan Heights and requiring the demolition of stores, businesses, and homes. In 1967, the neighborhood was further obscured from the rest of San Diego with construction of the high-arching San Diego–Coronado Bay Bridge overhead. Squeezed between the waterfront industrial complex, freeway, and bridge, Barrio Logan is three miles long and just six blocks wide. Because of its proximity to the port the neighborhood was mostly zoned industrial, creating a cacophony of uses: the bougainvillea-draped Mercado Apartments and the neighborhood's colorful bunga-lows and historic wood-frame storefronts uneasily coexist "hoof-by-jowl" with metal plating shops, junkyards, an electrical generating plant, and a bridge-maintenance facility.

> Barrio Logan's residents are among San Diego's poorest; 40 percent of households have incomes below the poverty level. The community is almost 90 percent Hispanic and is sur-rounded by other low-income Hispanic and African-American neighborhoods. Because of the port and the industrial uses, Barrio Logan is plagued with some of the worst air pollution in San Diego County, which probably accounts for the high incidence of asthma and other respiratory illnesses among children—28 percent among children in Barrio Logan compared to 7 percent among children nationwide. The city probably assumed that the residents of Barrio Logan would eventually move out. But the city had not taken into account the neighborhood's historic and cul-tural significance to the Latino community. And the 144-unit Mercado Apartments, which opened in 1994, soon became the epicenter of efforts to reclaim the neighborhood.

> The apartments were developed by Richard Juarez and the Metropolitan Area Advisory Committee (MAAC), a nonprofit social services agency with a staff of 350, an annual budget of $20 million, and a mission "... to help individuals and families become self-sufficient ... to provide more than housing ... to build community." MAAC executive director Roger Cazares, like Juarez and Mercado architect Carlos Rodriguez—and many other Latino leaders in San Diego—grew up in Barrio Logan or Logan Heights. MAAC maintains an office on-site, and provides job training, assistance in small business start-ups, adult education classes, even a food bank. There is a Head Start preschool program, after-school assistance with homework and child care, and lots of activ-ities, including field trips to baseball games, a Christmas *posada,* and Friday night movie screen-ings. Tenants—who attend standing-room-only monthly tenants meetings—are encouraged to get involved in the community and are employed in management and maintenance.

> The apartments were designed by Lorimer-Case Architects and are extraordinarily attractive even by market-rate standards. Built to serve the "working poor," rents in 2002 ranged from $389 for one bedroom to $841 for three bedrooms. The apartments were offered to residents of Barrio Logan first and then to residents who lived in ever-widening concentric circles out from the com-munity—thereby ensuring that the project served the neighborhood. Prospective tenants were required to bring their entire families to a lengthy interview with MAAC, management, and other community organizations; once chosen they were required to sign a binding agreement that fam-ily members would remain drug- and crime-free. This was no deterrent for prospective tenants: the tenant population is stable and there is a long waiting list. Juarez, then community develop-ment director for MAAC, involved the community from the beginning, soliciting extensive input from prospective tenants who requested, for example, more storage space instead of dishwash-ers, gas stoves instead of electric (better for heating tortillas), and architecture that respected their Hispanic heritage.

> At thirty-two units per acre the development is less dense than the fifty-two units per acre permitted by the city's TOD guidelines; the higher density would have required that the units be constructed over a parking garage, driving up costs. The development is pedestrian-oriented, and built so as to promote personal interaction and public safety by allowing for what author Jane Jacobs—who pioneered the concepts of New Urbanism in *The Death and Life of Great American Cities* in 1961—called "eyes on the street." The apartments, which have porches and upper-floor balconies, are oriented toward the street or around private, semi-private, and two large public courtyards. The 212 parking spaces, many of which remain empty, were located in the interior of the development so as not to impede pedestrian flow or interaction with the community. The gates are seldom locked, intended more to extend the living space out to the street than to keep people out.

How the Apartments Got Built and the Retail Center Didn't

Impetus for the Mercado del Barrio can be traced back to 1970, a flashpoint in the history of Barrio Logan: the city reneged on a promise to provide the neighborhood with a park under the bridge, assigning the land to the California Highway Patrol for a maintenance facility instead. While the community had borne up under the zoning, freeway, and bridge, this was too much. Grandmothers and little children stood in front of the bulldozers, and construction of the new facility ground to a halt. It was at the height of *La Raza* movement, and the birth of Chicano Park—lying kitty-corner from what would become the apartments and shrouded in perpetual shadow under the bridge, its pylons covered with murals that garnered Barrio Logan international attention—galvanized the movement to save the barrio. But two more decades passed before the city did anything.

> In 1990, the city redevelopment agency made Barrio Logan a redevelopment project area, allowing the use of tax increment financing—which meant any increases in property taxes as a result of redevelopment could be invested back into the neighborhood—and making it eligible for federal grants. The focal point of the redevelopment plan was the Mercado del Barrio mixed-use project. But Barrio Logan had never been a high priority for the city, and then the recession hit. Juarez, then a development consultant, spent $20,000 of his own money and raised $50,000 from relatives to pay a consultant to prepare an application for an Urban Development Action Grant to help purchase the site. The city was awarded $875,000, but when Juarez encouraged the city to go after another federal grant for street improvements he was again told by the city to hire their consultant. And he did.

> Acknowledging his commitment, the city gave the project to Juarez, who enlisted the help and resources of MAAC and Roger Cazares, who agreed to take on the project and hire Juarez to manage it. Juarez and MAAC assembled $10,000 from the San Diego Community Foundation and $600,000 from the Local Initiatives Support Corporation (LISC), a national community

development intermediary, for the planning and engineering studies and other predevelopment work required to secure a construction loan. The San Diego Housing Commission provided a significant first piece of financing with a $1.5 million loan from its Housing Trust Fund, and a long-term silent second loan—"silent" because the loan payment can be deferred for the life of the loan and does not count as debt when lenders calculate a client's total debt—of $1.1 million. The Federal Home Loan Bank provided $800,000 from its Community Investment Program, which funds affordable housing and some nonresidential projects. Bank of America provided $3 million.

> Forty percent of the project was funded with low-income housing tax credits, which have become the single most important source of capital subsidy for affordable rental housing in this country. California allocates both federal and state tax credits to qualified projects through a competitive process, and the credits are sold to investors who use them to reduce their tax liability, thus generating equity. LISC's California Equity Fund syndicated tax credits for the Mercado Apartments, raising $5 million. The San Diego Redevelopment Agency provided gap financing for the remaining $1 million needed for the total $12.4 million cost. But if it was a challenge securing financing for a risky apartment complex in a neighborhood where no housing had been built in fifty years—in the early '90s when all real estate projects were experiencing a credit crunch—securing financing for the 6.6-acre retail complex proved even more difficult.

> The city used the federal government's HUD Section 108 Loan Guarantee Program, which allows cities to borrow against current and future allocations of federal Community Development Block Grants, to purchase the $7.1 million Mercado del Barrio retail site. Unfortunately, there was nothing like the low-income housing tax credit program to raise equity for a retail project. Banks will typically loan up to 70 percent of the money for a shopping center, as long as there are loan guarantees. But a "major credit tenant" like a supermarket or drug store chain usually provides the loan guarantees and promises to continue paying rent even if the business closes its doors. But no major credit tenant was interested in Barrio Logan.

> It has been argued that banks and retailers underestimate the buying power of inner-city neighborhoods, where higher densities can compensate for the lower median income. Assessing buying power in low-income neighborhoods, however, is complicated because residents are often undercounted in the census—and census data is often used to determine buying power—especially if they are new immigrants or living more than one family to a house. A supermarket typically needs to draw on a population of 9,500 in order to be successful, and MAAC had two market studies indicating the Mercado's market would likely draw on a population of 55,000. But the major retailers were not persuaded and came up with other reasons not to come to Barrio Logan, arguing, for example, that because of the location next to the port the store would not draw on a wide enough service area. Juarez said he got a more candid explanation from a major video chain that said Barrio Logan's residents were not their "target population." "That's redlining," said Juarez, "but it's only illegal if you're a bank. As long as banks depend on major credit

tenants to give them the comfort level they need to make loans, then neighborhoods like Barrio Logan are out of luck."

> At one point Juarez was going to create his own Mexican supermarket—Mercado del Sol—to anchor the center, and Bank of America agreed to provide $2.4 million for the market and another $7.2 million for the retail center. "Latinos are the most potent and fast-growing consumer and political force in the country, and San Diego is the only major U.S. city with no retail district serving the Latino community," Juarez said. Because Bank of America would not have been able to sell their Mercado loans on the secondary market—major credit tenants are standard criteria for sales on the open securities market—the bank agreed to "hold the paper," putting the loan in its portfolio instead. Bank officers agreed to do it "out of the goodness of their hearts," Juarez said, adding they were probably also eager to prove—having just undergone a highly scrutinized merger with Nationsbank—that being a megabank was not a bad thing.

> The Bank of America loan officer who structured that deal, Mitch Thompson, had worked for MAAC in 1977. "It took an inordinate amount of time and knowledge to come up with a financial structure that worked," Thompson said. "But it was a one-off deal. It was too darn complicated to do again." The deal fell through because Landgrant Development, MAAC's development partner in the retail venture, did not want to move forward without a major credit tenant to help shoulder the risk. Landgrant, a suburban shopping center developer, was working with the Redevelopment Agency on other projects, including the mammoth Las Americas International Gateway shopping complex on the U.S.–Mexico border. Las Americas had opened around the time of the 9/11 terrorist attacks and was struggling, and Landgrant was financially stretched.

Back to Square One

So after six years the Mercado project was back to square one, with no financing and no anchor. Meantime, Juarez had moved on to other jobs as a developer, though maintaining a 25 percent interest in the project; MAAC had 25 percent, and Landgrant 50 percent. In 2002, Juarez was working on transit-oriented development around bus in the nearby neighborhood of City Heights, again putting together a supermarket-anchored shopping center, this time with much more luck. Meantime, Mitch Thompson had moved from Bank of America to the California Equity Fund, and then back to MAAC, where he helped complete three more affordable housing projects and rehabilitated a strip mall into a mixed-use office-retail-charter-school complex for at-risk teens, and had developed a loan fund for first-time home buyers.

> By the end of 2002, Landgrant succeeded in getting a small regional chain of Mexican markets called El Tigre to anchor the shopping center and Thompson had aroused the interest of the Enterprise Social Investment Corporation, a national financial intermediary for community development. President Clinton had signed into law the Community Reinvestment Act of 2000 before leaving office, which created the New Markets Tax Credit program, designed to help

finance retail in low-income neighborhoods. Similar to the low-income housing tax credit program, the New Markets Tax Credit program provides investors with tax credits if they invest in community development entities (CDEs) like Enterprise, which would in turn invest in commercial and real estate projects in low-income neighborhoods.

> Enterprise had applied to the Treasury Department for tax credits, which would be used to help finance the project. "The Mercado is the quintessential New Markets project," said Thompson. But the renewed interest in Barrio Logan had to do with more than the New Markets Tax Credit. The decline in the stock market in 2001 and 2002 had reinvigorated the real estate market, and property in downtown San Diego was hot and getting hotter with construction of the downtown ballpark. The Mercado was already 70 percent preleased. In addition, MAAC, which had had no experience as a developer when the agency undertook building the Mercado Apartments, now had a track record and could draw on Thompson's extensive background in lending.

In the Shadow of the Downtown Ballpark

Barrio Logan had always been a self-sustaining family-oriented neighborhood where people both lived and worked; it provided skilled labor to the shipyards and service industry workers to downtown. But as the new downtown ballpark began casting a long shadow over surrounding neighborhoods and land values continued to climb, investors who didn't necessarily have the community's interests at heart began eyeing Barrio Logan. "There's always been tremendous political pressure to get something built that brings the neighborhood back," said Todd Hooks, assistant director of development for the Redevelopment Agency. "But the new challenge is to do that in a way that protects Barrio Logan's integrity in spite of what will be tremendous pressure to gentrify, and to make it an anonymous, high-density adjunct to downtown."

> In this new context the Mercado shopping center became even more important as a way to provide high-quality goods and services and several hundred jobs—"to help hold the fabric of community in place," said Hooks. Nobody was more interested in getting the project built than the city redevelopment agency, which had sunk $13 million into Barrio Logan but could only prove it on paper—aside from the Mercado Apartments there had been few tangible improvements. The retail center planned at this juncture, however, was not the Mexican-style Mercado that had been envisioned by MAAC: large stores combined with smaller spaces and market stalls for start-up businesses, room for retail carts, public space for gatherings and cultural activities, and maybe an open air market and other festivities on weekends. That project, Juarez believed, would have become a destination for tourists and people from all over the city, and a draw for those who wanted to have dinner and park their car before taking the trolley to the ballpark.

> Instead, Landgrant was building a suburban shopping center in Barrio Logan. It would wrap around three sides of the two-block site—requiring the vacation of a street down the middle—

turn its back on one street, and locate truck delivery bays facing the vacant property between the center and the trolley station. Parking would be in the middle and on the backside of the site— away from the trolley—but the stores would open onto the parking lot. There would be 3.5 parking spaces per 1,000 square feet of retail space—compared to the 2 allowed under the city's TOD guidelines and the suburban standard of 5, which is what Landgrant wanted. A well-known neighborhood restaurant named Chuey's would be moved onto the adjacent vacant property from its current site across the street. The existing Chuey's was a cavernous structure that drew a large crowd of downtowners for owner Luis Garcia's well-turned-out home-style Mexican cooking. Plans for the new restaurant were proudly displayed above the long and lively lunch counter. But what looked in the drawing like a large public plaza fronting the trolley was in fact a huge parking lot.

> The city had adopted an array of zoning code amendments to encourage TOD—including an urban village overlay zone, a transit area overlay zone, a townhouse zone, and a mixed-use zone—and there were the TOD design guidelines, which were in effect within a quarter mile of all trolley stops, including Barrio Logan. But the zoning code amendments had not yet been implemented in an updated community plan for Barrio Logan and were therefore optional. Both Juarez and the city planning department had sought to make the retail center more transit- and pedestrian-friendly, but Landgrant and the redevelopment agency applied tremendous pressure to keep the project moving forward.

> "I like to use the technical term 'freaking out' to describe why we're trying to push this one through," said Pat Hightman, the Redevelopment Agency's Barrio Logan project manager. "The land has been vacant for years, we haven't been able to collect on our $875,000 grant from HUD because we aren't building anything yet—and we need that money because some of it has already been spent—there are political pressures to generate property and sales taxes, and on top of that there are financing deadlines. The problem is that the city wants a, b, and c, the developer and the lenders want x, y, and z, and the community wants something else. And we at the Redevelopment Agency are expected to reconcile all the conflicts and make it happen."

The Future of TOD in the City

The San Diego City Council, at the end of 2002, adopted the City of Villages strategy as a new element of the city's General Plan. But council members directed staff to remove all planned density increases—fearing this would arouse the ire of their constituents—and made it harder to change densities and zoning through the community plan amendment process. And the MTDB, which made Transit First its official policy at the end of 2000, did not put forward any initiatives to fund it. MTDB would ask voters in 2004 to approve an extension of the half-cent county sales tax used to fund transportation projects. But unless the tax was restructured, only a third of the money would go to transit—with the remainder funding roads and freeways—while Transit First would require a three-quarter-cent sales tax with all proceeds going to transit. The city, meantime, had calculated a $2.5 billion shortfall in funding for the infrastructure required to accommodate its projected population increase—either with or without City of Villages. Both City of Villages and Transit First would require tax increases.

> So while San Diego was poised to make a tremendous leap forward in terms of changing land-use patterns at the turn of the century, the mood had turned cautious, generating no small measure of cynicism among some residents, including former state Senator Jim Mills, who had authored the legislation that created the MTDB and built the trolley system. "San Diego has suffered over the course of years from an indolent city council that is content to merely make it from one election to another without stirring up controversy," he said. "And Transit First was nothing but a pipe dream." Former MTDB planner Bill Lieberman, who'd left the agency to become a consultant, was less caustic but no less pessimistic. "It was always my feeling that what was proposed in Transit First and City of Villages was a real stretch for the region. Both documents provide vision, but I'm not sure there is the political will to provide all the funding that would be necessary."

> And there was a step back at the regional level from efforts to promote the coordination of transportation and land-use planning and decision making. Legislation had been introduced in 2000 that would have combined the regional council of governments, the county's two transportation agencies, the port authority, air quality management district, and a new border infrastructure agency into one regional superagency—to be run by popularly elected regional officials with land-use authority over regionally significant transportation projects. The initiative encountered so much opposition that it evolved into a bill in 2002 that merely consolidated the planning functions of the MTDB, North County Transit District, and the San Diego Association of Governments (SANDAG) under one roof, at SANDAG.

> SANDAG planner Carolina Gregor remained optimistic, nonetheless, about the direction in which the region was headed. She pointed out that the city would have to revisit the issue of density: every California city is required by state law to show how it will provide for its share of the regional housing need—determined by the regional council of governments working with the California Department of Housing and Community Development, and the California Department of Finance—in a housing element to the city's General Plan that is updated every five years and that identifies adequate sites with appropriate zoning and infrastructure. SANDAG, for its part, was incorporating Transit First projects into its regional transportation plan, setting aside a special $25 million fund for transportation projects that supported smart growth, and revising funding criteria so that projects supporting smart growth would score higher. "It's an incremental step forward, not a leap," Gregor said. "Slowly but surely smart growth and transit-oriented development are becoming part of the political consciousness."

Lessons Learned

While there has been great effort to get banks and investors to loan money for affordable housing projects, there needs to be a similar effort to make money available for retail in low-income communities because of the shortage of financing sources, patient, long-term capital, and loan guarantees for retail. Rich Juarez and Mitch Thompson agreed the crux of the problem in financing the Mercado retail center was that it needed a major credit tenant. Even loan funds and venture capital funds set up specifically to encourage the development of retail in low-income neighborhoods—like the Local Initiative Support Corporation's Retail Initiative Fund and Fannie Mae's American Communities Fund—use the same lending criteria as major banks: they require major credit tenants, which are publicly traded companies that have credit ratings and operate under rules about public disclosure, which means that investment bankers can look at their financials and readily assess their strength. And major credit tenants do not operate under any of the federal guidelines and constraints—against red-lining, for example—that banks do. "You've got to have a major credit tenant—that's how these projects get financed. Because it's not about the project, it's about the credit statements of the people who sign the leases," Thompson said.

> Thompson said the chances of convincing a bank to provide financing for a project like the Mercado were slim. "Bank of America agreed to do the deal for other than standard business reasons," he said. "They did it because of the Community Reinvestment Act, and because the project was in an Enterprise Zone and would have been eligible for low-cost industrial bonds—which would have been re-loaned to the developers through Bank of America at lower-than-market-rate interest. And they did it because Rich had been working with a community development corporation (CDC) that was a subsidiary of Nationsbank at the time of the merger with Bank of America—and the CDC strongly supported the project and was able to provide Bank of America with in-house expertise. If we really deem that projects like these are important then we need to write more definitive language into the Community Reinvestment Act to get banks interested. Because the lesson is that we still need more resources if we want to cause these things to happen."

> Juarez had been able at one point to get San Diego National Bank to agree to loan the Mercado $8 million if the developers could have come up with a $4 million loan guarantee—which would have been possible, he said, if the amount of the guarantee could have been reduced after one or two or three years when it became evident that the retail center was not going under. After five years of success, the project's track record would have made it salable on the private market. "The problem," he said, "was getting the building built, and getting past the bank's fears that it would be unsuccessful." He suggested that a loan guarantee could be made available for a short period of time, backed by a revolving loan fund, and suggested that a foundation could set aside as little as $10 million to leverage financing for three or more projects at a time in a metropolitan area.

> Juarez was working in another low-income neighborhood with the non-profit San Diego Revitalization Corporation (SDRC), which was endowed by Price Club founder Sol Price, who had grown up in this neighborhood, called City Heights. SDRC had already invested $80 million in affordable housing, townhouses, mixed-use office and retail projects, a childcare center, library, park, swimming pool, and police substation, and was in 2003 proposing advancing funds to the city redevelopment agency to purchase a block where Juarez could build a retail center, to be anchored by an Asian market, and 150 residential units. SDRC would leave the money in the retail project until it got off the ground, and the redevelopment agency would reimburse SDRC from the tax increment funds the project would generate. "San Diego National Bank told me that I needed a Sol Price when I tried to get financing for Barrio Logan," said Juarez. "The involvement of San Diego Revitalization has made it as easy to arrange financing in City Heights as if we had a major credit tenant. Every developer in a low-income neighborhood needs a loan guarantee or patient capital to provide a bank's loan officers with the comfort level they need to take that loan to their board for approval."

The New Markets Tax Credit will help, but there are limitations. The New Markets Tax Credit will help provide financing for commercial projects at lower interest rates in the early years, which will translate into lower lease rates, thereby making projects in low-income neighborhoods more attractive to retailers. Charlie Werhane of the Enterprise Social Investment Corporation's new Enterprise Community Fund, which will use these tax credits to underwrite supermarket-anchored retail projects like the Mercado, said it has been a problem nationwide getting supermarkets to commit to low-income neighborhoods, partly because higher construction costs translate into higher lease rates and partly because the supermarket chains have no reliable means of determining disposable income in these neighborhoods. "The feedback we get from community development corporations locally is that the market information on low-income neighborhoods is unreliable," he said. "Information about the buying power of these neighborhoods hasn't yet been put in a usable format to take to retailers."

> He noted, however, that unlike the Low-Income Housing Tax Credits, the New Markets Tax Credits alone will be insufficient to drive investments—their relatively modest size means that the projects they generate will have to provide substantial economic benefits on their own to attract investors. The New Markets Credits have a present value of about 39 percent—5 percent of equity invested for the first three years and 6 percent for the next four years—compared to 70 percent for low-income housing tax credits or up to 90 percent in very distressed and high-cost areas. Equity investments will be returned to investors after the seventh year.

> The New Markets Credits will be a source of "patient" capital to grow a business before a return on funds is due to the investor. The credits function much like "mezzanine" debt or bridge loans, which are shorter-term than permanent loans and therefore require a smaller interest rate

to cover interest-rate risk. Risky projects are likely candidates for this kind of debt, and can use the mezzanine financing until they prove their value and are able to secure long-term loans at reasonable rates.

> Werhane agreed that the national commitment to financing retail in low-income neighborhoods lags behind the commitment to affordable housing, and said the Enterprise Foundation, too, had focused on housing. "We have always relied on the individual cities to come up with incentives for retail," he said. "But our view of community development at Enterprise has always been much broader. We have always believed in the need for ancillary development—of commercial real estate including retail and office—to support housing. The New Markets Tax Credit will allow us to broaden our mission."

Development partners should share the same vision and values. Juarez and Thompson stressed that the number one lesson they learned was that it is very important to be careful when choosing a development partner. While Landgrant President Sam Marasco was sympathetic to the original Mercado vision for the retail center, Landgrant the corporate entity—as represented by the project manager and Landgrant's financial partners—was not. "We learned that a suburban shopping center developer has certain experiences that don't necessarily carry over to an urban site in a high-density, low-income, inner-city neighborhood where there could be much more intense uses," Thompson said. Todd Hooks of the Redevelopment Agency added that the city had believed it would be a good partnership because MAAC had the commitment to carry the project through, while Landgrant had the "horsepower." "But we knew it was going to be a weird marriage," he said, "and that it would continue to be a really difficult relationship."

The City of San Diego's TOD implementation strategies have not been strong enough to encourage widespread TOD. While the city adopted the TOD design guidelines and a number of TOD-supportive zoning code amendments, by the end of 2002 these had not yet been incorporated into and implemented through more than a few of the city's forty community plans. When the city council adopted City of Villages, the planning department was directed to apply the TOD guidelines in all of the potential "villages" identified in the Strategic Framework Element so as not to miss any opportunities while the community plans were being updated. But the planning department was told not to apply those TOD guidelines that referenced either parking or density. Those changes still required a community plan amendment.

> The city had tried putting a number of innovative parking strategies in place—low maximums in downtown, shared parking, and reductions for mixed-use developments in transit corridors and for projects incorporating transportation demand management—but these were proving politically untenable. Downtown's parking maximums, for example, were replaced with low minimums as the result of pressure from the business community. "Parking remains a very

11.4

The apartments are oriented
to the street, and to private,
semiprivate, and public
courtyards. (Photo: David Lorimer,
architect-principal, and Carlos Rodriguez,
architect-designer/associate,
Lorimer-Case Architects.)

11.5

The mission of the developer was
to "build more than housing,...
to build community." (Photo: David
Lorimer, architect-principal, and Carlos
Rodriguez, architect-designer/associate,
Lorimer-Case Architects.)

political issue," said city planner Nancy Bragado. "We're definitely not pushing the market when it comes to parking." Regarding density, the TOD guidelines recommended minimums, with maximums to be determined by the community plan or zoning. "We have traditionally provided density maximums not minimums," explained Bragado. "We are beginning to introduce low minimums mostly to get communities used to the idea."

>   The planning department continued to urge more transit- and pedestrian-friendly designs and codes wherever a discretionary permit review process was required—for larger developments and anything other than what was permitted by right—although there had been only limited success in negotiations with Landgrant in Barrio Logan. Where the city was able to take a more proactive role—developing a master plan for Rio Vista, for example, and a master environmental impact report for downtown San Diego—there was much more success. And projects

like Barrio Logan and the City Heights urban village, downtown San Diego, and the very promising San Diego State University transit village were made possible because the redevelopment agency was involved and able to bring along its toolbox of tax increment financing, land assemblage, and public subsidies—strategies that made TOD more affordable and/or more convenient for developers compared to other sites.

REFERENCES

Affordable Housing Finance Magazine. 2002. $2.5 billion available in New Markets Tax Credits. February. At www.housingfinance.com.

Blair, Tom. 2001. Spicing up Little Italy. *San Diego Magazine* August. At www.sandiegomagazine.com.

Bragado, Nancy (Senior Planner, City of San Diego Planning Department). 2001–2003. Interviewed by the author.

———. Transit Joint Development in San Diego. *Transportation Research Record* 1669. Paper No. 99-1514.

California Department of Transportation. 2002. Statewide Transit-Oriented Development Study: Factors for Success in California. May 3.

California Housing Law Project. 2001. Housing Element Law. At www.housingadvocates.org.

California Office of the Treasurer. 2000. The Double Bottom Line: Investing in California's Emerging Markets. May.

California Tax Credit Allocation Committee. 2001. A Description of California Tax Credit Allocation Committee Programs. April 17.

Cazares, Richard (President and CEO, Metropolitan Area Advisory Committee). 2002. Interviewed by the author.

Chase, Carolyn. 2002. City of parks—or city of parking? *San Diego Earth Times* September 2002. At www.sdearthtimes.com.

City of San Diego. N.d. City of Villages. At www.sannet.gov.

City of San Diego. N.d. Municipal Code. At http://clerkdoc.sannet.gov/Website/mc/mc.htm.

City of Seattle. 2001. San Diego Trolley Case Study. February.

Clark, Cathy. 2002. The Neighborhoods: City Heights. *San Diego Magazine.* At www.sandiegomag.com.

Donoho, Ron. 1997. Hillcrest: Uptown and Offbeat. *San Diego Magazine* February. At www.sandiegomagazine.com.

Flanigan, James. 2002. Building Inner-City Equity: A Decade After the L.A. Riots a New Financial Order Is Directing More Investment Dollars to Low-Income Areas As Nonprofit Groups Act as Intermediaries between Capital and Communities. *Los Angeles Times* April 21.

Goldberg, Gail. 2002. City of Villages—Our Best Alternative. *San Diego Union Tribune* September 22.

Gregor, Carolina (Senior Regional Planner, San Diego Association of Governments). 2003. Interviewed by the author.

Hightman, Pat (Deputy Director, San Diego Redevelopment Agency). 2001. Interviewed by the author.

Hoffman, Alan (Principal, The Mission Group). 2001–2002. Interviewed by the author.

Hooks, Todd (Deputy Director, San Diego Redevelopment Agency). 2002–2003.

Initiative for a Competitive Inner City. ICIC Research Facts. At www.icic.org.

Local Initiatives Support Corporation. 2002. How New Markets Tax Credits Will Work. February 15. At www.liscnet.org.

Inzunza, Ralph (San Diego City Councilman, District 8). 2003. Interviewed by the author.

Juarez, Richard (Urban West Development Consultants). 2001–2003. Interviewed by the author.

King, Patricia (Loan Officer, Bank of America). 2001. Interviewed by the author.

Kirshner, Miriam (Senior Planner, Metropolitan Transit Development Board). 2002. Interviewed by the author.

Laufik, Jan (Development Director, Metropolitan Area Advisory Committee). 2002–2003. Interviewed by the author.

LeSar, Jennifer (Senior Vice President and Investment Manager, Bank of America). 2001. Interviewed by the author.

Lieberman, William (Transportation Consultant, San Diego). 2002–2003. Interviewed by the author.

Metropolitan Transit Development Board. 2001. Transit Works. January.

Metropolitan Transit Development Board. 2000. Metropolitan Transportation Survey Statistics for the San Diego Metropolitan Area FY 2000. At www.sdcommute.com.

Mid-America Regional Council. 2002. Case studies: Uptown District. August. At www.marc.org.

Morgan, Neil. 2000. Peace at War: Senator Links RITA Bill with Funds for Cities. *San Diego Union Tribune* June 15.

Nathanson, Chuck. 2002. Financing Smart Growth. Major San Diego Employers Worried About Area's Deteriorating Quality of Life. *San Diego Dialogue Report* April/May. At www.sandiegodialogue.org.

National Association of Housing and Redevelopment Officials. 2002. Resources for Affordable Housing. 2002. At www.nahro.org.

Novogradac and Company LLP. 2002. New Markets Tax Credit. At www.novoco.com.

Ortiz, Rachel (Executive Director, Barrio Station). 2003. Interviewed by the author.

Peters, Scott. 2002. Region Needs a Transportation Plan. *San Diego Union Tribune* February 17.

Roberts, Benson. 2001. New Markets Tax Credits: The Next Tool for Community Development Financing." April 18. Local Initiatives Support Corporation Online Resource Library. At www.liscnet.org.

Rodriguez, Carlos (Rodriguez-Simon Design Associates). 2001–2003. Interviewed by the author.

San Diego Association of Governments. 2003. Draft Preliminary 2030 Forecast Process and Model Documentation. February.

———. 2003. Mobility 2030: The Transportation Plan for the San Diego Region. Draft Final. February 2003.

———. 2003. Preliminary 2030 Cities/Counties Forecast. February.

———. 1999. INFO: A Million More People in the Region by 2020. May–June.

———. 1997. INFO: Land Use in the San Diego Region. July–August.

San Diego Dialogue. 1999. Towards Smart Growth for San Diego County. Briefing paper prepared for San Diego Dialogue's Quarterly Plenary Session. January.

Sanada, Glen (Senior Vice President, Bank of America). 2001. Interviewed by the author.

Small Business Association. 2002. Certified Development Company (504) Loan Program. August 2002. At www.sba.gov.

Smith, Chris (Executive Vice President, Landgrant Development). 2001–2002. Interviewed by the author.

Stepner, Mike (Dean of the New School of Architecture). 2001. Interviewed by the author.

Thompson, Mitch (Senior Vice President of Housing and Community Development, Metropolitan Area Advisory Committee) 2001–2003. Interviewed by the author.

Urban Land Institute. 1998. Mercado Apartments Case Study. September ULI Project Reference File, vol. 28, no. 15. July–September.

U.S. Department of Housing and Urban Development. N.d. Section 108 Loan Guarantee Program. At www.hud.gov.

U.S. Treasury Department. 2001. New Markets Tax Credit: Spurring Investment for Business Growth in Urban and Rural Communities. April. At www.treas.gov/cdfi.

Weisberg, Lori and Susan Gembrowski. 2002. Commuting a Longer, Lonely Drive. *San Diego Union Tribune* May 26.

———. 2002. Planners Say It Takes Villages to Grow a City. Blueprint Aims to Combat San Diego's Housing, Traffic Problems with More Compact, Community-Oriented Building. *San Diego Union Tribune* January 6.

Werhane, Charlie (President, Enterprise Social Investment Corporation Realty Partners). 2003. Interviewed by the author.

Williams, Leon. 2002. Exploding Myths about Public Transportation. *San Diego Union Tribune* May 9.

Zion, Lee. 2002. It Takes a Village...or Two. *San Diego Business Journal* August 12.

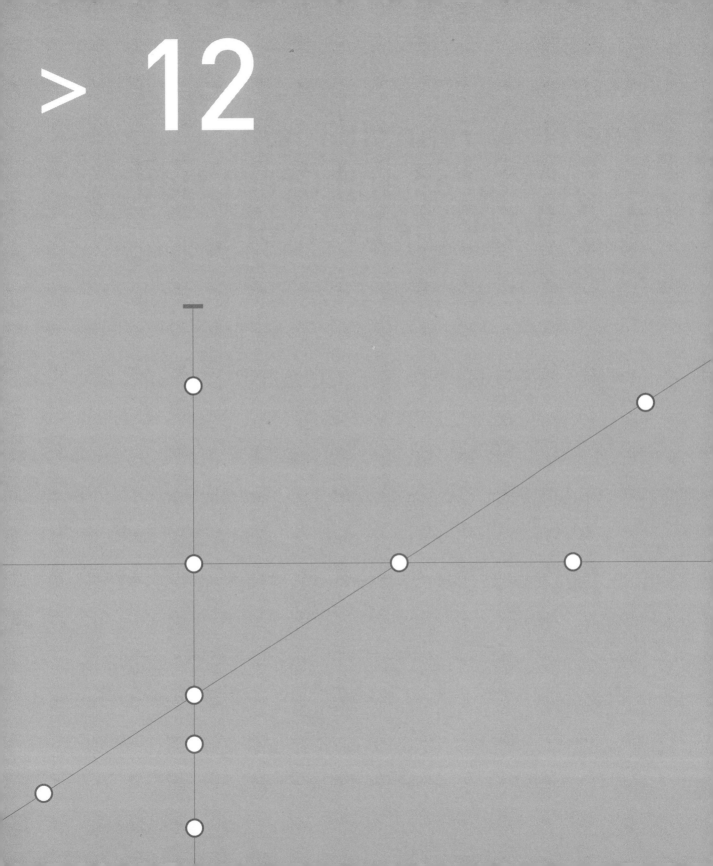

The New Transit Town: Great Places and Great Nodes That Work for Everyone

Scott Bernstein

This book is about investing in smarter development of our community assets. "To develop" comes from a French verb that originally meant "to unwrap." "Assets" meant "of sufficient estate." "Community" speaks to things that must be done together. And "to invest" is to make a conscious act of sacrifice in expectation of a return.

> We write within a context of urgency. Transit-oriented development (TOD) represents a kind of complex proposition, a subset of the general proposition that some things really are more worth doing together than separately. The marketplace for real estate development cannot meet the urgent needs of today or tomorrow's generations without realizing this. The most common form of transportation provides a good example.

> Our society has made it possible to acquire personal rapid transit in the form of motorized vehicles. This brings "push-button" accessibility, what planners call "on-demand" or no-wait transportation. But this comes at a very high cost. We spend almost a trillion dollars a year on passenger transport in America, the overwhelming majority of it ($836 billion per year) on personal motor vehicle ownership and operations; we spend perhaps $100 billion per year on highways and mass transit.[1] We have effectively dumped the cost of traveling on the traveling public and allowed the marginal cost of acquiring that access to be very low. It is much easier to put a few dollars down on a finance contract for a car than it is to organize to create mass transit. The first is something that can be done on a personal or household level, while the second requires establishment of areawide authority, acquisition and control of rights-of-way, supermajority approval of new taxes and/or innovative financing obligations for the life of a very-long-lived project, interconnections with existing and other proposed mass transit projects, and so forth.

> And yet, people and communities are lined up to start new transit systems, to build great stations and great communities around them, with an estimated backlog of at least fifty years under current funding formulas. This is true not only in areas that traditionally grew up around mass transit but also, and perhaps more important, in the Sunbelt regions of the West and the South. In the absence of dedicated funding sources, voters at the state and local levels are, where

possible, developing local option referendum campaigns and voting to tax themselves to advance these agendas. This is prima facie evidence that given the motivation, people will organize to get around the split incentives—the car and the suburb—that have prevented these logical investments.

> The opposite of a split incentive is a joint incentive, and both history and this book are rich in examples. American and European cities grew up around an inherently efficient land-use pattern served by public transportation systems; for a very long time this combination served to minimize the cost of development and personal expenditures.

> The advent of the automobile and public policies that encouraged decentralization caused a divergence between America and Europe. As a result, traditional American cities and suburbs have struggled to hold on to their location efficiency, while European cities have been more successful in maintaining this benefit. American cities and suburbs developed after World War II are coping poorly with the costs of sprawl and inefficiency.

> American metropolitan areas decentralized at rates that were up to thirteen times faster than population growth from 1970 to 1990, and in general, at least three times faster from 1982 to 1997. As a result, the cost of transportation as a portion of household expenditures rose from one dollar out of ten in 1950 to almost one dollar out of five in 2000.[2] Whereas metropolitan air pollution was traditionally dominated by power plant and manufacturing emissions, after the 1990s it was clearly dominated by the growth in transportation. Air quality gains that resulted from vehicle efficiency standards and fuel quality improvements were overshadowed by the growth in vehicle miles traveled.

> For every 1 percent increase in metropolitan land use, annual vehicle miles traveled increased by at least 1.25 percent.[3] However, this formula works in the other direction, too. For each doubling of density within communities and within metropolitan areas, annual vehicle miles traveled are reduced by 20 to 40 percent.[4] This latter finding has been shown to be a reliable function of the combination of density, frequency, and quality of mass transit, quality of the pedestrian environment, and access and proximity to everyday amenities, including shopping, services, and recreation.

> Transit-oriented development describes both the patterns that American communities traditionally exhibited and patterns that many newer communities never have had but are clearly striving for. It is a method of achieving location efficiency and community livability, and a potential major contributor to metropolitan environmental quality. Because transportation expenditures for automobiles now constitute the second largest household expenditure in America, TOD also represents a pathway to lower expenditures, increased household savings, and increased household, community, and national wealth.

> America stands at a crossroads. Vehicle miles traveled (VMT) increased by 3 percent annually from 1950 to the mid-1990s; but the rate of increase started dropping in 1996. It was down

to 1 percent annually in 2000. The tragic events of 9/11 resulted in a major reduction in intercity travel by aviation, and a likely increase in intercity travel by automobile, which is probably the reason that the annual rate of VMT increase jumped back to 1.9 percent in 2001. If we remove intercity travel from the picture, we are indeed at a crossroads: Americans are driving much less than they did in previous decades.

> *If* the major development question facing America today is, are we sprawling or are we reinvesting?, the answer is yes—we are doing both simultaneously.

> We can grow efficiently only if our cities and suburban communities provide location efficiency. This can happen if we make the most of our existing assets and communities, and make it work for everyone.

> The topics and case studies in this book were selected to provide a review of one of the most important tools for achieving this kind of vision. Transit-oriented development is being attempted in older American cities and suburbs, as well as in postwar metropolitan areas. It appears to be popular, and is being tried with some success by nonprofit affordable housing developers and the nation's largest commercial developers.

> But what is this development form? Is there a standardized definition or product type that can be consistently applied? Does it work better for one type of developer or another? Is there a logical scale for these developments? Why isn't it a development priority in more places? Does it only work well in upscale developments or can it work for everyone? If it is the right thing to do, what will it take to deploy it rapidly in as many places as possible? Can we learn to sustain a culture of transit-oriented development and inclusively beneficial livable communities?

Land Use, Infrastructure, and Regional Investment

The history of real estate development in America underscores the importance of providing choice in the kinds of housing that people can buy. This choice is even more important because of significant demographic changes highlighted in chapter 1. American households over time are likely to be older, smaller, and significantly more foreign-born than the market assumed to be the case through the 1990s. These changes have profound importance for planned development, and for the role of TODs in housing a growing population. Since the census first measured household size in 1790, American household size has dropped almost continuously, from 5.8 persons to 2.6 in 2000. From 1965 to 2000, while household size dropped from 3.3 to 2.6 persons, average home size shot up from 1,450 to 2,100 square feet. For the past several years, the market has been completing 1.7 million new homes per year, of which 321,000 or 20 percent are in dwellings of five units or more, and the balance are overwhelmingly single-family.[5] The growth in American households is outpacing the growth in population, driven by the aforementioned demographic changes and the growth in single-parent families. The marketplace is not producing the kinds of housing that can effectively house the population that needs it.

12.1
When done right, as in this photo in Brisbane, Australia, transit becomes an extension of the community.
(Photo: Hank Dittmar.)

> The kind of communities we are building—with single-family homes on large lots—are consuming land at a rate that is not likely to be sustainable. These acres come from conversion of farmland, ranches, and forest, and require a significant investment in infrastructure to meet the transportation, energy, water, drainage, sewage, telecommunications, and municipal service needs of these new developments. It costs approximately $50,000 more per dwelling unit to meet these needs in a greenfield area than it does in a built-up brownfield or grayfield; the net costs are even less when infill occurs in a suburb that may have overbuilt infrastructure carrying capacity.

> In just one metropolitan region, Chicago, the thirty-year expected growth of 800,000 households, if accommodated in the existing footprint, might bring net savings of $35 billion.[6] Nationally, the "swing" in these investments is easily in the trillions of dollars over the next three decades. Continued rapid decentralization is in effect "redlining" public investment in existing communities' schools, streets, and facilities and is no small part of the upward pressure on property taxes.

HOUSING SUPPLY VERSUS DEMAND

If we map the growth in housing versus the growth in households by county for each year of the 1990s, a very interesting pattern emerges. Approximately one-third of all counties had rates of housing growth that exceeded population growth; one-third had population growth rates that exceeded available housing; and one-third had housing and household growth rates that were approximately even. The group in which household growth clearly exceeded available housing is composed of all the cities and communities experiencing rapid price escalation; the rates of escalation are very high in "central counties" (in urban affairs literature these are the counties in metropolitan statistical areas where the largest cities are located), where the overwhelming majority of America's mass transit is located. This shows a very high and underserved demand for transit-served communities and implies that, far from being a primary cause of gentrification and displacement, transit-oriented communities are in demand and the market has yet to provide a product at sufficient scale to meet it.

FIG 12.1

Relative Difference Between Rates of Growth in Households and Housing Units from 1990–2000 (Source: Center for Neighborhood Technology.)

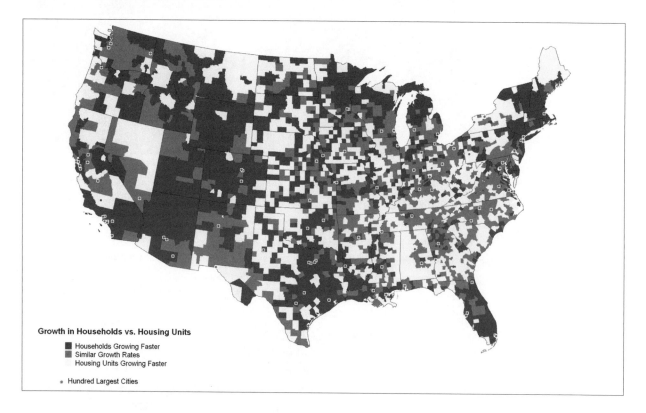

Growth in Households vs. Housing Units
- ■ Households Growing Faster
- ■ Similar Growth Rates
- □ Housing Units Growing Faster

◦ Hundred Largest Cities

LOCATION EFFICIENCY AND HOUSEHOLD EXPENDITURES

TOD has the real estate characteristics of a "home base," a livable community for residents and a workable community for businesses and service providers. These attributes are the place-making qualities of the kinds of communities that TOD can both create and support and in turn be supported by. TOD also has to serve other functions.

· First, it needs to function as a destination, not just as an origin. This means it must be accessible to people traveling from other communities within the region, and even to people traveling between regions.

· Second, it must function as a gateway to the regional transportation network and to the network of communities in that region served by the larger transportation system.

> As a functioning gateway, TOD must work for pedestrians, bicyclists, buses, and on-demand transit vehicles such as shuttles, vans, and taxicabs. If motorized vehicles dominate the general character of available transportation in the region and in the surrounding community, TOD may have to work as a bridge between two very different kinds of worlds and lifestyles (see chapter 8 on Dallas's TODs).

> A functioning access point to the network requires a relatively high frequency of service (or short waiting times between service availability). Cities and suburbs originally grew in the United States with spectacular service frequency. In the case of surface streetcars, under one-minute headways (time between cars) were limited only by street congestion; streetcar suburbs in Chicago had up to 200 intercommunity trains per day if you include both the steam commuter railroads and interurban electrics. A relatively high density was necessary to support this level of service, but if you have this level of service it can help support the investment needed to produce high-density, mixed-use communities. Reid Ewing and Todd Messenger of Rutgers University, for example, calculate that increasing densities in Sunbelt communities from 8.4 to 11.2 dwellings per acre (or 25 percent) justifies doubling the frequency of bus service from twice to four times hourly.[7]

> This interplay between frequency of service and land use plays out regionally in very important ways. As noted in chapter 2, the location efficiency studies have found that in cities across the United States each doubling of residential density is associated with a decrease of 20 to 40 percent in annual vehicle miles traveled, and a similar reduction in average household vehicle ownership. If this were a description of a financial investment, then imagine being able to put your money in a dependable savings account or security and getting a 20 to 40 percent annual rate of return! A recent study at UCLA corroborates these findings.[8]

> Recent research suggests that a principal benefit of working mass transit and location efficiency is reduced automobile dependence. This is more than an intangible or psychological benefit. Owning one less car per household in higher density areas near amenity-rich communities with frequent and convenient transit is worth $400 per household per month, net, of transit expenditures. Median household automobile expenditures measured regionally (on a metropolitan statistical area basis) run between $6,000 and $10,000 annually. Owning fewer cars and driving less clearly provides a stream of consumer expenditure savings, or to say it another way, more disposable income. We estimate that achieving this level of savings is the equivalent of a

5 to 10 percent increase in disposable income for the first three quintiles of household income in metropolitan America.

> Parking expenditures and strategies to reduce these could play an important role in large-scale TOD (parking cash-out, trading employer-provided parking for employer-supported transit, reduction in minimum parking requirements, and provision of parking shared between multiple users). Employer-provided parking has been estimated to cost at least $36 billion annually. Estimates of the cost of providing an extra parking space (i.e., the marginal cost of parking) vary from $6,700 to $50,000.[9] Under these circumstances, (a) it costs much more to provide enough parking for cars than the cars cost themselves, and (b) space for parking is scarce in high density situations by definition. Will Rogers once noted, "On the road to success, there are many tempting parking places."

> In Arlington Heights, a northwestern suburb of Chicago located on a Metra commuter-rail line, the city adopted a strategy of promoting downtown redevelopment that is both transit- and pedestrian-oriented. The city assumed the responsibility of redirecting automobile traffic flows around a complex street and passenger rail station intersection and of financing the parking requirements for new mixed-use developments. The developers received access to parking and expedited plan reviews in exchange for sharing these structures (which are internal to each of twelve mixed-used buildings) with shoppers and offices in the downtown community—in effect, the city became a "parking utility" with control over design guidelines. The city's efforts were recognized in 1999 with the annual Daniel Burnham Award from the Metropolitan Planning Council in Chicago.

> In Chicago and many other cities, it was recognized that transit would thrive best if surrounded by a market of transit users. This in turn provided an incentive for dense mixed-use development around the stations and for providing a pedestrian-friendly environment. Evidence that expenditure density occurs in lower- and mixed-income communities has been accumulating over three decades of academic and market research. The importance of this was recognized in transit plans well before the adoption of municipal zoning in 1923 and before the adoption of sales taxes in the 1930s. In a sense, high density communities are concentrated and congested by design. For example, Chicago was developed around the confluence of a river system and a major lake and became the terminus for twelve trunk railroads, each of which, starting in 1856, spun off passenger railroad operations, local commuter facilities, and incentives (including the invention of the monthly transit pass) around which developed street grids, street railways, and later elevated railroads. These kinds of infrastructures facilitated the rapid growth of American cities and simultaneously supported the patronage and finance of the transportation systems that made them possible. This, in turn, created an investment climate of anticipation. In an evocatively titled 1925 essay, "Our Stake in Congestion," planner Frederick Ackerman noted "... as a general proposition the purpose for which credit is used in the case of purchase of urban lands and the erection and purpose of buildings is to capture the appreciation of value which is

a function of growth, concentration and even congestion ... paper securities carry face values that represent nothing more tangible than this prospect."[10]

REAL ESTATE VALUE CAPTURE

In 1903, it was estimated that the addition of electric streetcar service in Chicago was saving the average rider fifteen minutes in each direction, making possible a journey of three more miles in the same time span; Richard M. Hurd's estimate of the increased value of this benefit, capitalized into real estate value, within the three-mile semicircular zone of Chicago, was $456 million.

>   All of the case studies touched upon this phenomenon. Billions of dollars of value were added to the Rosslyn-Ballston Corridor in Arlington; in fact, Market Common, a high-density, mixed-use TOD project that opened in late 2001, was sold by its development partners to a teachers' pension fund for $166 million on March 3, 2003—the largest transaction of its type in recent years.

The Challenge Ahead

It has become a routine cliché to talk about how public subsidies lead to excessive land uses without necessarily describing how. It is worth taking the time to reflect on the historical roots and characteristics of transit-oriented communities.

>   The major characteristic of the real estate production system that has developed in the last five decades has been commodification. Financial services products have reduced the down payment barriers for single-family home purchasers, and a thriving secondary market for the mortgages used to finance single-family homes and risk-reduction products have made these investments relatively easy to finance. By contrast, multifamily housing and mixed-use development are at the other end of the curve. These products are not standardized and neither are their associated methods of design and of financing.

>   The historians Kenneth Jackson and John Stilgoe point out that railroad and streetcar suburbs produced exclusive enclaves, but more important, at scale they produced affordable housing for the "common man." Prior to the introduction of self-amortizing mortgages, capital was usually available only in very short-term notes requiring up to 50 percent in down payment or equity. This encouraged development by small builders of homes on narrow lots or amalgamation of interests into entities large enough to sell securities. On the public finance side, there was not enough funding to produce separate streets for streetcars, and the mass transit they made available was a real asset. Taken together, these factors helped encourage the development of the kind of rectilinear grid we are used to seeing today.[11]

>   Planned communities today occur most likely in either single-use, relatively low density subdivisions, or in very high density downtown developments; too much of the latter is being planned for an upscale population in the upper two income quintiles of earning power. A very

sophisticated real estate investment equity market has emerged that pumps approximately $200 billion per year into nineteen standard real estate products, none of which are specifically intended to be transit-oriented development.[12] Only 6 percent of this equity capital was used in 2002 for mixed-use real estate.[13]

> America's population is projected to grow by 76 million persons between 2000 and 2030, and at 2.5 persons per household the market will need to produce another 30 million homes to meet this need. If household size continues to drop, as some have projected, this could grow to 38 million homes, and there will be a likely loss of housing stock over this period of another 22 million dwellings. The resulting net need of 60 million dwellings will require annual production of 2 million homes per year; we are already running short by at least 300,000 dwellings per year. If we continue to produce housing in the pattern experienced from 1982 to 1997, we can expect to consume another 50 million acres of land for development.

> Transit-oriented development can offset this considerably because a great deal of growth can be accommodated around rail stations. As pointed out in chapter 1, there is an existing inventory of about 2,400 rail stations, with another 130 to be constructed soon. At the writing of this chapter in early 2003, the Center for Transit-Oriented Development was preparing to conduct a market study to assess the development potential around station sites, confident that the analysis would confirm the existence of a substantial market for new multifamily residential development within a quarter-mile to half-mile radius of these stations. This development will begin to define the armature for densifying communities that are served by transit or are connected to transit by virtue of walkable streets.

> In chapter 2 we identified six ways to array this TOD: urban downtown, urban neighborhood, suburban center, suburban neighborhood, neighborhood transit zone, and commuter town center; and in the case study chapters, these TODs had actual densities ranging from 7 to 120 units per acre. This is but one of a large number of ways that the geographic distribution of development could occur; it's not a likely scenario if business does occur as usual, but it's a direction that we could move in, if certain kinds of conditions are met, as outlined in table 12.1.

> Transit-oriented development is joint development. No one party is responsible for it, and it provides not a single function but multiple functions with multiple costs and benefits for the many users and investors and operators that are party to it. These kinds of investments can potentially provide economies for their surrounding communities and regions and, in the aggregate, for the nation as a whole.

> But the "joint-ness" referred to is a more subtle and richer concept than is traditionally implied by the notion of "economy." In a typical "economy of scale," unit costs drop as a function of increase in production. This is an attribute shared by automobile manufacturers and large-scale developments of single-family tract homes alike.

> TOD represents a different kind of economy, one that is often referred to as an economy of scope or a network economy. In this kind of economy, the benefits to each produce returns to

TABLE 12.1—FUNDAMENTAL SHIFTS NECESSARY TO A CULTURE OF SUCCESS

TODAY	TOMORROW
Auto-oriented and transit-related development	Transit- and people-oriented development
Surrounded by parking and plazas	Part of a streetscape
Value capture is rent seeking	Value capture is multipurpose
Managed tightly by a single entity, e.g., transit operator or developer	Jointly managed with broader community
Financing tied to physical design	Financing tied to performance measures
Seen as a subsidized liability	Formally credited as a local and regional asset
Transportation benefits are defensive, e.g., for congestion management	Transportation benefits are affirmative, e.g., household savings, local economy, healthy environment
Promoted primarily for certain upscale markets	Promoted to achieve sustainable mixed-use, mixed-income communities
Clever exceptionalism (i.e., it really does look like rocket science)	A way of life

scale. For example, if developers learn to produce multi-use structures within TODs, we would expect their unit costs to decline over time with experience and improved methods and technologies. Similarly, it is clear from the chapters on regulation and finance that the urge to streamline does eventually overcome the burden of rules and plan requirements. And unit costs—including time—do drop accordingly. But economies of scope and of networks function differently.

> Cities are systems within systems of cities, and transit-oriented communities are systems within systems of transit-oriented regions. Both the transit systems themselves, and the stations, and the intangible rights-of-way and plans and rules that link these assets together are public assets providing public utility.[14] This is true whether the asset is owned by a public entity or by a private entity whose ownership is spread in the marketplace.

> This is also true of the pedestrian amenities that are part and parcel of TODs. Philosopher of walking Rebecca Solnit notes, "Walking focuses not on the boundary lines of ownership that break the land into pieces but on the paths that function as a kind of circulatory system connecting the whole organism. Walking is, in this way, the antithesis of owning."

> Transit-oriented development could no more function without a good walking environment than a body could function without a circulatory system. And what goes for walking goes for the connections and proximity between people and what they do and the social aspects of living. This is beyond the simplistic view that value capture is all about taxable real estate value. It is this covariance and codependence and the resulting synergies from these combinations that produce the ultimate value of transit-oriented development.

TABLE 12.2—ASPECTS OF LEARNING PROCESSES

OLD LEARNING	NEW LEARNING
Closed: Inputs are carefully controlled.	Open: We are provided a rich variety of inputs (immersion).
Serial-Processed: All learners are expected to follow the same learning sequence; learners only learn one thing at a time.	Parallel-Processed: Different learners simultaneously following different learning paths; many types of learning happening at the same time for individual learners.
Externally Referent and Designed: Both knowledge and the learning process are predetermined by others.	Self-Referent and Emergent: Knowledge is created through the relationship between the knower and the known. The outcome cannot be known in advance.
Controlled: The teacher determines what, when, and how we learn.	Self-Organized: We are active in the design of curriculum, activities, and assessment; teacher is a facilitator and designer of learning.
Discrete, Separated: Disciplines are separate and independent; . roles of teacher and student are clearly differentiated.	Messy, Webbed: Disciplines are integrated; roles are flexible.
Static: Same material and method applied to all students.	Adaptive: Material and teaching methods varied based on our interest and learning styles.
Linear: Material is taught in predictable, controlled sequences, from simple parts to complex wholes.	Nonlinear: We learn nonsequentially, with rapid and frequent iteration between parts and wholes.
Competing: We learn alone and compete with others for rewards.	Co-Evolving: We learn together; our intelligence is based on our learning community.

(Source: Julia Parzen et al. 1996.)

> Successful TODs can be understood only against the test of time. In Europe and in America, communities have been developing around, nurturing, and benefiting from public transit systems for centuries. The ones that have lasted have the attributes of learning communities, as is shown in table 12.2.

> How do these observations and classifications help us understand how to address urban and regional challenges in effective ways? One perspective that is gaining currency is that people and firms maximize their asset-seeking behavior. If people and organizational leaders recognize opportunities or threats, they will work to address these in the best ways they can. This kind of analysis leads to the application of continuous improvement theory and practice in large corporations, in some large public institutions, and in the private sector, and is increasingly at the root of business and manufacturing networks. Accordingly, the success of these perspectives in driving organizational change is a function of the quality of what different interests can do better together than what they do separately—and this is a way to view the value of social capital in the broader economy.

> An intriguing prospect is that social capital plays a similar value-added, cohering, and performance-oriented role in the life of communities and regions. Literature, discussion, and practice in urban and regional organization are increasingly based on a sense of the importance of assets. Notable efforts are focusing on community assets, household assets, and natural capital assets.

> Our view is that achieving desirable outcomes of quality of life or livability or urbanism takes investment, investment takes maintenance, and maintenance takes accounting for existence

value and a set of reinforcing norms, whether in law and regulation or, more informally, to guarantee a sense of permanence.

Getting Started

It is the evolving nature of the American urban economy to provide access to specialized services. Community development of the sort that TOD represents requires the application of ideas, technologies, and approaches that have heretofore been considered too large and too complex to apply at the scale of location, place, or community. Service providers are assemblers of knowledge and of approaches that no single developer or community could expect to have competency in on their own; in some cases, this knowledge and these services function in the public interest, and so it would not be in the public interest to have this knowledge reside in only a small number of practitioners.

> This helps define the need for an "intermediary" service provider, to provide a form of specialization of organization and to enable investment in both the tangible and intangible aspects of transit-oriented development. The right kinds of resulting institutions will be a curious sort of "weaver" or investment banker, pulling together many different other institutions and competencies into a system that can lend or rent its reputation in a universally recognized way, which in turn makes it easier to know what the goals of good community design and investment are, and once achieved, to acquire the resources to get there and sustain the outcomes successfully.

> Such organizations are agents of diffusion, and as such, they enable rapid learning—and a shortened time cycle for adoption of innovations and new ways to overcome seemingly insurmountable hurdles. Early transit engineers Bion J. Arnold and William Parsons served as nationwide agents of diffusion for the idea that statistics could solve the transit problems of a city.[15]

> Real estate development in many ways is the primary business of America. Of $31 trillion in tangible wealth in America in 2001, $11 trillion was in residential assets, $6.7 trillion in private nonresidential real estate, and $6 trillion in government structures and in highways, streets, and mass transit systems.[16] Where we choose to put these investments makes all the difference to economic and environmental sustainability.

> At the end of World War II, model communities were developed in New York (Levittown), Chicago (Park Forest), and southern California. These ideas were diffused rapidly and successfully, as were many innovations in the financial services market that led to standardization of the wrong kinds of real estate investment products.

> The new "transit town" is intended to be the new model community for the new millennium. The chapters in this book on zoning and regulation and on financing TOD show that determined, capable, and inventive teams can meet the challenge of "new learning" demonstrated in table 12.2; the case study material demonstrates that this has actually been going on for a long time. The "new transit town" is a work in progress, somewhere at the early end of the continuum stretching from research and development to the desired set of functionally replicable products.

12.2
The striking train station in Solana Beach, California activated the sleepy beach community.
(Photo: Rob Quigley Architects.)

What is needed to get there is a set of supportive conditions for the desired marketplace to emerge, including the following:

·   Defining transit-oriented development as a set of products meeting a set of performance measures.
·   Standardizing and providing systematic approaches to implementation.
·   Removing public policy barriers.
·   Removing barriers in standard marketplace practice (e.g., creating new ways of accepting risk, as is discussed in the chapter on financing TOD).
·   Expanding the range of demonstration projects.
·   Standardizing performance measures and publicizing evaluations of real projects against these standards.
·   Broadly diffusing the resultant standards and practices.
·   Getting broad alignment around support of these products and their supportive policies and practices, region by region, across the United States.

> Functionally, there is an agenda for improving the state of the art. This agenda is largely a matter of getting important knowledge and capacity disseminated and providing supportive policies; the policy agenda is largely one of providing incentives to minimize short-range investing and to maximize collective investment behavior.

> For example, making retail work remains an enormous challenge for mixed-use development in general. Several firms and organizations have emerged in the last decade to specifically address the challenges of helping the marketplace see the retail potential in mixed-income communities. No low-cost, generally recognized service yet exists "on demand" to provide the kind of geographic information and mapping that could drive a new generation of investment products backed by the new spatial awareness of retail demand.

> There is a similar story around location efficiency. The tools to measure location efficiency are now available, and in many jurisdictions the data is in the public domain. For much of the country, however, the data is unnecessarily restricted and so the transaction costs of constructing usable location efficiency maps is artificially inflated.

> Real estate value capture has the longest history of any of our proposed performance measures; the standard tools were worked out by Richard M. Hurd in 1903 and have been refined continuously ever since then. There is an emerging critical literature on traffic and parking that can be applied to standardized performance measures for the network connectivity or "node" aspects of TOD; much work remains to gain broad acceptance in the transportation planning and community development fields, and to integrate this knowledge with the reemergent knowledge of the value of and supportive conditions for physical activity and the pedestrian environment.

> The dominant pattern of settlement in America is metropolitan and regional.[17] The vision of regional networks of transit-oriented communities cannot work unless the rich benefits of TOD are formally credited for their full tangible and intangible benefits. This will require honing our methods not only of developing real estate but also of democratizing participation in the planning of our communities. Effective public participation will require skilled assistance, both to buy room at the table for traditionally excluded community leaders and to perform complex decision making effectively.

> In the last ten years, creative work has gone into the design and deployment of computer-aided decision support tools. The idea is to help skeptical audiences or even supportive ones more quickly learn the benefits of better urban design.[18] These visual preference–oriented tools are slowly being merged with a kind of simulation tool that can start to measure the outcomes of changed design. In particular, we still need to work both at building better urban physical designs for TOD, and at helping residents, businesses, government, and investors "unwrap" the hidden economic, social, and environmental impacts of these investments.

> Suppose that, collectively, residents of a region had the choice of shifting some of their personal transportation expense and some of the excess investment in new infrastructure together

toward a certain future in which their commuting and shopping time was shorter, their access to capital and wealth higher, and their feelings of community satisfaction higher? Developing better TOD means unwrapping a very big package indeed.[19]

> Ultimately, working communities are both great nodes and great places. To capture and distribute fairly the benefits of high-performance transit orientation is a matter of social, economic, and political invention. If we take the time to make it everyone's business, it will lead to a future we can all afford.

NOTES

1   Author's calculations, based on Roslyn A. Wilson, Transportation in America. Washington, D.C. Eno Foundation, 2003.

2   Scott Bernstein and Ryan Mooney Bullock. 2002. *Driven to Debt*. Chicago: Center for Neighborhood Technology.

3   Author's calculations based on data supplied by the Chicago Area Transportation Study.

4   John Holtzclaw, Robert Clear, Hank Dittmar, David Goldstein, and Peter Haas. 2002. Location Efficiency: Neighborhood and Socioeconomic Characteristics Determine Auto Ownership and Use. *Transportation Planning and Technology* Winter: 1–25.

5   Author's analysis, data from U.S. Bureau of the Census, at www.census.gov and from historical sources.

6   Staff analysis, Center for Neighborhood Technology. See also literature review in The Costs of Sprawl Revisited. Transit Cooperative Research Program, National Academy of Sciences, 2001.

7   Todd Messenger and Reid Ewing. Transit Oriented Development in the Sunbelt: Get Real (and Empirical). Florida Atlantic University/Florida International University Joint Center for Environmental and Urban Problems, 2000. In 1977, Boris Pushkarev and Jeff Zupan found in *Urban Rail in America* that doubling of service frequencies for rail rapid transit could result in up to 79 percent more revenue ridership (Bloomington: University of Indiana Press).

8   Daniel Baldwin Hess and Paul Ong. Traditional Neighborhoods and Automobile Ownership. *Transportation Research Record* 1805: 35–44.

9   Todd Littman, www.vtpi.org, and Don Shoup. 1999. "In Lieu of Required Parking," *Journal of Planning Education and Research* 18:307–320.

10   I'm grateful to Professor Sam Bass Warner for pointing me in the direction of this article.

11   Sam Bass Warner Jr., *Streetcar Suburbs: The Process of Growth in Boston 1870–1900*, especially chapter 6, "Regulation Without Laws; General Motors president Alfred P. Sloan acknowledged the growth of installment credit for consumer purchases as the principal reason for their success in *My Years With General Motors*; and Edwin R. A. Seligman showed how modernized credit provided a kind of "inverse savings account," leading to the rapid growth in automobile sales in overtaking furniture and musical instruments—neither of which, as far as I can tell, had the land-use influences of credit for buildings and for cars. See *The Economics of Installment Selling: A Study in Consumers Credit* (New York: Harper, 1927).

12   Christopher Leinberger. 2001. *Financing Progressive Development*. Washington, D.C.: Brookings Institution Center on Urban and Metropolitan Policy. At http://www.brook.edu/es/urban/capitalxchange/article3.htm.

13   PriceWaterhouseCoopers and LendLease. 2003. *Emerging Trends in Real Estate 2002*. REIT Capitalization by Project Type, page 30.

14   Jeffrey Richards and John M. MacKenzie. *The Railway Station: A Social History* (Oxford: Oxford University Press, 1986). Attributes many historical social and community benefits to rail stations; one of the more interesting in England was that by providing book stalls for the working class, literacy rates increased.

15   Paul Barrett and Mark H. Rose. Street Smarts: The Politics of Transportation Statistics in the American City, 1900–1990. *Journal of Urban History* 25(3):405–33; Carl W. Condit, *Chicago 1910–1929: Building, Planning and Urban Technology* (Chicago: University of Chicago Press, 1973); and personal communications, pp 237, 262, 267; Bion J. Arnold. *Report on the Engineering and Operating Features of the Chicago Transportation Problem* (New York: McGraw Publishing, 1905). Similar studies performed for several dozen cities between 1902 and 1920. Also Bion J. Arnold. The Urban Transportation Problem: A General Discussion. *Annals of the American Academy of Political and Social Science* 37,1, (January 1911):3–13.

16   Bureau of Economic Affairs. United States Department of Commerce. 2002. Fixed Assets and Consumer Durable Goods 1925–2001. Survey of Current Business, September. At http://www.bea.gov/bea/ARTICLES/2002/09September/0902FixedAssets.pdf.

17   Scott Bernstein and Bruce Katz. The New Metropolitan Agenda: Connecting Cities and Suburbs. *Brookings Review* October 1998; The Metropolitan Initiative, at http://info.cnt.org/mi; Partnership for Regional Livability, at www.pfrl.org; Scott Bernstein, Bruce Katz, Rob Puentes. TEA 21 Reauthorization: Getting Transportation Right for Metropolitan America, at http://www.brook.edu/es/urban/publications/tea21.htm; DeWitt John, *Building Better Communities and Regions: Can the Federal Government Help?* (Washington, D.C.: National Academy of Public Administration, 1998).

18   See www.placematters.com for descriptions; and same website for Terry Buss and F. Steven Redburn, Modernizing Democracy.

19   See "Gains that Endure," chapter 5 in Robert H. Frank. *Luxury Fever: Money and Happiness in an Era of Excess* (Princeton: Princeton University Press, 1999), 75–93 for several versions of this suggested exercise.

REFERENCES

Ackerman, Frederick L. 1925. Our Stake in Urban Congestion. *Survey Graphic* 7:141–142.

Albrecht, Donald et al. 1995. *World War II and the American Dream: How Wartime Building Changed a Nation.* Cambridge Mass.: MIT Press.

Bernstein, Scott. N.d. Using the Hidden Assets of America's Regions to Ensure Sustainable Communities. At http://www.cnt.org/hidden-assets/.

Bernstein, Scott and Robert Soden. 2002. *Analysis of Household vs. Housing Growth.* Chicago: Center for Neighborhood Technology.

Berry, Brian J. L. 1964. Cities as Systems within Systems of Cities. *Regional Science Association Papers* 13:147–164.

Bertolini, Luca and Tejo Spit. 1998. *Cities on Rails: The Redevelopment of Railway Station Areas.* London and New York: Routledge.

Fulton, Bill and Rolf Pendall. *Who Sprawls Most?* (Washington, D.C.: Brookings Institution, 2002). At www.brook.edu/urban. Based on USD National Resources Inventory. Census comparison by author.

Hurd, Richard M. 1903. *Principles of City Land Values.* New York: The Record and Guide.

Illinois Central Magazine. 1926. Suburban Service for 70 Years. August 19.

Jackson, Kenneth T. 1985. *The Crabgrass Frontier: The Suburbanization of the United States.* Oxford: Oxford University Press.

Kretikos, Eleni. 2003. Market Common Fetches Rare Price. *Washington Business Journal.* March 3. At http://washington.bizjournals.com/washington/stories/2003/03/03/story1.html.

Kretzmann, John and John McKnight. 1998. *Building Communities from the Inside Out.* Evanston, Ill.: Northwestern University.

McDonald, Alan and Leon Schrattenholzer. 2001. Learning Rates for Energy Technologies. *Energy Policy* 29:255–61.

National Association of Real Estate Investment Trusts. 2003. Chart Book. At www.nareit.com.

Nivola, Pietro. 2000. *Fit for Fat City.* Washington, D.C.: Brookings Institution Surface Transportation Policy Project. 2002. Transit Growing Faster than Driving: A Historic Shift. Washington, D.C. At http://www.transact.org/library/Transit_VMT.asp.

Oliver, Melvin and Thomas Shapiro. 1997. *Black Wealth, White Wealth.* New York: Routledge.

Parzen, Julia et al. 1996. *Staying in the Game: Strategies for Urban Sustainability*. At http://www.cnt.org/publications/staying-in-the-game.pdf.

Prugh, Thomas et al. 1995. *Natural Capital and Economic Survival.* New York: Chelsea Green.

Randall, Gregory C. 2000. *America's Original GI Town: Park Forest, Illinois.* Baltimore: Johns Hopkins University Press.

Sherraden, Michael. 1995. *Assets and the Poor.* New York: Armonk Press.

Solnit, Rebecca. 2000. Wanderlust: A History of Walking. New York: Viking.

Stilgoe, John R. 1988. *Borderland: Origins of the America Suburb 1820–1939.* New Haven: Yale University Press.

ABOUT THE CONTRIBUTORS

Gerald Autler is an associate at Strategic Economics, a consulting and research firm specializing in urban and regional economics and planning. He has co-authored articles on transit-oriented development with Dena Belzer.

Dena Belzer is founder and principal of Strategic Economics. Her expertise lies in transit-oriented development as well as strategies for attracting local-serving retail and fostering mixed-use districts.

Scott Bernstein is the founder of the Center for Neighborhood Technology, which develops resources and systems that promote sustainable communities. He co-founded the Surface Transportation Policy Project, is co-director of the Reconnecting America's Transportation Networks project, and has worked with the White House and Congress on transportation and sustainability issues.

Shanti Breznau is an associate planner at Strategic Economics, where she specializes in the intersection of land-use policy and urban real estate economics.

Peter Calthorpe, a founder of the Congress for the New Urbanism and principal of Calthorpe Associates, was named by *Newsweek* as one of "25 innovators on the cutting edge" for his work in redefining urban and suburban models of growth.

James M. Daisa is project manager for the nationally renown engineering firm Kimley-Horne, and is an expert in pedestrian and transit-oriented development, neo-traditional town planning, downtown revitalization, and conventional highway and urban street analysis and design.

Hank Dittmar is president and CEO of Reconnecting America, formerly known as the Great American Station Foundation. Reconnecting America is a national non-profit that seeks to integrate transportation systems and the communities they serve, and bring transit-oriented development to scale through the Center for TOD, one of its core programs. He is the former executive director of the Surface Transportation Policy Project, the nation's leading advocate for transportation policy reform.

Judith Espinosa is the director of the Alliance for Transportation Research Institute at the University of New Mexico. She was formerly the New Mexico Secretary of the Environment and Secretary of Transportation and is nationally known for her advocacy and public interest work.

Sharon Feigon is manager of research and development for the Center for Neighborhood Technology, where she has specialized in developing innovative market-based solutions to the problem of urban sprawl.

Ellen Greenberg is director of policy and research for the Congress for New Urbanism, where she has investigated issues ranging from the adaptive re-use of shopping malls to the design of walkable streets.

David Hoyt is a writer and researcher for the Center for Neighborhood Technology.

Dennis Leach is a senior associate with TransManagement Inc. where he is engaged in a broad array of assignments covering multimodal and intermodal transportation policy, planning, and management. He is a resident of Arlington County, Virginia, where he currently chairs the county's Transportation Commission.

Gloria Ohland is a former journalist and a senior editor with Reconnecting America. She did extensive media work while heading the Surface Transportation Policy Project's Southern California office, garnering headlines for issues ranging from pedestrian safety to the amount of time mothers spend driving.

Julia Parzen co-founded Working Assets Money Fund and Working Assets Funding Service, co-authored *Credit Where It's Due: Development Banking for Communities*, and has provided strategic planning, evaluation, and program design to a wide range of clients.

Shelley Poticha is the executive director of the Center for Transit Oriented Development. She is an urban planner and was formerly the executive director of the Congress for New Urbanism, where she guided CNU's growth into a coalition with a prominent voice in national debates on urban revitalization, growth policy, and sprawl.

Abby Jo Sigal specializes in real estate analysis and valuation and is currently working with the Enterprise Social Investment Corporation.

INDEX